THE FUTURE CHURCH OF 140 BCE

A Hidden Revolution

BERNARD J. LEE

THE FUTURE CHURCH
OF 140 BCE

A Hidden Revolution

with
"Two Kinds of Power"
by
BERNARD M. LOOMER

Crossroad | New York

1995

The Crossroad Publishing Company
370 Lexington Avenue, New York, NY 10017

Printed in the United States of America

Library of Congress Cataloging-in-Publication Data

Lee, Bernard J., 1932–
    The future church of 140 BCE : a hidden revolution / Bernard J.
Lee.
        p.   cm.
    Includes bibliographical references and index.
    ISBN 0-8245-1529-3 (pbk.)
    1. Catholic Church–United States–Teaching office.
2. Hermeneutics–Religious aspects–Christianity.   3. Laity–
Catholic Church.   4. Catholic Church–United States–History–20th
century.   5. Laity–United States–History–20th century.
6. Pharisees.   I. Title.
BX1407.T4L44   1995
282'.73'09045–dc20   95-22257
                                                        CIP

To My Marianist Brothers and Sisters
Lay and Religious
Who Love Me and Who Do Not Love Me
Who Challenge Me and Support Me
Who Are My Community and My Story
From Whom I Have Learned
Most of the Things
That Today I Believe
Matter Most
And Have Consequences
That Are Full of Grace

CONTENTS

PREFACE

In a preface an author should state the major premise of the book and say a little about why and how the book got written. I shall try to do both of those things.

The Catholic Story

The premise of the book is simple. It is very important for the praxis of the Christian community in the United States Catholic church to find ways to *include lay interpreters in the pattern of authorized interpretation that defines the Catholic story.* They are not currently numbered in what W. Dow Edgerton calls the "guild" of authorized interpreters. Only ordained members of the community belong to this guild, which means that all of them are men with celibate commitments. The contribution of lay interpreters is essential but partial. Clerical biases are seldom nuanced through corrective and/or balancing dialogue with lay biases. No one interprets bias-free.

I think of "lay" less in terms of canonical and/or theological definitions and more in terms of a person's social location. Making it in the world on a daily basis is the social location of lay experience. It includes family, friendship, business, leisure, economics, politics, and so on. I think of "cleric" equally in terms of social location, determined in large ways by the fact of ordination. Clerics have organizational responsibilities for the operations of church as an institution and the delivery systems whereby sacramental life and pastoral exigencies are attended to.

In his analysis of the Jesus movement, Gerd Theissen notes that there were two social forms of discipleship: the itinerant disciples who moved around with Jesus and the resident disciples who formed the first house churches and have always been the great majority. (1985, 8–23) You can tell an itinerant not to worry about the next day, because even Solomon in all his glory was not arrayed like the lilies of the field. But you cannot tell parents with a house and three children not to worry about what food they will have on the table tomorrow. Jesus also advises that no one going into battle should fail to size up the other side. Generals, I take it, are supposed to worry about tomorrow. Theissen says that Jesus gives both kinds of advice because sometimes he is speaking to the small group of itinerant disciples and sometimes to the larger circle of resident disciples. There is one kind of living praxis for one group, another for the other group. They overlap but do not coincide. The analogy, I hope, is obvious.

The official interpreters have come, and still do come, from only one social location. That is one of the clearer meanings of "clericalism." The "-ism" names not the rich and necessary contribution of the clerical interpretation of what defines the Catholic story but the exclusion of lay interpreters from the guild that does the defining. At best, lay interpreters have sometimes squeezed some words into the interstices of the web of official interpretation.

How accountability functions is one of the ways in which interpretive power can be indexed. There are structured ways in which priest-pastors are accountable to the bishop. When a priest is ordained, he places his hands in the hands of the bishop and promises obedience. However, there is no formal structure whereby a priest is accountable to the community for the exercise of leadership. There are no evaluational procedures. That gives a priest far more power than the community in shaping how parish life is conducted. People are accountable to whoever hires them. Members of the parish community do not "hire" the pastor; the bishop "hires" the pastors. The members of the parish are not guaranteed any voice whatsoever in the selection of the one who is to lead them. If there is a consultation, it is gratuitous, not required. The bishop chooses.

There are no structured processes by which the lay people of God in a local church are consulted in the selection of the church's bishop. The key figure in recommending episcopal appointments is the pope's delegate in Washington, D.C. Once appointed, the bishop of the local church must report in regular visits directly to the pope. But there is no ordinary evaluational procedure whereby a bishop is required to render an accounting of his leadership to the priests and lay people of the local church. Accounting "upward" in the chain of command is structured. There is no accountability "downward." This is one of the more unfortunate expressions of clericalism. Only those who can demand accountability have an assured position as collaborating author of the Catholic story.

The guild has so defined the Catholic story that the story does not seem to admit of lay interpreters into the guild. It will not be easy to get that story told differently. The premise of this book is that the story should be told differently and can be told differently; and I hope to propose some of the reasons why, as a conversation starter.

When I speak about how the Catholic story gets interpreted, I do not mean only doctrinal and moral issues—though those too, of course. But the Catholic story is also about our ritual life; about holiness; about relationships; about sexual love; about gender; about how community is organized; about how leadership functions; about how our faith can have children (our faith is losing its children fast in our times); about responsibility to the earth and the need for reconciliation with the earth; about the need to give faith an effective public life in the propagation of God's mercy and justice in our social systems; about an animated, mutually respectful, and critical dialogue between faith and culture; and so on. The clerical interpretation of the story is not up to many of those issues, not as a lack but as a function of social location. Equally, lay interpretation is not up to some of the tasks of keeping the larger *ecclesia* effective, holy, and healthy, not as a lack but as a function of social location. But we have had an overabundance of the latter, which preoccupies the church with itself, and too little of the former, which would keep the people of God "peopley," if one may say so. The Spanish expression *iglesia popular* carries the sense of church as owned by the people. All the baptized people of God are shareholders in the incorporate Body of Christ and need to be at the board meeting or be represented at the board meeting, *with a vote*. This book is an encouragement to rethink who really must be at the board meeting.

Lay Gifts, Lay Delights, and Lay Pain

I have taught religion and theology for many years now, undergraduate and graduate, lay and religious, seminarians and priests. Among the seminarians and priests are so many truly extraordinary people, for whose gifts the entire People of God can count themselves graced. I hear from them both the rapture and the pain of being a priest in today's church. In some ways Dickens's words about the French Revolution speak for the ecclesial revolution today. It is the best of times and the worst of times. Ordained people of God are often very close to the best and the worst. They differ from lay women and men in that, when all is said and done, they have a place where they call tell the story and have it counted.

When I began teaching at St. John's University in 1977, there were about a hundred seminarians and perhaps a dozen lay and religious students. By 1985 there were about fifty seminarians and over fifty lay students. Those were the years when the great shift began. Today there are about three times as many men and women in graduate programs in religion, theology, and ministry who are not on an ordination track as there are seminarians in the four years of theology before ordination. There are over twenty thousand non-ordained, paid professional women (80 percent) and men in the nineteen thousand parishes in the church in the United States in ministry and leadership.

I can only tell you what an array of gifts I encounter and what generosity abounds concerning them. We are not shy of extraordinarily gifted vocations to ministry. I wager that the Holy Spirit is forcing systemic change by altering the numerical balance among the kinds of vocations called forth.

Sometimes I hear utter delight from people whose gifts are welcomed and appreciated, who have a place under the ecclesial sun to be received and valued. They are sometimes the true pastors in parishes that do not have a resident priest-pastor (though canon law does not allow them the official title *pastor,* for that is how the Catholic story is written today). They are sometimes the directors of religious education for an entire diocese, though they cannot give an *imprimatur* to a textbook, even when they possess more theological acumen than the one who does. Sometimes they are leaders in base communities, who have discovered that there is in the Word a presence as real as the Eucharist's real presence – different, and not interchangeable, but real as real can be.

Sometimes I hear the deep pain. I know a woman with a doctorate, with a wonderful background in biblical studies, a storyteller par excellence, an engaging preacher who can speak as wife and mother, who moved out of the Catholic story and into another story where she has received a most incredible welcome. The move was anguishing for her, for the Catholic story is deep in her insides even as another story surrounds her outside. The sadness is poignant, much that is hers, and some that is mine too.

There is the pain of lay people with leadership and/or ministry positions who have been told "to stop reading so many books." There is indeed a power issue here around knowledge and competence. There is pain over how low salaries tend to be, not just at the low figure, but often over the need to leave ministry because it does not provide a living wage. This would not happen if the lay voice were a regular member of the guild of authors who create the Catholic story.

I could continue the tales. These are anecdotal, to be sure. For a more empirical sense of where satisfaction and dissatisfaction are experienced in lay ministry, consult the study *New Parish Ministers* by Philip Murnion, published by the National Pastoral Life Center (1992, 97–103). When the gifts of the laity are welcomed, that is the right thing to happen. But the welcoming has not yet found its way into operative structures.

This book is primarily about the Catholic church in the United States, although ramifications beyond us abound. What is unique about the U.S. Catholic church is the level of education among Catholics. We are about 25 percent of the general population but over 40 percent of the college population. What is also unique and more portentous is the number of lay Catholic women and men getting graduate degrees in the sacred sciences. No other church in Christian history has been so well educated generally and had so many lay people educated in Scripture, theology, church history, pastoral counseling skills, and so on.

We must find a way in our *pattern of authorized interpreters* of the Catholic story to include the lay interpretation. One need only look at steadily declining church attendance to guess that too many people are not hearing their story told "at church." Those of us who are not lay are no less impoverished for not having our lay sisters and brothers at the "board meeting" where policy is formulated and decisions are made. The Spirit of God operates without privilege or prejudice within the whole People of God. There is normative hearing of God's Spirit everywhere in the church. There is also distortion, from which no part of the church is exempt. At the end of this book, I will be proposing "dialogic community" as a serious model for ecclesiological reflection on a suddenly evolving praxis in Catholic life: lay women and men, learned in the tradition, effectively leading and ministering in Catholic community, whose interpretive voice is desperately needed in retelling the Catholic story for the twenty-first century.

I have emphasized the importance of the education of Catholic laity and the interpretive competencies they are developing. I value equally the knowledge that comes without education but from caring and being perceptive. There is an interpretation that comes from the margins and from exile that knows some things that no one else knows, that we all need to know. It is possible to be both educated and in the margins or in exile. Catholic women know a lot about this.

Why this book? I want the great gifts of lay men and women to become as constitutive of the Catholic story as the great gifts of those who are ordained. And for that to happen, they must gain some form of admission into the guild of authoritative interpreters.

A Metaphor from 140 BCE

As a way of exploring the future church, I am suggesting throughout the book that a phenomenon in Judaism a century and a half before Jesus could serve as a guiding metaphor, maybe even a root metaphor, for some of the transformations that I believe are urgent. What happened in Judaism was a hidden revolution, "hidden" because no one saw it coming until it was there. It was the introduction of lay interpretation into the telling of the Jewish story. The power base for the lay movement was lay learning.

After developing the metaphor, I discuss a pile up of revolutions— paradigm shifts—in Western culture, and then present three of them one by one. Each of these three chapters ends with a particular pastoral response to the central thrust of the revolution. I believe this pile up would not have occurred had there been a way for these cultural changes to be processed by the larger Catholic story. But a church that felt itself under siege became, in fact, preoccupied with its institutionality; and since the guild of interpreters was structurally inside the besieged institution, its agenda controlled the Catholic story. Lay experience, grappling with the paradigm shifts and having a formal point of entry into the writing of the Catholic story, could have made a difference. In the closing chapter I commend the model of dialogic community to the praxis of Christian life as a process that gives the lay inter- pretation a point of entry into the guild, or, to change the image, a voting place at the board table. I offer no specific suggestions about how to do it. I think no one knows how to do it. People who think it ought to be done, cleric and lay, are the designated explorers, and the journey will be long and tedious because 1,900 years of historical mapping has never charted this ter- ritory.

A Working Instance

I have a working model to cite. It is small and it is imperfect. It struggles. But I experience that it works. I cite it because it is part of the reason why the thesis of this book has seemed to me workable, not merely fanciful. The instance to which I shall refer is, I believe, a result of an appropriate response to the paradigm shift in Western culture in which the French Revolution was situated.

I begin with some weeks spent in Paris in the summer of 1989, the bicentennial of the French Revolution. While there I was reading Simon Schama's history of the French Revolution (1989). He interprets this period as the final disintegration of the feudal system, in which a few people were kings and queens, or lords and ladies, and the great majority of remaining people, which was nearly everybody, was their subjects. The new momentum in the Western soul, says Schama, was to be a citizen who participates in society. It was a move from subject to citizen. The call to arms in behalf of citizenry was *liberté, égalité, fraternité*. These are the trademarks of citizenhood: freedom, equality, and brother- and sisterhood. It was a violent and messy revolution.

The church might have sought institutional means to incorporate this paradigm shift in ways appropriate to its soul, but it did not. However, some of the religious orders that sprang up at this time did respond. That is the experience I know, and about which I speak. The Marianist Sisters were founded in 1816 by Adele Batz de Tranquelleon and William Joseph Chaminade; the Marianist Order of Brothers and Priests by Chaminade a year later. Both orders grew out of a fifteen-year-old movement of lay communities in southern France. I will speak of the men's order.

We are a community of brothers and priests. Brothers have always outnumbered the priests, sometimes seven or eight to one, other times three to one. There is only one formation program for all. A person can indicate his interest in priesthood. When he asks for final vows all of the Marianists with whom he has ever lived are consulted about both Marianist membership and priesthood. At the time when he would begin seminary studies, there is another consultation of the community. No one enters seminary without the strong support of the community. This relational connection is vital to our tradition. The community's voice has a structured place.

Leadership in Marianist communities and ministries is open equally to ordained and non-ordained Marianists. The non-ordained brothers are sometimes as well or better educated in theology than priests. Sometimes not. What carries weight is knowing the tradition, not being either a priest or a brother. I think a priest who tried to "pull clerical rank" would get a smile and a shrug and not much else. I know that equality, in the limited context of one specific religious order, has worked well. The ministry of the priests is deeply appreciated, but a priest carries no additional power as an interpreter of the Marianist story because he is a priest. We are citizens together.

Equal access to being in positions that create the Marianist story is guaranteed. If the provincial is a brother, the assistant provincial is a priest. If the provincial is a priest, the assistant provincial is a brother. Elected delegations to provincial and general chapters must be comprised of both brothers and priests. They have the same voting rights.

There has always been a solid, profoundly collaborative relationship with lay people and with smaller groups more intimately associated with Marianist religious. In the years since the Second Vatican Council, lay Marianists have become an autonomous and interdependent member of the Marianist family, with their own international structure and fiscal support. There are about 2,400 Marianists in the two religious orders and about 8,000 lay Marianists in a vast network of lay communities.

I can assure anyone that we have done some things well and some things poorly and that we struggle every day. But I have experienced herein a place where lay and clerical interpreters have equal voice in the structure of authorized interpretation, a place where lay and religious exercise a joint stewardship for the Marianist charism.

I am not suggesting that this model is replicable in the same way in ecclesial structures (or that it is not). I cite it for two reasons. First, it is a place where non-ordained and ordained have a structure that assures both of an interpretive voice in the praxis of Marianist living. I know, therefore, that something like this can work, and I know of nothing (except the power of a long history to the contrary) that prevents Catholics in the United States from working on some new models of ecclesial polity.

The second reason for citing the Marianist example is that it is part of the reason why these issues matter to me in the first place, and therefore part of the reason why all the things in this book came together for me the way they did. We see things from the vantage point of our experience (which is also why we miss some other things). My concern for some new ways of being together in church reflects my experience as a priest in a particular religious community. I am nearly compulsive about our need to welcome lay women and men into responsible coauthorship of the Catholic story in this country. And every other country.

I

THE HIDDEN REVOLUTION

OF 140 BCE

Introduction

There is a hidden revolution going on in the Roman Catholic Church in the United States for which a hidden revolution in Judaism in the middle of the second century BCE is a remarkable parallel. This revolution is deeper by far than even the incredible shifts in church life that are visible to the naked eye—and the visible indicators are substantial indeed. The revolution is not just about positions now held by lay people instead of by priests and/or religious. The hidden revolution is occurring in the intellectual and affective life of the People of God, and it is about who interprets Catholic Christian identity and how and why it happens.

A revolution is a sudden realignment of power, and that fits. By "power" I do not mean crass, popular connotations about coercion, but the whole system of relationships that guide how a social system exerts influence and receives influence. One of the most important social locations of the hidden revolution is the infrastructure of ministry and leadership, because lay Catholics are increasingly in positions where their voices are informed, articulate, and convincing.

In an institution like the Roman Catholic Church, it is no minor event that in the 19,000 parishes in this country there are 20,000 paid non-ordained women (about 85 percent of the total) and men (15 percent) in parish ministry (Murnion 1992, 9). Lay Catholics hold key chancery positions, occupy leadership positions in (arch)diocesan offices, tribunals, and so on. Lay theologians direct religion, theology, and ministry programs across the nation. There are more lay people in graduate ministry education than those preparing for ordination. According to the Center for Applied Research for the Apostolate (CARA), there were about 2,900 men in the four years of theology leading to ordination (*National Catholic Reporter,* Feb. 11, 1994, p. 5). Recent research on graduate programs in ministry in Catholic colleges and universities indicates over six thousand students in forty-two of the member institutions (Topper et al., 1993, 1). There are some twelve additional institutions offering graduate ministry programs that are not included. There are also numerous academic masters programs in theology or religion, many of whose students are preparing for ministry in the church, and these are not counted. Nor did we have access to the numbers of Catholic students in these areas in non-Catholic institutions. Though this is not a scientific count, I would surmise that there are probably three times as many non-ordination track women and men in institutions of higher learning preparing for ministry and leadership in the church as there are seminarians.

More and more of the educational texts used in colleges and universities are written by lay theologians. It is not just a matter of arithmetic, that is, of greater numbers here or there or everywhere. It is a matter of *the power of a voice that interprets* who we are and what we are about.

Juridical perspectives on power are concerned with who holds what positions. Functional perspectives on power are concerned with who has what kind of concrete influence on how large a group, or how many parts of a group, and how deep and enduring is the hold of that influence on such groups. Designated leaders are often not the community members with the most power. Few careful observers of Catholic life in the United States, for example, would contest the incredible influence of religious women upon ecclesial sensibilities in the postconciliar church. They have done this without occupying designated positions of juridical ecclesial leadership.

Functionally, a great transfer of power is afoot. Different kinds of people are in power than used to be in power. It may be, however, that in the final analysis the transfer of power, as significant as that is, will not be remembered as having been as significant as the transformation of *how* power functions. The "how" of power counts as much as the "who" of power. But in the hidden revolution, it is the "who" that is transforming the "how"!

Many of us wonder with awe at how the mystery of church will appear on the yonder side of these developments in the deep story of the Christian People of God. We like to guess at what it might be like. I am suggesting for consideration and for extrapolation that a hidden revolution in Judaism that occurred in the mid-second century BCE holds instruction for us today. I would like to think of Judaism's hidden revolution as a metaphor for our Catholic experience in the final years of the second millennium.

That Word!

The word I have thus far avoided is "Pharisees." It is very difficult for Christians to hear "Pharisees" with positive emotion, so contaminated has been the Christian interpretation of this religious group. In *The Galilean Jewishness of Jesus,* I attempted to revise the traditional Christian interpretation of the Pharisees, convinced as I am that Jesus remains largely inexplicable without a positive evaluation of the Pharisees and their influence on his religious soul (Lee 1988, 96–118).

The Pharisees suddenly appeared in Jewish life a century and a half or so before Jesus. There is precious little exact knowledge about their origins and their early history. How and when and why they begin are obscure. When they appear for the first time in recorded history, they are a full blown, taken-for-granted movement within Judaism, with whose existence and character the reader is presumed to be familiar. It is clear that they are largely a lay movement of educated Jews who had a decisive impact on the evolution of Judaism in the spheres of religion and politics alike. More to the point, their influence was revolutionary. It renewed and reshaped Judaism through and through.

Horizons

The first commandment tells the Hebrews that they must not have strange gods before them. Having this commandment at the head of the decalogue is revealing. It is there at the beginning, and it is first for a reason. Hebrew history is a relentless encounter with other tribes and other nations. How, then, does this people maintain the relative purity of the Hebrew soul before YHWH, except by making traffic with other gods the foremost prohibition. Heading off cultural traffic is not an option. But religious fidelity in the flow of cultural traffic is no easy option.

The plot thickens during four and a half centuries of Greco-Roman traffic. In 331 Alexander the Great conquers the area of Palestine. After his death a short time later, the larger region of which Palestine is a part is divided between two of Alexander's generals, Ptolemaeus in Egypt and attendant regions, Seleucus in Syria and attendant regions.

Until about the beginning of the second century BCE, the Jewish people in Palestine are under the Egyptian Ptolemeus and his successors. The burden of taxation is not ruinous, and there is a relative autonomy. When the Seleucids to the northeast replace Egyptian control around 200 BCE, there is a sustained effort to hellenize the Jewish nation, and not without the complicity of Jews as well. Not satisfied with attempts at Greek inculturalization, the Seleucids attempt to establish worship of Greek gods in Jerusalem itself.

Revolt against this religious imposition is led by the Maccabees, who in a period of some thirty years establish a Jewish nation once again, the Hasmonean dynasty. By 142 BCE the Jewish nation has basically reconstituted its former borders and is trying to come to terms with the inevitability of some kinds of Greek influence.

Keeping one's religious soul intact is not as simple as living in religious abstraction from the religious instincts of the Hellenistic world, while rubbing elbows with the remainder of Hellenistic culture. People cannot live in packages like that. Bumping into the otherness of other cultures always calls some of our presuppositions—our cherished convictions about what is really real—into question and leaves us no choice but to reinterpret. That, then, is the profound challenge: not to keep one's religious soul intact by repeating only an ancient interpretation of faith, but to reinterpret so that the ancient faith lives in new incarnations with its integrity honored and the first commandment obeyed.

The Pharisees, whatever else they also might have done, played a very significant role in moving Jewish religious faith through this tedious territory by the creation of a process which, in its turn, fashioned a new Judaism. The parallels between that time of Jewish transformation and our own are partial, to be sure, but there are sufficient analogical bonds to make that older history a helpful metaphor for a newer history; at least, that is the story I am undertaking to tell. After discussing the Pharisees, I will venture to describe modern analogues to the ancient resistance to hellenization and the ways the church has fended off what it felt would be a cultural hijacking of its faith.

The Pharisees make a rather sudden appearance in Jewish history, already a group with power and influence when they show up on stage. Josephus, a first century CE Jewish historian, documents their presence during the leadership of John Hyrcanus (134–104 BCE). There is no concrete information about their origins. They have to have some history before their appearance with John Hyrcanus; therefore, I arbitrarily locate their origins somewhere in the 140s BCE. As we shall see shortly, Ellis Rivkin believes that they make an appearance before the time of John Hyrcanus, a position that would locate them in the 140s. Therefore, I choose 140 BCE as the symbolic node in a time of tortured and upending ferment.

There are three sources of information about the Pharisees: Josephus, a first century CE Jewish historian, the Christian Scriptures, and rabbinic materials written between 200 and 600 CE. These sources, each in its own way, are both problematic and revealing. But that is all the basic information there is. After that it is interpretation and method. Perhaps an initial glimpse into the Pharisees from an account in Josephus will set the mood.

Josephus on the Pharisees

The historian Josephus is a Galilean Jew from the generation right after Jesus. Josephus played on both sides of the table with Jews and Romans (finally, more with the Romans). He is highly approving of the Hasmonean leadership of Hyrcanus, who was a disciple of the Pharisees. Josephus reports that at a banquet Hyrcanus indicates his commitment to be a righteous man and notes his desire to please the Pharisees. In fact, he invites critique whenever it is necessary. The Pharisees decline criticism.

Because of intrigue on the part of a malevolent Pharisee named Eleazar, the details of which are not important, there is a rupture between Hyrcanus and the Pharisees. Hyrcanus transfers his loyalty to the rival group, the Sadducees. The Pharisees retain significant influence among the populace and provoke continuing unrest. Emerging after a struggle for power following the death of Hyrcanus, Alexander Jannaeus becomes the new king (103–76 BCE), and the agitation of the Pharisees continues.

In his final hours of life, Alexander confides to his wife, Alexandra, that much of his grief as king was caused by his shoddy treatment of the Pharisees. He advises her that when she becomes queen (reign 76–67 BCE), she should court the favor of the Pharisees, because of their influence over the people. This she does, and the Pharisees "became administrators of everything, to banish and recall whom they wished, to loose and to bind. In short, the advantages of royalty were theirs; the expenses and burdens were Alexandra's" (Saldarini 1988, 91). Anthony Saldarini concludes that Alexandra gave the Pharisees whatever they asked, including some direct power in the daily affairs of the nation (1988, 94).

The presence of the Pharisees in the Gospels (with all of the critical nuancing that those texts require) makes clear their continuing importance in the time of Jesus and in the early years of Christian life. They were influential religiously and politically.

I propose to start a discussion of the Pharisees by tracking with three of the better-known attempts to interpret them. One of the scholars, Anthony Saldarini, is Christian; and two of the scholars, Jacob Neusner and Ellis

Rivkin, are Jewish. I will then propose why I think the Pharisaic movement provides some insight into current developments in the Catholic Church.

Saldarini: The Pharisees as Retainers

In *Pharisees, Scribes and Sadducees,* Anthony Saldarini pursues one of the more fruitful contemporary methods of understanding ancient cultures—the use of sociological models (1988, 11, 14, 287). He is careful not to impose categories on another age that reflect only a more recent experience. In his deliberately functional approach, he stresses the social and political activities of the Pharisees and pays far less attention to their thought and beliefs than do Neusner and Rivkin.

The general context for the Mediterranean world is that of an agrarian society. Most people belong to a peasant class of farmers, and the remaining 5 to 7 percent are part of or closely connected with the governing class. Saldarini interprets the Pharisees as retainers in this social system:

> The governing class maintained its position with the assistance of what Lenski calls retainers, whose roles in society were military, governing, administrative, judicial and priestly. These retainers were mostly townspeople who served the needs of the governing class as soldiers, educators, religious functionaries, entertainers and skilled artisans; it is here we will find the Pharisees and scribes. The governing class and its retainers seldom exceed 5–7% of the population. In modern society the Retainers' roles are fulfilled by the middle class, but in antiquity they were not a middle class because they lacked any independent power. (1988, 37–38)

Following Bryan Wilson's typology of seven different kinds of sects, Saldarini judges that the Pharisees best fit the category of the *reformist* who "seeks gradual, divinely revealed alterations in society" (1988, 72). This fits the general picture that Josephus gives. They are a social movement with a power base, and it is their expertise in Jewish law and observance that grounds their power.

Saldarini rejects a common reading of the Pharisees as a sect of learned lay people who succeed in replacing traditional leadership (1988, 284). He is indeed correct that the Pharisees *did not replace* the traditional leadership structure. They did, however, become a new voice that created a dialectic with traditional leadership to which their knowledge was important. In so doing, they moved into leadership, not in place of, but along with. The conflicts between the Pharisees and the Sadducees symbolize the dialectic between the priestly tradition that defends the written Torah (Sadducees) and the creation of a second trajectory, an oral tradition, which carries equal weight. Saldarini acknowledges the relation of the Pharisees' learning to their power: "any literate and learned people who knew and interpreted the social and religious traditions of the culture were also looked to as leaders" (1988, 52). While Josephus has indeed an imperial bias, Saldarini accepts some of the broader strokes with which Josephus depicts the Pharisees, that is, that they interpret the laws more accurately than others, and that they are an intellectual force because of how they are able to interpret (1988, 91, 87).

Saldarini has been clear about his methodological commitments (the interpretive use of sociological paradigms), their scope and their limitations. The use of this approach provides some groundbreaking insight into this movement in Jewish life. There are, however, some blank spaces. He indicates that while the category of "retainer" is a helpful typology, the unanswered question is: Exactly who retains them? When Hyrcanus distances himself from the Pharisees, what keeps them operative? There seems to be no information on this, especially in regard to Galilee (1988, 294–95).

Saldarini also indicates that his methodological commitment does not concern itself with the thought of the Pharisees. He does not concern himself in any sustained way with the Pharisees as interpreters who create a new oral tradition. But he indicates clearly the context for that development: "the social, political and economic situation of Palestinian Jews underwent a number of upheavals in the Greco-Roman period which demanded adaptation of Jewish customs and a reinterpretation of Jewish identity fashioned by a Biblical tradition" (1988, 281–82).

Neusner: The Pharisees in Politics and Religion

The written materials concerning the Pharisees are such partial and often biased records that Jacob Neusner says "practical skepticism" is about the only adequate attitude toward historical knowledge of their origins and activities (1973, xx). He, like other interpreters, works his way through the texts and interpretations. Methodology makes all the difference in the historical judgments at which one arrives. Neusner has a central concern for the texts themselves and the trustworthy information that they might yield. There are abundant materials in the rabbinic literature concerning the Pharisees, but they are written centuries after the fact. Neusner's meticulous textual criticism is especially accessible in his three-volume study of the Pharisees (1971). In much of what follows I will be following the more popularized presentation in his book *From Politics to Piety* (1973).

The Pharisees are a manifest political presence already in their early history, as we saw above, during the time of Hyrcanus and following. Around the time of Herod's rule and the lives of Hillel and Shammai (the generation that immediately preceded the life of Jesus), the Pharisees' religious presence is more keenly felt. To whatever extent the rabbis are successors of the Pharisees after the destruction of the Temple in 70 CE, their influence is both political and religious. Having said that, any scholar of that period will warn against using a contemporary distinction between secular and religious realms. The Pentateuch was at once both civil and religious law for the Jews, but they also had to contend with Greek and Roman political structures.

The social situation for the emergence of the Pharisees is an interlude of Jewish nationhood, barely free of foreign domination, but preoccupied with questions of power in Jewish religious life. The Pharisees are one of a number of sects making power claims.

Egyptian and Seleucid domination are on the back side of this history, previous to 142 BCE. Roman domination will occur on the new side of this history, beginning with 63 BCE. Neusner says that one of the accomplishments of the Pharisees is their ability to compromise with foreign power as long as "Torah was the binding law on the Jews. . . . In effect they were saying, 'We shall rule the country in collaboration with whatever foreign power is willing to make possible our dominion over the life of Israel'" (1973, 50). Jesus, in fact, responds in this spirit when he says it is permissible to give Caesar what is Caesar's so long at God gets what is God's.

While there are priests among the Pharisees, as a group they are not members of the priestly class—they were primarily a lay movement. In fact, they are in lively contrast with the Sadducees, whose fidelity to the Temple and Temple priesthood is their defining characteristic. The basis of Pharisaic power claims is knowledge of the Torah. The Sadducees defend the Torah too. The Pharisees, however, claim minute knowledge of an oral Torah as well as the written Torah, while the Sadducees acknowledge only the written text. It would be difficult to overestimate the impact of the oral Torah upon the future of Judaism. As soon as there is normative truth outside of the Scriptures, the way is open, as Neusner indicates, "to the accommodation of new ideas and values within the structure of inherited symbols—holy words, holy deeds, holy doctrine. The 'oral Torah' opened the Judaic tradition to the future" (1973, 54).

The Pharisees are not theologians in the Western sense. They do not intend to spin out a rational system, but they are concerned to reflect on life from the perspective of the written and oral tradition, to organize their reflection around major themes, and to develop guidance for daily living.

They are only quasi theologians, or, perhaps, theologians in a different and far more practical mode.

Today we recognize more consciously that every theologian theologizes from a social situation and that the social situation tinctures the product in method and in content. The social situation for the production of the written Torah is the return from exile in the sixth century BCE. After a century in captivity and a return to a Sion without a Temple, the need and desire for stability and a secure identity are very substantial. Under priestly direction the Temple is rebuilt and the central traditions are collected and redacted into the Pentateuch. One important aspect, therefore, of these great written traditions is that they have a rather priestly origination and are responsive, obviously, to priestly concerns, for that is the social location of their interpreting activity.

The lay status of the Pharisees is part of the social situation that creates their social agenda, or perhaps better, their socioreligious agenda. From their "seeing place," they see the holiness of home and of daily life. "One must eat secular food (ordinary everyday meals) in a state of ritual purity, as if one were a temple priest. . . . The table of every Jew in his home was seen as being like the table of the Lord in the Jerusalem Temple" (Neusner 1973, 82–83). Granted that ritual too easily loses most or some of its double moorings in the sacred and the secular through thoughtless daily repetition, it is yet ritual's ability to sacralize life and intensify the meaning of lived experience that makes it so important in the first place. In his analysis of religion as a cultural system, Clifford Geertz notes that the power of religion in culture comes from religion's ability to locate everyday actions upon a horizon of ultimate meaning (1973, 122). If rituals that infer the holiness of the Temple are located in one's home as well, the holiness of daily life is inferred. I would venture that the sacralization of marriage, family, and home, which the Pharisees help instigate, is no small part of the valued role they played in Jewish life. The lay social location of the Pharisees cannot but have facilitated the social construction of a holy laity in which they engaged.

Though larger discussion is reserved for later, I would at least note here that the emergence of a large body of educated, articulate lay people in the United States church is part of the reason for such an outpouring of books and centers for lay spirituality. Vatican II reminded us that all Christians are called to perfection. It is not fair to the Christian to call canonical religious life "the life of perfection," as we did for so very long. The implication has been that other vocational choices are a lower calling. The recognition that marriage is a charism of perfection no less than celibacy is a recognition or a "knowing" that married people know best, and it is from the social location of married experience that this mode of union with God is being celebrated in many ways for the first time. Canonized married saints are few and far between compared to the martyrs, priests, religious, and virgins.

The Pharisees did not co-opt the Temple, but they provided another important center of religious interpretation that constituted a dialectic between the priestly and the lay experience. In one of the articles in a two-volume study of Jewish people in the first century, M. Stern observes that "the teaching of the Torah and the direction of the spiritual life of the people ceased to be the prerogative of the priest and became the province of men who did not belong exclusively to the priestly class" (Safrai and Stern 1976, 620). That is one of the parallels between Judaism in the second century BCE and Catholicism in the United States church edging into the twenty-first century CE: lay interpretation of Catholic Christian identity has entered into a strong dialectic with hierarchical interpretation.

The notion of a truth outside of Scripture is one of the momentous achievements of the Pharisees, for it is that, as Neusner said, that opened the tradition to new ways of being Jewish in a changing world. While the word "interpretation" could not have been part of their vocabulary, the Pharisees were, as I spelled out in *The Galilean Jewishness of Jesus,* the grand interpreters (1988, 112–18).

The matter of table fellowship and fellowship meals, *havurot,* needs attention. The Pharisees are an identifiable body. Neusner says it is an avocation and not a vocation, that is, not a full-time job but a role played in Jewish life in addition to one's regular occupation (1973, 8). The bonding between them is noted by Josephus: The Pharisees are affectionate to each other" (*Jewish War* 2.166). Neusner understands that the table fellowship among the Pharisees was given a large impetus under the Pharisee Hillel, during the early part of the first century CE (1973, 14). While the abundance of rabbinic materials about the Houses of Hillel and Shammai are profoundly shaped by later history, one can at least read *some* historical memory in a tradition that so affirms the reality of table fellowship, for of the 341 references to legal positions of these two Houses, two-thirds concern table fellowship (Neusner 1973, 86). The fact that Jesus was invited to table by Pharisees is an indication of some basic comfort level between them over issues of politics and religion. But the nature of such table fellowship accounts as well for the chagrin of Pharisees that Jesus also ate with the unseemly.

No phenomenon as loaded as that of Pharisaic origins suddenly appears without precedent. A continuing transformation of the Law of religious life is endemic to Jewish life. The covenant itself undergoes repeated transformation—from Noah's covenant rainbow, to that with Abraham [and Sarah], then with David, and the relocation of covenant from stone tablets to heart in Jeremiah. When the Pharisees, therefore, become far more articulate about their interpretive development of an oral Torah, they are making explicit what has long been implicit: the openness of tradition to creative transformation. A glance at a specific instance of the interpretive tradition will help.

No sooner is the written Torah redacted under the direction of Ezra the priest than interpretation is a fact of life:

> In the view of all the people—since he stood higher than them all—Ezra opened the book. . . . Ezra read from the book of the Law of God, translating and giving the sense so that the reading was understood. (Ezra 8:5–8, passim)

As anyone familiar with interpretation theory realizes, every translation is itself an interpretation, because language systems are never interchangeable. The need to interpret is not new, therefore, for Ezra does that. But Ezra is a priest, and during the period from Ezra to the Pharisees, stewardship for Torah was a priestly duty. The Pharisees do not initiate interpretation; they initiate a new social location for it (i.e., from the viewpoint of lay learning) and restructure Judaism so that it now must entertain an internal dialectic between priestly and lay interpretation. We easily recognize this hermeneutical dialectic between the Pharisees and the Sadducees in our Christian Scriptures.

The title of Neusner's book, *From Politics to Piety,* underscores the multifarious power presences of this group. When they first appear they are more visible in the politics of the nation, but not without reference to their expertise in interpreting the twofold Law. By the time of Jesus, their power is more manifest in the religious sphere, but not without their moderating influence on the Jewish relationship with the Romans. If the rabbis of Jabneh (70 CE and later) and Usha (135 CE and later) are not simply the successors of the Pharisees, there certainly are strong continuities. In both cases the rabbis are trusted by the Romans to guide Jewish life, and they initiate the rabbinic genius of Mishnah and Talmud. Our contemporary distinction between secular and religious (e.g., all the issues around the separation of church and state) is no guide to the ancient Jewish distinction between politics and piety, because for the ancient Jewish nation politics and piety both had their source in the same one book. Politics and piety, therefore, are matters of emphasis more than clear distinction.

Rivkin: The Pharisees and a Hidden Revolution

Ellis Rivkin's historical research into the origins of the Pharisees first suggested to me parallels between that period and the present and future of the Catholic Church in the United States. He called his book *The Hidden Revolution,* and I have used that for a subtitle of this book in tracking developments in the United States Catholic Church. I believe, of course, that the Catholic story is larger than the United States Catholic story. As Jung observed, if you tell anyone's story at a deep enough level, it is Everyman's story. The United States Catholic story is inserted into a welter of motion in which the church-at-large is caught up. The motion is focused by the Second Vatican Council, but its causes were well at work long before, and these same causes have affected other religious traditions as well. According to the 1992–1993 report *Religion in America* "survey evidence indicates that the Church of the Future will be shaped from the 'bottom up' rather than the 'top down.'. . . One would have to conclude that if church leaders are not sensitive to the growing demands of the laity to have a role in leadership, organized religion could show further signs of slippage in the years ahead" (Gallup 1993, 4). It is my contention in this book that "the growing demands of laity to have a role in leadership" is not primarily about leadership positions, but about a defining voice, engaged in a dialectic with other defining voices, concerning Catholic Christian identity.

Because revolution is the theme of Rivkin's historical reconstruction of Pharisaic origins, the place to begin is with his description of revolution:

> Revolutions are occasions of heightened social interaction; of decisive decision making; of disintegrative and reintegrative processes; of the displacement of previously dominant forms of social organization; of the transfer of power from one class to another and from one type of leadership to another. Revolutions are the culmination of changes and developments that have been long in the making and which have gradually built up into situations breeding conflict and demanding decisive resolution. Revolutions mark the end of one dominant mode of social organization and the inauguration of some novel form of cohesiveness. A revolution, in essence, is that process by which one system of authority is replaced by another. (1978, 211)

It is my intention here to reflect the process by which Rivkin proposes his understanding of Pharisaic origins and then to indicate the social location of the movement and its intent. Rivkin asks, When is there clearly a presence of Pharisees, and when is there clearly a time when they are not yet on the scene, and then—the critical search into origins—are there any clues to what might have occurred during this middle time between their absence and their first appearance?

We know from the Jewish historian Josephus that the Pharisees are a strong, active presence during the reign of John Hyrcanus (134–104 BCE). At the other end, it is clear from Ben Sirach that the priests are the only interpreters and that there is no indication of any other Torah than the written Torah.

The book of Sirach was translated by Ben Sirach's grandson in the thirty-eighth year of the reign of King Euergetes (170–117 BCE), therefore around 132 BCE. Ben Sirach would have lived some sixty years earlier. Therefore, the time of composition is somewhere between 190–180 BCE, at which time there were no Pharisees.

Ben Sirach's esteem for the priesthood is evident in the way he eulogizes Simon the High Priest, who died shortly after 200 BCE: "the leader of his brethren and the pride of his people." For Ben Sirach, although Moses is of blessed memory and is equal in glory to the holy ones, it is the priest Aaron who receives the covenant:

> Yahweh exalted Aaron, the brother of Moses, a holy man like him, of the tribe of Levi. He made an everlasting covenant with him, and gave him the priesthood of the people. He blessed him with splendid vestments and put a glorious robe upon him. (Sir 45:5b–7)

The authority to instruct in the Torah is given to Aaron (Sir 45:15) and the Aaronide priesthood after him (Sir 45:20). Control over Law belongs to the Aaronide priests, and to them alone. Nor is there is any hint of a twofold Law.

In Ben Sirach there is multiple mention of scribes, the *soferim*. They are learned in the Law. Because they are among the wealthier, they have leisure for study. But Rivkin notes that "no matter how the verses are twisted, the *Sofer* is not a legislator; he does not arrogate to himself authority over the Law; he does not challenge the Aaronide supremacy" (1978, 200).

It is interesting that this word *sofer* is indeed used later for the Pharisees as well. But in Ben Sirach there is no sign of learned interpreters of the Law who know an oral Torah. Nor do the Sirach *soferim* have any claim that diminishes the authority of the priests.

The logic, then, is that there are no Pharisees before 180 BCE, and there are Pharisees in the reign of Hyrcanus; therefore, we must look to that interim period for the origins. For Rivkin the question is: Are there any activities or events that disclose anything like a second kind of Law? He concludes from history presented in 1 Maccabees that there is indeed evidence for Phariseelike religious and political behaviors.

In 197 BCE the Seleucids wrest control of the Jewish nation away from the Egyptians and embark upon a project of forced hellenization, not without collaboration from Jewish hellenizers. The hellenization includes efforts at urbanization. Rivkin notes that

> the on-going process of urbanization had so altered the structure of experience of merchant, shopkeeper, artisan and peasant alike that the Pentateuch no longer resonated with their deepest needs and their innermost yearnings. For the Pentateuch had been designed for a relatively simple agricultural-priestly society and not a complex urban-agricultural society embedded within a world of poleis. . . . When, therefore, a crisis of leadership occurred with first Jason and then Menelaus violating the Law by buying the High Priestly office from Antiochus IV, the people were ripe, not merely for rebellion, but for revolution. (1978, 206–7)

In 1 Maccabees 45 we learn that there is a Great Assembly of priests, elders of the country, rulers of the nation, and the [lay] people. This assembly makes Simon Maccabee both leader and high priest because of his valor in fighting against the hellenizing Seleucids. All the people agree with this decision and give Simon the authority to act.

There is a Great Assembly for which there is no provision in the Pentateuch. The Pentateuch requires that the high priest always be from the line of Aaron, Phinehas, and Zadok, but this assembly approves a man for the high priesthood who is not a Zadokite because he appears to be the person best suited for both civil and religious leadership. Rivkin takes this as clear evidence that a revolution has occurred in the power structure: there is a recognized body with authority that is not provided for in the Pentateuch, and there is a decision that sanctions behaviors contrary to the pentateuchal directives concerning the high priesthood. Clearly some kind of revolution has occurred, albeit that its dynamics are well hidden from historical eyes. We note the end of one form of social organization and see the start of another. Power is redistributed and exists in a new form in the new place:

> the Pharisees carried through one of the most stunning revolutions in the history of humankind—a revolution they never acknowledged and of which they left no record other than their transmutation of Judaism. (Rivkin 1978, 15)

Reprise on the Pharisees

The origins of the Pharisees are obscure, and their character is complex and shifts emphasis in different eras. I have tried to present some of the insights from three different interpreters. All three share the same data, that is, the information provided by the Scriptures, by Josephus, and by the later rabbinic materials. Anthony Saldarini makes use of the social sciences and gathers much insight from the sociological types of "sect" and "retainer." Jacob Neusner focuses on textual criticism and is especially attentive to the later rabbinic materials that reliably reflect late second-Temple experience. Finally, we looked at a more speculative model in which Ellis Rivkin engages in some historical reconstruction based on hints from the period between which there is clearly no oral Torah and the period when the historical record is clear that the Pharisees are on the scene.

I am drawing some summary points together that reflect my generalizations. I am interested in the ways that the transformation of Jewish religious life under the influence of the Pharisees has parallels with the contemporary experience of the Catholic Church in the United States. That interest accounts for both what I select and what I neglect in the eight points that follow.

1. The appearance of the Pharisees is a watershed in Jewish history. They are produced by a tradition and they produce a tradition. In the religious organization of the Jewish people there is a profound transformation, at the center of which is an oral Torah. It is a matter of the authorship of ongoing religious and political life. And "author" and "authority" are finally the same thing in this context. There is a transfer of power and a transformation of the power model.

2. The power base is learning. As Saldarini has indicated, the economy of agricultural cultures like those in Palestine does not have a true middle class. The Pharisees appear to be well connected with the upper class, often as retainers in that system. And they are affluent enough to have the leisure for study. They excel in their knowledge of the oral Torah.

3. The Oral Torah provides for a truth and an authority outside of the Scriptures. To this Judaism owes the openness of the tradition to ongoing critical self-transformation through interpretation.

4. The Pharisees are fundamentally a lay movement, even though there are priestly members among them.

5. Because lay experience is the social location of their interpretation, they recognize the sacredness of daily life and family, and they ritualize the sacredness of home with ritual appropriated from the Temple.

6. The Pharisees break the hold of clerical interpretation but they do not replace it. They introduce a healthy power dialectic between lay and clerical interpretation. The debates between the Pharisees and Sadducees illustrate

this dialectic. When the Temple is destroyed and the Sadducees no longer exist, the notion of a dialectic continues to shape rabbinic tradition, where interpretations vie with interpretations in a tradition-opening dynamic.

7. All groups need boundary experiences to maintain their identity. Table fellowship is such an inclusion ritual for the Pharisees. They know who they are together through their *havurot*. This practice does not dominate the whole of Pharisaic history, but it is operative in the time of Jesus and is a backdrop for some of the eucharistic instincts operative in Christian origins.

8. The Pharisees are dealing with issues that are about four and a half centuries old (since the return from captivity in Babylon): how to be in a culture that in many ways appears at least foreign and often hostile to one's essential religious passions. The issue is to live effectively and interactively in that culture and not lose one's religious soul.

There are many developments in the contemporary Catholic Church that resonate with developments in Judaism around the rather sudden appearance of a highly educated, articulate laity who are engaged in the social construction of Catholic reality. This occurs in a religious world aggravated by four and a half centuries of fundamentally ineffective interaction with culture. The Second Vatican Council stands alone among the church's councils, called not to fight error but to come to terms with today: *aggiornamento,* Pope John XXIII called it.

Christians and Pharisees

In the Catholic world generally, it is a shock to suggest that the Pharisees are a helpful metaphor for our shared life today, because we have been reared believing that "Pharisee" names the opposite of what any sane Christian would ever choose to be. The *Webster's New Collegiate Dictionary* says that "pharisaical" means "marked by hypocritical censorial self-righteousness." It is certainly true, as Walter Benjamin says, that "every work of civilization is at the same time a work of barbarism" (cited in Tracy 1987, 69). The Pharisees too, then, certainly live from a narrative that is not only creative but also destructive. The Christian tradition has dwelled on the negative aspects and rarely alluded to the creative transformation put in place by pharisaic imagination. We Christians have less often been clear about the destructive interpretations that have been played out in our own history. The holocaust is surely the most visible of those tragedies. It is time to let the pharisaic movement offer us a metaphor for self-understanding today.

For many of the reasons presented above, Jewish experience generally understands the Pharisees to be one of the finest flowerings of Judaism, for out of the Pharisees the rabbinic tradition flowed. There is little in Jesus' teaching that is in serious conflict with the deeper instinct of the Pharisees. This is difficult to decipher, however, since the Christian Scriptures are ambiguous. If you read Luke with no other Gospel in mind, you have a very different sense of the Pharisees than when reading Matthew as though that were the sole source of information about the Pharisees.

The ambiguity shows up in these ways. On the one hand, the Pharisees often call Jesus teacher/master. In Acts, Luke reports that there are Pharisees among the post-Easter disciples. There are multiple instances of Jesus appearing at table with the Pharisees, and given the tightness of their *havurot,* it is not likely that Jesus would be there without their overall comfort with his teaching. Jesus is often invited to read Scripture in the synagogue and then teach about the text. Given the religious influence of the Pharisees on Jewish life, it is not likely that Jesus was at vicious odds with the Pharisees (he certainly was not aligned with the Sadducees, who, with the Pharisees, were the major influences on Palestinian Judaism).

There is without doubt a tensive relation between Jesus and the Pharisees on some issues—concerning Sabbath observances, for instance, or over Jesus' equal willingness to be at table with those who are culturally undesirable. But these are not such as to cause a rupture within Judaism. Jesus' differences with the Sadducees are, in fact, far more pronounced.

There are numerous sects in Judaism in Jesus' time, the best known being the Sadducees, Pharisees, Essenes, and Zealots. After the destruction of the Temple in 70 CE the Sadducees no longer have the Temple for their sacred place in Jewish life. Those who would take the Romans by violence are eliminated. And the Essenes are destroyed. Pharisees survive in their transmutated development as the rabbis of rabbinic Judaism.

They are thus "mainstream" Judaism and not just the principal antagonist for Christians; they are virtually the only one. The polemics between Pharisees and Christians are embittering during those three decades when the Gospels are being redacted. Much New Testament scholarship concludes that the polemics of this later period are retrojected into many of the Gospel narratives. As a result, Christians have never known and appreciated the religious and cultural genius of the Pharisees.

I want to conclude this chapter restating my intention to see the emergence of the Pharisees in the second century BCE as a metaphor for developments in the Catholic Church in the United States. If a metaphor works, it is because one thing is truly like another thing. But they are not identical.

Therefore, the thing that is like another is also *not* like another. I am concerned with the *is like,* but we shall retain our awareness of the *not like* as well.

The major *like* is simple. The Pharisees introduced a lay hermeneutic into Judaism that was forceful enough to constitute a dialectic with the Temple hermeneutic. The dialectic became constitutive of Jewish religious culture. The power base for the Pharisees was in their learning, in their command of the texts of their tradition as they interpreted, from the social location of lay experience, the reality of Jewish identity. They added oral text to written text and opened the tradition to a normative process of interpreting, interpreting the interpretation, interpreting the interpretation of the interpretation, and so on.

It remains to be seen whether Catholic Christianity will open itself to the inclusion of dialogic community in its essential structure, the major justification of which is pneumatological: the Spirit of God is a gift to the entire community and works in every part of it equally.

II

THE PILE UP
OF REVOLUTIONS

Deep Story: Continuities and Discontinuities

Aggiornamento was the way Pope John XXIII described the most crucial homework the church needed to do. This is the Italian word for "updating," and never before in the history of the church and its councils was a worldwide council called for precisely that purpose. In fact, the needed updating was and still is massive. In this chapter we will look at the pile up of revolutions that makes the updating so urgent. Each revolution is a very large paradigm shift in the structures of Western culture. The differences in culture before and after each of these piled-up revolutions are easy enough to justify a comparison of the ancient Jewish struggles with the otherness of the cultures all about them and to remember the specific innovations of the Pharisees in this regard.

When there is no choice but to intermingle with other cultures, the challenge is to learn what there is to learn while keeping one's soul intact, one's deep story integral. We struggle to determine what continuities must be guaranteed and what discontinuities are allowable.

Realistically, we must acknowledge from the start that any real conversation with otherness puts us at risk because we cannot control ahead of time where we shall be on the other side of the conversation. We cannot know ahead of time what our commitments to fidelity shall ask of us once we have put ourselves at risk through genuine conversation. And there is no true conversation without putting oneself at risk. No small part of Pharisaic genius was learning to do this. It is not as though one's soul remains untouched in the process. That is too facile, because one cannot genuinely encounter otherness and have one's own interpretive world utterly unaffected. The real challenge is to learn to be faithful even within new interpretive frameworks.

After a long history of cultural conversation with Egyptians, Assyrians, Sumerians, and so on, the most taxing situation for the ancient Hebrews is the Babylonian Captivity when the dislocation lasts a century. Upon their return, and under priestly leadership, the written Torah is produced, so that remembered history, especially a recalled and recreated covenant, can be on everyone's lips and in everyone's heart. In times of experienced threat, we try to get the essentials of our story clear once and for all. In a community's new and early life there is normally a clarity and an attendant freedom. But time moves on and the freedom of one time becomes the restraint of another.

The problem with any written text is that you cannot canonize it unless you canonize the worldview in which it was incubated, and that would be intellectual suicide, for time moves and worldviews change.

The Pharisees introduce an oral Torah and with it a principle that opens the deep story and the soul of a people to an ongoing process of self-reinterpretation. The Pharisaic intervention in Jewish religious history is in the wake of about four and a half centuries of fending off the threat of the otherness of other cultures. This was the Jewish experience from the return to Jerusalem after the Babylon Captivity to the latter part of the second century BCE.

For Christians in the last four and a half centuries, the foreign culturalizers are not hellenizing nations (the task of Pharisees) but large, epochal movements in Western culture that were ecclesiastically perceived as dangerously other, hostile, that is, to dominant ecclesial culture. I would like to name three of these "foreign" influences, identify the threat their "foreignness" poses, describe some institutional Catholic responses, and address the massive disorientation that these accumulating, piled-up revolutions are spawning as they hit all at once in our contemporary institutional Catholic experience. It will be work of the following chapters to indicate the ecclesial importance of the new culture of learned laywomen and laymen in creating a more profoundly mutual conversation with culture and reopening an ancient tradition to creative transformation.

I want to take note of these revolutions in Western culture. The first is the scientific revolution, which brought about a new method for acquiring knowledge and new knowledge content about the world that scientific method made accessible. The second revolution is the shift from feudalism to modern governance models that are participative. The French Revolution is the symbol *par excellence*. The third revolution is the rise of historical consciousness and the rise in our sense of historical responsibility. These are somewhat different phenomena, but what they have in common is taking history very seriously. The Modernist controversy at the end of the last century and the beginning of the present one is a sustained resistance toward historicized interpretation. Historical consciousness recognizes the historical conditioning of all experience, all understandings of experience, and all articulations of our understandings of experience. Historical consciousness was coming into its own in the latter half of the nineteenth century and was concomitant with the church's experience of being beleaguered by the loss of great secular resources and power and the reduction of church territory to the quite small Vatican state. Once again finding itself in a defensive mode, the church reacted in what we know today as the Modernist controversy.

The other half of the historicizing revolution is a shift in Western anthropology. In the Greek tradition, the splendor of human reality was found in human rationality. We are made for the contemplation of truth, beauty, and goodness, and we find our deepest fulfillment in that contemplation (beatific vision). Our tradition has centered more upon truth, but not to the exclusion of the others. For sometime now, and especially in recent generations, we have begun to think of the splendor of human reality as the responsibility we bear as shapers of history, as makers of the worlds we inhabit.

The so-called secular world has absorbed the portentous impact of these revolutionary influences, sometimes critically and sometimes uncritically. The ecclesial hermeneutic has resisted these influences, sometimes critically and sometimes uncritically. One way of noting the divide between secular and religious culture, beginning with the scientific revolution in the early sixteenth century, is to recall names of people who have been major influences in Western culture. On any list of the "famous" from the time of Constantine until the sixteenth century, the majority of names will be church-related people, few of them women: Ambrose, Augustine, Benedict, Boethius, Cassiodorus, even Charlemagne as a church reformer, Gregory the Great, Bonaventure, Thomas Aquinas, Duns Scotus, Abelard and Heloise, Francis and Clare, Dominic, Catherine of Siena, and so on. In the monastic libraries the classical texts of Western culture were preserved. The university itself is a flowering of the church's love of learning in the Middle Ages.

But how quickly things change. From the sixteenth century on, the new list of the "famous" is dominated by men and women (mostly men, and that too will change) who are not religious figures: Descartes, Einstein, Freud, Galileo, Hegel, Jung, Marx, Pasteur, and so on. The great centers of learning in the United States are secular universities, not Catholic colleges and universities, albeit many Catholic institutions of higher learning are reputable. In a word, the world's "symbol-making factory" changed its address. It is not a church address anymore.

There is tragedy in the intensifying polemic between academia and ecclesia in this country because it reflects renewed ecclesial discomfort with secular learning and its claims and with speculative, theological dialogue with this learning. It is not as though there are no problems in the institutional culture of the university, for there are. Whether they are any more serious than institutional problems in ecclesial culture is an open question. The recent Roman document *Ex Corde Ecclesiae* attempts to intensify institutional church influence over Catholic colleges and universities. What is right about the document is its assertion of the importance of the university to Catholic life. What is right about the document is also its awareness that the church has truth it must affirm. What is missing is a sense of the importance of mutually critical dialogue between church and secular learning. Secular learning also has truth claims that it has a right to affirm. History makes clear that secular truth claims and ecclesial truth claims have sometimes modified each other's interpretations.

Once upon a time Catholic colleges and universities maintained their Catholic identity primarily through the large numbers of priests, brothers, and sisters who taught all the subjects. Today most subjects, religion and theology included, are taught by lay scholars. The tension between academia and ecclesia is in part the dialectic between a lay hermeneutic and a clerical hermeneutic. That may not be all of it, but it is a lot of it.

Many of us in universities hear our Catholic colleagues call themselves, with tongue in cheek, "Catholic *emeritus*," or "a recovering Catholic." In this morning's paper here in New Orleans there was an article on writers who create aphorisms that catch on. The article quotes the actress Susan Sarandon as saying, "If you want to become a lapsed Catholic, go to a Catholic university!" I find this kind of language painful to hear, but I recognize that it names the equally painful rift between church learning and secular learning. Catholic colleges and universities are, in fact, places where the pile up of revolutions in the ecclesial courtyard is often felt very deeply by lay Catholic scholars, and young students feel the tensions through their teachers.

Some of my colleagues are people who have read *Ex Corde Ecclesiae* because, underneath it all, they do care deeply. They are chagrined at the church's claims to be a teacher of truth when those claims are not qualified in two important ways. First, good teachers must also be good learners, willing to be in open dialogue, and ready to be taught by other teachers. The United States episcopal conference has sometimes done this very well, but Rome has been uneasy with bishops who, as teachers, openly learn from the ones whom they also teach.

The second area of discomfort in respect to church claims to truth in *Ex Corde Ecclesiae* is the fact that the church has sometimes held very firm positions that were later altered. Three examples of the latter are important to recall, given the mood in the church today.

The first can be noted simply, because it is familiar. Galileo was condemned by the church for positions that the world generally accepts today. John Paul II has publicly acknowledged the church's serious mistake.

The second is the less-known case of Fr. Henry Poels, a professor at Catholic University, dismissed from his position by the board of trustees (Fogarty 1986). Wary of new biblical studies, Rome established the Pontifical Biblical Commission in 1903. In 1906 the commission issued a position statement that Moses was substantially the author of the first five books of Scripture, the Pentateuch, a position that new historical-critical scholarship was seriously challenging. There is not a serious Catholic biblical scholar today who would hold for Mosaic authorship of the Pentateuch.

Poels was actually a consultor to the Pontifical Biblical Commission and indicated personally to Pope Pius X his difficulty with the commission's position on the authorship of the Pentateuch. On his own initiative, he indicated that he would not teach this position in his classes and not even teach in that area of biblical studies. Poels met in Rome with Cardinal Merry del Val, who insisted that he swear "a solemn affirmation of my personal belief—in conscience—that Moses was the author of the Pentateuch" (Fogarty 1986, 182). He could not, of course, swear to this. In 1910 the board of trustees of Catholic University terminated Poels's relationship with that institution.

Today there is a basic consensus in biblical scholarship that the Pentateuch was redacted in the period after the return from the Babylonian Captivity, some thousand years after Moses. A number of strands of oral tradition are redacted by an editor (or several editors) into these texts, so basic to solidifying Jewish identity in a period much in need of identify formation and intensification following the disorientation of the Babylonian Exile. It is healthy to remember at this time how secure a judgment there was at very high levels regarding a position that has been reversed by historical scholarship a few generations later. There have been victims of ecclesial overcertainty about where truth lies.

The third example concerns abortion. The church has always had a clear position against abortion. Pope John Paul II has been increasingly insistent about Catholic opposition to what he rightly calls the "culture of death"—and the culture of death is broader than the issue of abortion but counts abortion as one of its flagrant, daily expressions. If the Catholic position has always been clear, the rationale behind the position has not always been the same. I think it helpful and honest to confront this development.

The church position today is that a human person is present from the first moment of conception. The language of "child," "infant," and "baby" to describe a fetus reflects this understanding. I do not want to argue positions, for I believe deeply that being "prolife" is Catholic to the core. For 1,500 years the firm teaching of the church was that there was a time lapse between conception and the beginning of personhood (between "animation" and "hominization") (Donceel 1985, 81–83). The argument of Thomas Aquinas is standard. Matter cannot receive form until the matter is suitable to the form. You cannot carve a sculpture in water—wrong matter; but you can carve one in ice—possible matter for the form of a sculptured figure. The soul is the human form, and the bodily material must be able to support the activity of a human soul, which requires physiological development. That, in a broad stroke, is the argument for delayed hominization: it takes time before the matter can receive a human soul.

The *Catechism of the Council of Trent* (1662) holds that through miraculous intervention the human soul was joined to the matter from the first instant in the case of Jesus. "Nobody can doubt that this was something new and an admirable work of the Holy Spirit, since in the natural order nobody can be informed by a human soul except after the prescribed space of time" (*Catechismus Romanus ex decreto Concilii Tredentini,* Lovanii, 1662, 36, cited in Donceel, 82). In a decision regarding the baptism of an aborted fetus, the Holy Office declared in 1713 that a fetus can be baptized "if there is a reasonable foundation for admitting that the fetus is animated by a rational soul. If, however, there is no reasonable foundation, it may by no means be baptized" (*Collectanea de prop. fide 1,* Rome, 1907, #282, cited in Donceel, 82). More recently, Catholic philosopher Jacques Maritain held that human nature is *virtually* present in a fetus, though not formally, and that deliberate abortion is tantamount to murder. Jesuit theologian Albert Vermeersch insisted that the metaphysical distinction between the possible (potential or virtual) and the actual is a crucial distinction: *Homo quomodo occidatur antequam existat?* (How could a human person be killed before a human person exists?)

I am not a moral theologian and do not have any eagerness to take up the cause of whether there is "delayed hominization" or not. I want to point out that on a topic about which the church speaks with solid conviction today, the personhood of a fertilized ovum *ab initio,* its firm teaching for 1,500 years was other than its present position. Opposition to abortion did not change, but the underlying rationale has changed.

As Joseph Donceel points out in his article on the topic, the most important issue is that the Catholic church has always opposed abortion, even when "delayed hominization" was its firm teaching. On what grounds, then, does one oppose abortion, even if the fetus is not yet a human person? Some of the most important prolife reasons may be found in answers to that question. All of those reasons from the earlier logic of the prolife position would certainly bolster the authority of the ecclesial voice today because there are more reasons than one for the position. In *Evangelium Vitae,* John Paul II holds to the personhood of a fetus from conception on. But he also draws on a wider logic: "What is at stake is so important that, from the standpoint of moral obligation, the mere probability that a human person is involved would suffice to justify an absolutely clear prohibition. . . ."

All three of these issues—Galileo, Poels, and delayed hominization—make informed Catholics today cautious about the kind of power the church wants to exercise over the teaching of theology in Catholic colleges and universities. Given a record of mistakes as well as successes, more modest claims to truth certainty, and an acknowledgment that hierarchy and higher learning need to muddle through difficult issues together in the search for truth—these would make for a marvelous dialectical and dialogic relationship between ecclesia and academia. Driving a wedge between them, as some aspects of *Ex Corde Ecclesiae* are likely to do, does not serve the world well, or the church.

It is no surprise that the institutional church experiences some apprehension. The accumulated weight of so many piled-up revolutions calls for the kind of open conversation that puts participants at risk. No one can emerge from a true conversation unchanged. The change need not be an altered position; it may be the same one, held with better insight. It is a chastened ecclesia, or should be, and a chastened academia, or should be, that together must negotiate the pile up of revolutions.

I am also suggesting here, with the Pharisaic revolution as a metaphor, that lay learning is likely to be the prime agent of social transformation in the contemporary church, for reasons that his book hopes to lay out. Let us glance at a few of the piled-up revolutions.

The Scientific Revolution

When we consider what religion is for [hu]mankind, and what science is, it is no exaggeration to say that the future of history depends upon the decision of this generation as to the relations between them. (Whitehead 1967, 181)

There is a double edge to the scientific revolution. One edge is the method of arriving at new knowledge, and the other is the new knowledge it brings. The method seriously involves the turn to experience, which is the name of Donald Gelpi's recent book which traces this steady paradigm shift in our culture (1994).

It would have been turmoil enough for the church to confront this revolution in more peaceful times. But, in fact, the implications of the scientific revolution begin to unfold as the church is responding with fierce defensiveness to the Protestant Reformation. William Bausch correctly observes that "Trent's close mindedness to science was a reaction to the reformers who, it was felt, went awry in misguided speculation," and "this set a conservative tone for many centuries" (Bausch 1989, 273).

The record of problems the church has had with scientific knowledge is widely enough known that it does not require a lot of documentation. I recall the stir caused by Bruce Vawter's *Pathway through Genesis* nearly forty years ago because it did not rule out evolution as a plausible and probable way it was and is. Not very long after that I remember the *monitum* that was placed upon the writings of Pierre Teilhard de Chardin. Today his work would not, I think, raise many eyebrows at all. But Teilhard was still under the cloud of the Modernist controversy.

The profounder dimension of the scientific revolution is methodological: how do we acquire accurate knowledge of reality? The philosophical tradition inherited from the hellenized world places primary trust in the deliverances of our rational processes and is fundamentally deductive in character. The scientific method depends upon the deliverance of experience and experiment and is primarily inductive in character. Whitehead sees Francis Bacon as a pivotal figure:

> The explicit realisation of the antithesis between the deductive rationalism of the scholastics and the inductive observational methods of the moderns must chiefly be ascribed to Bacon; though, of course, it was implicit in Galileo and all the men of science of those times. But Bacon was one of the earliest of the whole group, and also had the most direct apprehension of the full extent of the intellectual revolution which was in progress. . . . Bacon remains as one of the great builders who constructed the mind of the modern world. (Whitehead 1967, 42–43)

The British empiricists represent a sustained philosophical attempt to come to grips with the impact of scientific method on a theory of knowledge. Kant saw their problems and sought correctives in his philosophy. Phenomenology, at the beginning of the century, proposed an alternative to the British empiricist and to Kant. It sought a new way of getting back to things themselves to understand what they tell about themselves. William James sought to rescue a narrow empiricism by saying that what we know is what we can cull from our experience of the world. For James, however, that "experience" is a much broader and deeper phenomenon than sense experience. An empiricism based on sense experience alone gets religious reflection no place. But a Jamesian empiricism stands a chance, as James himself said, of being perhaps the best friend that religion ever had, as he demonstrated in *The Varieties of Religious Experience.*

Virtually from Trent onward, the institutional church has been in far too defensive a mode to engage itself in a dialectic with this scientific revolution in our sense of how we know and how that influences our sense of what we know. Especially in moral theology, which is where the rubber meets the road for much of people's lives, a deductive approach to natural law has not had an open conversation with an inductive method. The pressure to consult lived experience as a teller of the human tale comes largely from lay experience where secular science has taken a firmer hold of sensibilities. That does not mean that everything about secular science is to be embraced, only that it must be a respected conversation partner in the dialectic.

So what is the issue in practical living? Laywomen and laymen in the United States church have basically not accepted the church's teaching on birth control, and religious and clergy are in fairly strong sympathy with their position. On the surface this response might be interpreted simply as disregard for church teaching and church authority. In my judgment, the issue is methodological: how does anyone interpret what it means to live one's sexuality in the context of marriage? If the "how" is rational, deductive, one has traditionally arrived at the official church position. If the "how" is observational and deductive, then one asks married people for their report of the meaning of their sexual experience. The point here is that different methods arrive at different conclusions.

Let it be said that issues on the inductive, observational side are less than perfectly clear. Induction is misused if it purports to arrive at general laws. Whitehead notes that induction discerns the general characteristics of future experience from the observed characteristics of past experience (1967, 44). Observations of recurring experience provide insight into the character of what is observed, and that data must be reckoned with. One cannot simply go from statistics to norms. Yet it remains one of the tasks of moral theology to gain deeper insight into the methodological connections between empirical data and norms.

The scientific revolution introduced new knowledge into Western culture and new empirical methodologies for the pursuit of understanding experience, toward both of which the church has frequently shown considerable resistance. In their 1989 study, *American Catholic Laity in a Changing World*, sociologists William D'Antonio et al., say their data indicate that "an increasing number of Catholics believe that they should make their own decisions in moral matters based on empirical information, even when the latter may challenge traditional values and beliefs" (1989, 5).

I am suggesting that the issue is experience-based, inductive avenues to moral norms in contrast with deductive, natural law avenues to moral norms—the two avenues run either side of the scientific revolution. Lay Catholics are not being lax on the issue and are not crassly disregarding the church. The disagreement is not first of all about moral conclusions, but about the method for arriving at conclusions. But different methods may indeed arrive at different conclusions.

The Political Revolution

Polis is the Greek word for "city." *Political* is an adjective describing whatever has to do with how people in a city—a social system—can best live together. Politics is about how things get done in a social system. The French Revolution is a symbol of a movement much larger than itself, a political movement that rearranged how people choose for power to function among those who live together in a social system, be it city, nation, or Western culture. The French Revolution marks the dramatic termination of a feudal model and a move toward more participative, democratic structures.

With the exceptions of a fairly brief but stunning experiment with democracy in Greece and a shorter, less-stunning experiment in Swiss history, the working arrangement was that most of the people in the world lived as subjects under a few people in the world—emperors or pharaohs, kings or queens, princesses or princes. The people were subjects of the over-lords. Because this was culturally presumed to be how things are, there was no question about whether to be subject to some such leader, only which leader. If things got bad enough, there might be an uprising, the result of which would be another, and one would hope, better leader. But the political power arrangement would not vary greatly.

In his book *Citizens: A Chronicle of the French Revolution*, Simon Schama says that "if one had to look for one indisputable story of transformation in the French Revolution, it would be the creation of the juridical entity of the citizen" (1989, 858). The revolution in the body politic of Western culture is the move from *subject to citizen*. The benchmark of citizenry is participation. A citizen participates in the choice of leaders, shares in the exercise of power at least by being represented, and ideally, at least, has access to the resources of a nation. The power role is not delegated by a leader to the people. Power belongs within citizenship. Even today in the central parts of Paris, the "text" of the French Revolution is visible from one end of the city to the other, engraved in stone on lintel after lintel after lintel: *Fraternité, Égalité, Liberté.* "We are all brothers [and sisters], we are co-equal, and we are free."

This is not a mere rearrangement of power. The move from subject to citizen is a paradigm shift in the fundamental interpretation of what it means to be a human being. But we need some qualifying considerations. The shift from subject to citizen did not begin with the French Revolution. It has not occurred solely within French culture; a catchphrase from the American Revolution, "taxation without representation," is of a piece with the spirit of the French Revolution. And, to be sure, the shift from subject to citizen is still as much hope as it is achievement.

Major shifts like this never make a clean swipe through any culture. The first impulse is to tack the new arrangement on to the old. When the French Revolution was over, France had not finished with emperor or king. The function of leader under the old arrangement was modified by the new understanding, and only later was the *polis* structurally refounded. It took time to incorporate the new understanding into new and stable political structures. Spain still struggled through the civil war of the 1930s and had to await Francisco Franco's death.

The move from being subjects to being real citizens flourished more easily in the United States after the American Revolution, though even in our setting the struggle still goes on. A woman citizen's right to vote came much later. The struggle for black equality is far from finished. One of every eleven white Americans lives below the poverty level; four of every ten African Americans. That has been a stable ratio, the stability not enforced by law but by internalized cultural attitudes. A black person with the same education as a white person will make one-third less in a lifetime as the white person. In United States culture we have the language of citizenship, but we manage to create unequal citizens from contrary, internalized cultural attitudes. The situation of many unequal citizens is not much different functionally from the role of subject.

Given that the paradigm shift did take hold more quickly and more deeply in a new nation like ours, one would expect to see American Catholics concerned about the body politic of the Body of Christ, and that was indeed the case in many parts of Catholicism in the United States. Rome even identified these desires as the heresy of "Americanism." I will take this up more at length in the fourth chapter, "The Transformation of Power."

The shift from subject to citizen offers a resource for the hermeneutics of retrieval. Reconstructing power arrangements in the church is not a matter of aping new secular models of democracy that emerged after the French Revolution. It is a matter of retrieving a pneumatology that acknowledges the gift of God's Spirit to the entire church with no preferential allocation in any part of it. It is a matter of retrieving what Elisabeth Schüssler Fiorenza calls the discipleship of equals, which does not eliminate roles but precludes their honorification. It is a matter of remembering that Jesus offered no order to his community about how it should be structured. What he did do was offer three metaphors to guide the operations of power: servant, steward, shepherd. The servant metaphor is particularly relevant to the power issue.

In summary, then, *a transfer and transformation of power* occurs in Western culture in the eighteenth century, best exemplified and symbolized in the French Revolution, though long in coming and yet incomplete. It is the end of feudalism as the dominant form of social organization. The democratic spirit informs human yearnings for a distribution of power located in lords, princes, and kings among all the people, turning subjects into citizens. A new imagination invents new civil structures, but no new Catholic imagination invents analogous novel political forms for the body politic of the Body of Christ. There are intimations of how that should proceed in the Second Vatican Council and further hints in the new Code of Canon Law. But none of these offers to the laypeople of God a true deliberative voice in institutional decision making, and that is at the heart of power.

The Historicizing Revolution

Historical Consciousness

In the late 1700s, Hermann Samuel Reimarus published an essay called "The Aims of Jesus and His Disciples," in which he indicated that the aims of the disciples may not have been identical with those of Jesus, since the disciples brought their own agenda to bear upon their understanding of Jesus. Reimarus's essay begins a century of intense New Testament scholarship which recognizes that the Gospels themselves are not histories of Jesus but the record of how communities remembered Jesus and taught new generations what and how they remembered. This long search for the "real" Jesus came to be known as the quest for the historical Jesus. "Historical" in this context does not mean "biographical," but means "what can be known about Jesus through a historical method."

Very many lives of Jesus were written during the 1800s. They went up many blind alleys, but also made amazing discoveries. During most of the tradition up to that time it was presumed that Matthew's Gospel was the earliest. Research began to show that most of Mark's Gospel also appears in Matthew's Gospel, and about half of Mark appears in Luke. Scholars have almost universally concluded now that Mark is the earliest Gospel.

Further, there is a lot of additional material that Matthew and Luke have in common that does not appear in Mark. When these common materials are separated out, it becomes clear that they are basically sayings of Jesus. Scholars are in rather universal agreement that Matthew and Luke had access to a collection of Jesus' sayings and that any such original collection of sayings is lost to us, except as retained in Matthew and Luke. This sayings source is often referred to as "Q," which stands for "*Quelle*," the German word for "source." It is also clear that Matthew and Luke sometimes alter a borrowed text slightly to give it a tighter fit in their own text for their own purposes.

Mark, Matthew, and Luke are often together called the Synoptics because they see Jesus in somewhat similar ways. John's Gospel has long been recognized as quite different. In the Synoptics Jesus seldom refers to himself in his teaching, or refers his followers to himself. He is preoccupied with proclaiming the kingdom of God, and of relating his followers along with himself to the work of making God's reign unfold in the world. In John's Gospel Jesus himself is frequently the concern of Jesus' teaching, and the kingdom of God is not a leitmotif.

By the turn of the century (early 1900s) it became clear to scholars that they could not use scientific historical methods as they were practiced then and deduce the "real" or "original" Jesus from them. Each Gospel was forged out of an oral tradition within a specific community. Jesus appears through the experience and memory of those different communities and in the language and cultural worldview of the communities. Jesus spoke Aramaic, not Greek. So every Gospel is already a crosscultural rendering. We are unable to retrieve that "original voice" perfectly. We have to do our best to situate all spoken words within the culture and worldview in which they were uttered. Further, we often need to know what the concerns of a particular person or people were within that culture that made them ask the questions they asked, or defend the positions they defended.

Although the Jesus-event was a thoroughly Jewish event, the people who began to reflect systematically upon it were for the most part educated in

Greek philosophy, especially in Stoic and Platonic thought. As Arius strove to interpret the nature and meaning of Christ, he did so with categories from Greek philosophy. When his conclusions proved unsatisfying, they were couched in a Greek worldview, and those who responded to his questions had recourse to the same worldview. The Nicene Creed (actually a creed initiated at Nicea and finalized at the Council of Constantinople) addresses questions raised in the third and fourth centuries by people with Greek philosophical categories in their minds and hearts. For most of us today, the Nicene Creed does not express our living faith with strong immediacy. It makes us feel our community with the early church, and we recognize our faith in its words. But were we to build a late twentieth-century Christology into a creed, it would sound very different. Our challenges are different. Our worldview is different. Our language is different. Our experience is different. We are increasingly conscious of how thoroughly our experiencing, our perceiving, our conceptualizing, and our articulating are conditioned by our historical location in time and place.

Everyone who translates an ancient Hebrew sentence into an Indo-European language system must make a judgment about what tense to use. Often it is obvious from the content, but sometimes it is not. And a mistake in tense can be a mistake in meaning. YHWH did not tell Moses, "I am who am," a sentence which in that form has supported the philosophical description of God as pure act, or pure being. Those original Hebrew verbs are ones that indicate not completed or perfect action, but unfinished, "going on" action. It is more as though YHWH said, "I am still becoming who I will become." In ancient Hebrew experience YHWH was normally characterized by the history with which YHWH was associated: The God of Abraham, Isaac, and Jacob; God who led us out of Egypt; and so on. So YHWH might have been saying to Moses, "Since the history that tells you who I YHWH am still goes on, if you want to know who I am, keep your eyes on what is happening in history, for I am there for you."

Another take on historical consciousness is the expression "social location." Our country's socioeconomic well-being is interpreted very differently by people whose income is at the poverty level than by the affluent in the top 20 percent of families. Satisfaction that one's gifts and expertise are treasured by an institution would probably have a very different index depending on whether we are measuring the satisfaction from the social location of men in the church or the differing social location of women in the church.

I am not the only male in the church who experienced some embarrassment while reading for the first time Elisabeth Schüssler Fiorenza's book *In*

Memory of Her and noting how regularly I had missed the remarkable role that women played in the development of early Christian communities. A woman exegete, rare until very recently, interprets from the social location of feminine experience and is sometimes enabled to see what the many male interpreters have not seen. Christian art, for example, has regularly pictured the two disciples Jesus encountered on the way to Emmaus as male. However, the fact that two people heading home for the evening invite Jesus for supper and for the night and the fact that one of them prepares dinner certainly suggest that this is a married couple. That seems so obvious now. It was a custom in history writing of that period to name and count men, but not women unless they stood out for some reason, for example, Jesus fed five thousand, "not counting the women and children." The fact, then, that one of the two disciples on the way to Emmaus, Cleophas, is named, and the other not, is a further support that one is a man and the other is a women who goes unnamed. How simply obvious that appears now.

Southern Women is a much-read book by people in New Orleans, where I live. Susan Tucker has interviewed black women who have worked a long time in the homes of white families and then has interviewed white women in whose homes black women worked. These culturally contrasting narratives are a transparent example of how profoundly social location affects how we interpret and name reality.

One of the major points of this book is that the reality of church and of Catholic Christian identity has been very largely interpreted by men who belong to the clerical structure of the church. That is a social location that enables those there to see some points well and to miss others altogether. What is emerging is an equally well educated laity that is interpreting the same reality from a different social location in the world. A lay perspective is a different vantage point and leads from different concerns, and sometimes sees what has not been seen before, or corrects what has been claimed before. It also misses things. A lay hermeneutic is as biased as a clerical hermeneutic, only differently.

We always interpret "fact" through our presuppositions. We all have presuppositions. There is no way to interpret without being biased. "Bias" just names the slant our conditioning gives us. It is not wrong to be biased, but natural. But it is terribly dangerous not to recognize that we are.

These, then, are some of the implications of historical consciousness:

1. There is no uninterpreted fact. We always and only experience, feel, think, and speak from some perspective.

2. Of all the influences upon our interpretations of experience, none is as pervasive as the language we speak. Though we rarely, or perhaps never,

ponder it, even grammatical structures embody a sense of the world. The use of words like "man" and "mankind" for all human beings is a noninclusive bias built into accepted grammatical norms.

3. Because sociohistorical location always conditions experience, there can be no experience, no interpretation of experience, and no articulation of experience that is transhistorical, transcultural or utterly perennial. You cannot catch any event by the scruff of the neck and pass it along! The only imaginable way one could utter a statement that is unalterably intelligible for all time is to freeze the worldview in which the statement is uttered. If that were possible it would be death to original thinking; but it is not even possible.

4. It is from realizations such as these that "hermeneutics" has arisen. Hermeneutics is the science of interpretation. It has some guidelines that give us our best crack at interpreting as accurately as possible.

When Christian writers began to apply historical consciousness to our interpretation of Scriptures, and then of the church's own self-understanding, this was very threatening. Writers like Alfred Loisy and George Tyrrell were labeled "Modernists" in the latter years of the last century and the first years of the twentieth century. Both were excommunicated. Maude Petre and Baron Friedrich von Hügel escaped condemnation. It is a reasonable surmise that as a laywoman and a layman they attracted less attention from Rome.

These issues continue, as issues around the ordination of women attest. Jesus' choice of only men as apostles is often cited as evidence of God's intentions concerning gender and priesthood. This argument is innocent of historical consciousness. Jesus was a lay Jew and not a priest. The reference to the high priesthood of Jesus in the letter to the Hebrews is a Christological metaphor and not a biographical claim. There is no evidence that the apostles were ever ordained priests. As Raymond Brown long ago pointed out, the early Christian communities, like Jesus and the disciples, were a movement *within* Judaism, and there was already a priesthood in Judaism. They needed none. The Jesus movement was a lay movement. "The apostle is a charismatic and not an institutional figure: his are the new frontiers and the adventurism of spiritual conquest" (Brown 1970, 36). It is difficult to establish on any historical foundation that priests are direct successors of apostles, or in other contexts, that the college of bishops is a direct successor of the "college" of apostles. To speak of a college of apostles is a blatant anachronism. There is textual evidence, however, that the twelve apostles symbolized the twelve tribes of Israel, and thus indicated the thoroughly Jewish self-perception of the early Jesus movement.

Because arguments such as these have for a long time supported the social construction of ecclesial power structures, some of the needed historical deconstruction is more difficult from the social location of the hierarchy than from the social location of the laity.

The Holy Spirit has been as much at work in continuing history as in the history of Christian origins. To say that the original working arrangement does not support a current theological argument is not to say that it may not be valid for some other reason. But we must become increasingly sensitive to the complexities of historical interpretation.

Historical Agents

In ancient Greek anthropology the defining characteristic of human existence is rationality: the human animal is a rational animal. It is thus, then, in the fulfillment of rational faculties, finally, that the highest human happiness is to be experienced, in the contemplation of truth, beauty, and goodness. In Stoic philosophy, whose basic instincts were a powerful influence on early Christian self-understanding, reason knows and contemplates the essences of things, which are always more perfect than any concrete instance of them. To contemplate essence means taking leave of all historical particularities. Sense knowledge is lower knowledge, and rational knowledge is higher knowledge. This breeds a profound suspicion of the world and suggests trafficking with it only as much as is necessary.

For much of the church's life, priesthood and religious life have been interpreted as the life of perfection, lay life clearly below that. In *Lumen Gentium* there is still the position that the hierarchy is concerned with non-temporal matters and the laity with temporal matters. If a presbyter is a community leader, is it not quaint that the presbyter's foundational concerns differ radically with the community's foundational concerns! In *Gaudium et Spes* that distinction no longer appears, and in *Apostolicam Actuositatem* the church affirms that all baptized persons are called to the highest perfection. But those revolutions at the level of idea have a long way to go at the level of lived experience.

Part of the Marxist critique of religion is that Western Christianity has discouraged responsibility for how history goes by emphasizing that true fulfillment is in heaven not on earth. It is important not to get into the kind of tussle that substitutes one for another. Yet we must take into consideration the revolution in Western anthropology that understands human essence as a history-making essence. God has intentions for human history, and they include us as historical agents whom God needs as collaborators in the

becoming of the world. This final revolution we are considering also facili-
tates the retrieval of basic biblical instincts about our role in the world.

The historicization of the subject as actor got an initial boost at the beginning of the sixteenth century from the scientific revolution, which emphasized experience as the beginning of knowledge and required abstract
thought and conceptual frameworks to originate in experience and be faithful to it. These were the issues the British empiricists tackled: Berkeley,
Locke, and Hume. Kant tried unsuccessfully to extricate that kind of empiricism from its prison of subjectivity, and in his *Critique of Practical Reason,*
he promoted the value of practical reason, albeit with idealist strains that
Husserl and other phenomenologists sought to overcome.

In the nineteenth century, however, a new sense of the human person
begins to emerge, that we are not primarily to know, but to act, in the drama
of human history—and more than that even, to be playwrights of history as
well as actors. Early in the nineteenth century, Hegel, idealist that he was,
still thought of the process of thesis, antithesis, and synthesis as being
Bildung, that is, making reality. It was Spirit that was at work in *Bildung,* or
in the language of the later development of the sociology of knowledge, the
Spirit works through the social construction of reality in which we human
beings engage.

With a debt to Hegel but also with a shift from the ideal to the historical,
Karl Marx understood the need for human beings to take charge of the process of development, to become very deliberate about making history and
to assume responsibility for building the future. While the Marxist enterprise has proved a dismal failure, its attractiveness has much to do with its
call to take charge of history and with people's readiness to be history makers. Marx said that the purpose of philosophy is not to interpret reality but
to transform it. Marx is one of the landmarks in the shift from subject as
knower to subject as actor.

There is, of course, some untenable *hubris* in the Marxian sense of how
readily one can take control of events, and equally so in Western faith in free
enterprise. Current events in both the United States and in the former Soviet
Union should make for chastened history makers. That more chastened
sense would have to say, "yes we are responsible; but history has a movement
of its own, and that movement sets parameters of the possible and desirable."

Concomitant with this nineteenth-century movement was a biblical
recovery of eschatology as central to any true understanding of Jesus' teaching. During this present century, there has been an increasingly historicized
interpretation of the reign of God. Most of Jesus' teachings during his historical life were about how we ought to be in the world together with God

and with each other, because of who God is for and with us. Liberal Protestantism in this period almost ethicized Jesus' teaching so totally that the grounding of the ethical in the mystical was lost (the work of Johannes Metz has been to establish an organic connection between the mystical and the political). Jesus' metaphor for the eschaton was "the kingdom of God." It was not primarily about life after death, nor primarily about something after "the end of time." Those elements are not absent, but Jesus' preoccupation is with the claim that the age to come makes on us now in the immediacies of our lived experience.

Now a return to twentieth-century thought. Existentialist philosophy was and is about the human enterprise, and its effect upon theology has been substantial. José Ortega y Gasset once mused that we human beings have no nature, we have only our history. Jean-Paul Sartre and Albert Camus similarly present human beings as unfinished beings who are making themselves in history. We are always finishing ourselves. Sartre insisted that existence, therefore, precedes essence. I am not arguing for the fine points of existentialism in this century or for any parts of Marxism in the last, but I want to call attention to Western culture's turn to the subject as an acting subject. The Christian religious version of this is an emphasis upon human collaboration with God in making history according to the intentions of God in Jesus Christ.

I could further point to the work of Henri Bergson's vitalist philosophy and to Maurice Blondel's chef d'oeuvre, *L'Action*. The thrust in European philosophy has a counterpart in late nineteenth and early twentieth century American philosophy in the pragmatism of Charles Sanders Peirce, William James, John Dewey, and in the process philosophy of Anglo-American Alfred North Whitehead.

In a different vein let me name the insights of people like Peter Berger and Thomas Luckmann concerning the social construction of reality. Knowledge does not merely reflect a world, it helps construct a world. Our knowledge of the world is always also our interpretation of the world along with the webs of meaning we weave and in which we are suspended.

The expression "the turn to the subject as actor," to the maker of history, to the transformer of social systems, seems accurate to me. History making is no less a rational task than is knowing, of course, for they are internally bound together, but the revolution historicizes the human enterprise and disallows the impulse to disconnect from history, even while contemplating in the desert.

Praxis or practical theology is the educational "place" where this historicizing revolution is especially visible. Theology has not often been accused of being on the cutting edge of culture, but in this instance I believe that it is (Lee 1994, 35–36). Practical theology, especially as it is practiced in professional ministry education at the graduate level in Catholic colleges and universities, is an institutional experiment of responsiveness to Western culture's historicizing revolution in a way that the institutional culture of Catholic higher education is rarely doing elsewhere in its system. And it is precisely because of the number of laywomen and laymen receiving education in these programs that historical consciousness and large commitments to history making are likely to enter functional ecclesial consciousness. And too often it is a forced entry, but insistence can also be a creative part of dialogue.

Reprise

In our terminology we have long recognized major shifts in how people think and act by calling the period beginning with the sixteenth century the "modern period." The impact of enough of these paradigm shifts, or revolutions, has been warded off by the church in some very defensive moments of ecclesial life so that a council was called for the sole purpose of updating. Vatican II initiated the process. It has slowed down very much recently. The pile of revolutions is still tall.

I have tried to name three of these revolutions: the scientific revolution, which added new knowledge and a new method for arriving at understanding; the political revolution, the development within the human spirit that refused to continue being subjects of the wealthy and/or the nobles and aristocrats and asserted citizen rights to share power and resources; finally, there has been the historical revolution, a sense of the historically configured, and therefore contingent, character of all experience and knowledge, and the recognition of responsible "history maker" as fundamental descriptor of human nature.

In the next three chapters I hope to indicate some fuller implications of each of these revolutions for Christian life. It is also my position that the church's openness to a fuller engagement of these revolutions is most likely to emerge from the social location of lay experience, not unlike the hidden revolution in Judaism a century and a half BCE. But this will require for lay experience a fuller voice in the community, one that has honor in power arrangements within *ecclesia*. The final chapter will propose the fruitfulness of dialogic community as a resource for reconstructed ecclesiology. Dialogic community, though not in those precise words, is a retrieval of power arrangements visible in the earliest communities. It is a proposal grounded above all in a pneumatology. The Spirit is God's gift to us all and is active in the dynamics between us all.

III

REVOLUTION ONE:
THE AUTHORITY OF EXPERIENCE

The license plates in Missouri announce that this is the Show-Me state. Though not a native of Missouri, when I lived there some time ago I relaxed into its motto because it is part of my culture as an American, too. We consider ourselves plain-speaking folks who like the facts. We like to think that we pay honorable attention to the deliverances of experience. Missouri may be typical Midwest, but when you tell your story at a deep enough level, you tell everyone's story at some level. Requiring empirical evidence feels like part of the deep story of U.S. culture to which Missouri gives one possible expression.

There is no philosophy around, unless one counts the ancient Hebrew temperament, that is as respectful of experience as American pragmatism. This philosophical school is largely a child of New England, through Charles Sanders Peirce, William James, and John Dewey. Once again, they are folks from a different quarter who told the story at a deep enough level.

The first Soviet astronaut said from space that he had not seen God out there. The crudest sort of empiricism presumes that sense experience exhausts the meaning of direct experience. William James would have reminded Yuri Gagarin that "pure experience" is the whole world of causal influences that pour in upon us, only some small portion of which registers at a conscious level as sense experience. We believe, for example, that our present existence is derived from our past experience, but this fundamental relationship between our present and our past is not verifiable as a sense datum. Because "empirical" is often narrowly understood to refer to sense experience only, religious thought has not courted empiricism. But William James contends that empiricism is "a more natural ally of the religious life" than people generally imagine (James 1969, 325).

My personal fascination with process/relational modes of thought over many years has been with the empirical instincts at work here. Philosophy is like the flight of an airplane. You begin by observing all you can from the ground. Then you take off, and from that observational distance above the fray, you generalize what is there below. The only purpose of philosophizing, which has much in common with imaginative generalizing in this approach, is to elucidate experience. So you land again, and use your generalizations to interpret previous experience, to understand and enrich present experience, and to help create significant new experience.

If the generalizations do not seem to work after assiduous and careful applications, then you undertake new ground observation, follow this with a new reconnaissance flight, do some new work up there, and land again to check out this more recent effort at large understanding.

Whitehead philosophized in dialogue with mathematics and physics, and with great appreciative grasp of the history of Western thought. Peirce philosophizes in dialogue with mathematics and natural science; James with medical science and psychology; Dewey with social science. In each of these instances, the philosophical insight of these figures is nourished by the background in science.

The inductive temper is not the only tendency of American minds, but it is one of the principal traits of the dominant culture in the United States. People do not need to have studied science to require that you "show me" how you have staked out your truth claims. The industrial revolution, the technological revolution, and now the information revolution are all applications of knowledge gained through the methods of the scientific revolution—and through these applications, the scientific revolution has got inside us all.

I would like to take up two examples of empiricism: (1) what we are learning about the reality of marriage through the deliverances of married experience; and (2) approaches to speaking of God that are grounded in experience. Following that I would like to address the complex meanings of the word "experience." Fidelity to experience is far more demanding than meets the naked eye. Finally, I want to indicate some aspects of the education being received by laywomen and laymen in graduate ministry programs and the penchant of practical theology to keep itself fine-tuned by "obeying" experience. "Obey" is the right word. It comes from two Latin words, *ob* and *audire*. *Ob* means "there in front of." *Audire* means "to hear." The two together mean "planting oneself right smack dab in front of something or someone and listening like the dickens to what is happening."

The Experience of Marriage

One of the achievements of the Pharisees was to sacralize family life by transferring into the home rituals that observed temple holiness. This is a move that can come only from those who experience family life as no less sacred than temple life. Those whose professional social location is the temple are not likely to be the ones to expand sacrality beyond the temple territory. The impetus will come from those professionally outside the temple whose social location is precisely marriage and family, and who have the power to accomplish the ritual transformation. The power base for the Pharisees was their learning and their subsequent introduction into Jewish religious life of an oral Torah that had no less authority than the written Torah. The oral Torah made room for ongoing reinterpretation of Jewish religious identity.

The Christian Scriptures make clear the constant dialectic between the lay interpreters and the clerical interpreters, the Pharisees and the Sadducees. Later polemic (final decades of the first century) between Christians and Pharisaic Judaism has effectively covered over the many ways in which the teaching of Jesus is largely consistent with the original intent of Pharisaic transformation of Judaism. Jesus was a lay interpreter. The language may be anachronistic, but that was the reality.

The dialectical dance between the lay and clerical hermeneutic has begun in Catholicism, although it does not [yet] have an official ecclesial dance floor. Issues around marriage and sexuality instance the dialectic.

Reflecting a long history of discourse, the 1917 Code of Canon Law regards marriage as a contract (canon 1012). "Procreation and nurture of children" is the primary end of marriage, and "mutual help" and the "remedying of concupiscence" are secondary ends (canon 1013.1). While these are not intended as definitions, nonetheless, the omission of love and intimacy is indeed notable.

There is a new wind blowing in Vatican II. In the opening paragraph of *Gaudium et Spes* concerning marriage, marriage is called a *community* of love (§47), a *conjugal* covenant, and an *intimate partnership of life*. Community, covenant, and intimate partnership set a different tone than does contract (§48). Given the fact that our descriptive interpretations of reality engage in the social construction of reality, something new is in the making. There is no record of any marriage annulment having every been granted before 1969 on the basis of one or both parties' psychological inability to enter into an intimate partnership of life. Since 1969, most of the annulments granted in the U.S. Catholic church have been for that reason.

The new Code of Canon Law reflects the descriptive transformation that occurred between the older code and *Gaudium et Spes.* The new Code of Canon Law begins the chapter on marriage very differently:

> Canon 1055. The marriage covenant, by which a man and a woman establish between themselves a partnership of their whole life, and which of its own very nature is ordered to the well-being of the spouses, and to the procreation and nurture of children, has, between the baptized, been raised by Christ the Lord to the dignity of a sacrament.

What is especially noteworthy is that there is no longer a distinction between primary ends and secondary ends. And, in fact, the partnership of life and the good of spouses are mentioned before procreation, even though they are not prioritized.

In his book, *What Is Marriage?* Theodore Mackin asks how we got from one description of marriage to the other (1982, chapter 9). I will be following Mackin's analysis of the role of Fidelis Schwendinger, Dietrich von Hildebrand, and Heribert Doms in helping the church think freshly on marriage. To be sure, their influence was resisted! All of these men were influenced by phenomenology, a philosophical school that began to take shape in the early twentieth century with the work of Edmund Husserl.

We recognize today that no one can have a totally "objective" experience of something. But in its early season, phenomenology tried to bracket out all interpretive interference and let things disclose themselves. Our task would be to receive the disclosures, the phenomena, and then describe what we have experienced. That is the only way to get back to the original "thing in itself" (*Ding-an-sich*). While we recognize that we always interpret, the basic phenomenological instinct is correct: we have to let things disclose themselves as fully and accurately as possible. We know what something is by reading our experience of it, albeit interpretively.

Schwendinger, in an essay published in 1939, writes a straightforward description of what two people are really up to when they marry:

> Unless we are prepared to maintain that the Church consecrates sacramentally an institution which has no meaning (i.e., an unfulfilled marriage like that of Joseph and Mary), we are bound to admit that marriage has some other meaning besides procreation and that this other meaning is essential to marriage. Community of personal life between husband and wife is the only possible other meaning. If we consider the psychological process which leads up to marriage ("falling in love," etc.), we must see that community of life is the first thing which the man and woman desire.... The Me-You community still remains the first thing when one looks at marriage objectively. The first thing which the man and woman want to do is not to create a third thing distinct

from either. The third person is not what unites them and makes them say WE, nor do they fulfill and consummate each other through it. No, the first and most obvious characteristic of marriage is the direct union in love between a Me and a You. (cited in Mackin 1982, 227)

Schwendinger is not asking philosophical questions. He is saying: when I look at marriage, this really is what I think I behold. This is what I hear married people say about why they got married. This is what marriage discloses itself to be.

Von Hildebrand, in his essay "Marriage," posed the question in terms of meaning. He saw that when procreation is not possible, marriage does not have less meaning. The loving relationship between husband and wife has meaning in itself. He recalled the biblical reason for the two sexes: "It is not good to be alone. I will create a suitable partner." For Von Hildebrand, this "suitable partnership" is the first meaning. Mackin summarizes Von Hildebrand's position as follows:

As a marriage is in its nature fundamentally a community of love, so too the physical consummation of it is not to be interpreted fundamentally as a means to procreation. Procreation is neither the only meaning nor the primary meaning of intercourse in marriage. Its primary meaning is to be the most complete expression of the parties' love for one another, its fullest embodiment. And since marital love is one in which the partners give over their whole persons to one another, intercourse is the act in which this self-giving can be at its fullest. (1982, 228)

Von Hildebrand drew heavy criticism from the church.

Doms, too, opts for an examination of experience. Many arguments about the nature of sexuality proceed from a rather obvious fact that this is how the continuation of the species is guaranteed. But there is a very important difference between animals who mate during a rutting season and human beings whose love making is not correlated with physiological cycles of fertility. Doms also stresses what he feels is the basic reality, namely, that shared love is the main reason that people marry, not the desire for children. The shared love seldom precludes children and usually welcomes family. But people marry because they are in love with each other.

Each of these three finds, in the words of Mackin, "that the canonical understanding of marriage is phenomenologically empty" (1982, 229).

The point here is neither to defend nor default these positions but to say that these ways of thinking about marriage are founded in a commitment to the deliverances of the experience of married people themselves.

Beginning with the first half of the twentieth century, there is an accumulating body of literature about human sexuality that attempts to be descriptive, that is, that tries to generalize the human experience of sexuality based upon what sexual beings have to say, rather than reason about it as the starting point. Sigmund Freud, of course, is the one most responsible for opening the discussion professionally and publicly. Many educated Americans know what the Kinsey Report was, and they are probably familiar with Masters and Johnson. The Hite report has continued to open discussion. Michel Foucault's writing on human sexuality is read internationally. Responsible technical studies are digested and made readable for *Time* and *Newsweek*. Slightly more technical discussions of such research find their way into the *New York Times Book Review*.

There are two important issues here. The first is to recognize that experience carries an authority and demands a hearing. Second, statistics cannot be turned into moral norms. But moral and ethical discourse cannot simply exclude it.

Patrick and Patricia Crowley are familiar in the U.S. Catholic church for their leadership in forming the Catholic Family Movement. They were appointed by Pope Paul VI to the commission that studied the question of birth control. To gather experience they surveyed three thousand Catholic couples from eighteen nations who had used the rhythm method. They asked what the experience was like. In his biography of Pope Paul VI, Peter Hebbelthwaite cites the Crowleys' summary of the information they gathered from married people's experience (1993, 467–68):

Does rhythm have a bad psychological effect? Almost without exception, the responses were, yes, it does.

Does rhythm serve any useful purpose at all? A few say it may be useful for developing discipline. Nobody says that it fosters married love.

Does it contribute to married unity? No. That is the inescapable conclusion of the reports we have received. In a marriage husband and wife pledge themselves to become one in mind, heart and affection. They are no longer two, but one flesh. Some wonder whether God would have us cultivate such unity by using what seems to them such an unnatural system. . . . Instead of love, rhythm tends to substitute tension, dissatisfaction, frustration and disunity.

Is rhythm unnatural? Yes–that's the conclusion of these reports. Over and over, directly and indirectly, men and women—and perhaps especially women—voice the conviction that the physical and psychological implications of rhythm are not understood by the male Church.

The effect of methodology here, even though not explicitly named, is stunning. You can begin with a description of sexual intercourse as biologically directed to reproduction (as it is for animals) and then deductively conclude what is natural and what is not. Or you can begin with a report from married people on the nature of intercourse in their marriage and then inductively conclude what is natural and what is not. Most people who disagree with the church on birth control are not callously ignoring the church. They have a very different sense of how you get reliable information about basic human experience. This is not an issue of a statistical vote on a moral question. Voting does not belong to the logic of truth. But a wide consultation of experience and the dialogue between divergent reports does favor growth in our security about moral ground.

When one is pondering these issues, the social location of married women and men has very different experiential biases than does the social location of celibate men. No interpreter is without bias because no interpreter is without the scope and limit of social location.

Sociological Interlude

In any large institution it is easy to understand how the people in leadership positions are very influential in interpreting the life of the institution. Those who exercise leadership in institutions are concerned with efficient operations, with predictability, with stability, with structure and organization. Following the usage of Victor Turner, let us call the institution a *societas* and each of the member groups that make it up a *communitas* (1977).

Communitas comprises those groups who with some immediacy experience their social world (relationships with spouses and children, friendships, work, city, taxes, car payments, daily newspaper, poverty and job insecurity, affluence, and perhaps violence, whether they are rich or poor, and so on). Here is where the exigencies of lived experience impinge upon the human enterprise and make demands. *Communitas* is a social location from which institutional life is not a large concern, except insofar as it supports or does not support *communitas*. *Communitas* is more ready and sometimes eager to change and adapt so that new needs are met. "*Communitas* is of the now" (Turner 1977, 133). It is less protective of structure and less committed to structural maintenance.

Communitas is nearer the action. Communities are like the larger body's five senses. They are the church's major contact zone with daily life. This is where the activity for which the organization exists occurs. Here in *communitas* people tend to have a clearer experience-based sense of what works well and what works poorly. When change is needed, it is often experienced first at this level. People at this level are more likely to begin adapting behaviors and policies to exigencies, which is an anti-structural posture.

The institutional church can be interpreted in many of the categories that belong to *societas*. As such, it has much in common with large organizational structures. It is the role of organization to make the smaller units in the organization function effectively and easily. *Societas* likes order and predictability. It values and guards structure. It offers stability to the smaller unit, the *communitas*, and helps assure its survival.

Let us look at some contrasts between *societas* and *communitas*, as Turner describes them. While Turner is describing differences in tribal life, much sounds familiar. As with all typologies, these are consistent tendencies that are noted. They are descriptive, not prescriptive.

Communitas	*Societas*
Sense of becoming	Sense of settled order
Able to ignore structure	Likely to protect structure
Equality important	Distinctions and rank are important
Heterogeneous attire	Special attire
Simplicity	Complexity, bureaucracy
Obedience to community	Obedience to superiors
Values authority of people's experience	Values authority of experience tradition
Tolerates some "foolishness"	Rewards sagacity, common sense
Is "of the now"	Structure rooted in the past and continued into the future through language, law, and custom

A local church (diocese) is *communitas* to Rome's *societas*. A parish is *communitas* to the diocesan *societas* and to Rome. Small Christian communities are *communitas* to parish, to local church, and to Rome. *Societas* and *communitas* need each other, and each one is diminished if the other cannot be what it is meant to be. While there is always some tensive relationship between the two, most of the time *communitas* is valued by *societas* because it enables the organization to do well what it needs to do. There is in all organizations, however, a tendency for *societas* to co-opt *communitas*. Structure does not invite antistructure into its private quarters!

In times of great change, *communitas* takes on a sort of liminal character. Turner calls *communitas* members in this case threshold people—in between a former way and a new way. "In liminality," Turner says, "the underling comes uppermost" (1977, 102). Those without power in the earlier dispensation have the most to say about the new dispensation. "Coming uppermost" may not mean appearing in central leadership structures but in the power to create the agenda. In the Catholic church, laypeople generally and laywomen particularly have been at the bottom of the power tree. In many small Christian communities, as they appear across the globe, there is no power tree. An alternative is instanced, and it calls *ecclesia* to consider its experience. The instancing is an antistructural function. Precisely because this is a liminal time in the church, the "authority" generated by the experience of small Christian communities is a prophetic gift. The authority is not juridical but is one whose claims are rooted in the deliverances of experience and in the belief that God's Spirit operates throughout God's people—in *communitas* as well as in *societas*, and perhaps especially in the dialectic spaces they create.

In a time of rapid and profound change, the dialectic between *societas* and *communitas* is especially pointed. During such liminal time, *societas* tends to be more protective of structure and *communitas* tends to be more willing to be antistructural. "*Communitas* breaks in through the interstices of structure, in liminality; at the edges of structure in liminality; and from beneath structure, in inferiority" (Turner 1977, 128).

Basic Christian communities, especially the grassroots models, are a remarkable expression of *communitas* in today's church. In this movement, the underling lay voice and the underling feminine voice come uppermost. These communities are experimenting with new structure to meet new needs and to address unmet human hungers. The tension between base communities and the institutional church has been especially visible in the Latin American church. But it has been my experience in this country that members of the hierarchy are reluctant to support small communities out loud, and I would hazard a guess that this hesitancy is a reflection of Roman nervousness.

My plea here, and throughout the book, is for entertaining dialectic community as an ecclesial model. Neither *communitas* nor *societas* alone can be life-giving. *Communitas* needs the supportive structures of *societas*. *Communitas* needs the affective memory of *societas*. *Societas* needs the deliverances of front-line, lived experience from *communitas*. *Societas* needs the prophetic imagination of *communitas*. I agree with Turner's description of all "social life [as] a type of dialectical process that involves successive experience of high and low, *communitas* and structure, homogeneity and differentiation, equality and inequality" (1977, 97). We do not now have an effective structured process in the church so that the dialectic can operate.

The clerical interpretation claims ascendancy. Lay experience is seeping through the cracks and may yet wash through voluminously.

A Pastoral Application: The Experience of God

Abraham Heschel observes, "there are no proofs for the existence of the God of Abraham. There are only witnesses" (1962, 22). Experience cannot prove God. The experience of God is not about proving. It is about testifying. The witnesses to God are required to make their God-talk credible with reference to their interpreted experience (all experience involves interpretation).

There is a movement in contemporary spirituality and theology with affinity to Hebrew experience. Storytelling is one expression. Narrative theology is another. Our ancient Jewish foremothers and forefathers did not make philosophical statements about God. They named God by naming the events in which God was experienced or the people with whom God had a bountiful connection: YHWH who led us out of Egypt; YHWH who freed us from slavery; YHWH the God of Abraham [and Sarah]; YHWH who made the world.

At a time when we who are on both sides of change feel that our insights are godly, we need more than ever to ground our discourse about God in concrete experience. In a postmodern world where metanarratives are always suspect, we nonetheless need stories to live by. It is enough that they are megastories. I would like to use process/relational modes of thought as such a megastory upon which to found some guidance for discourse about God.

This century will never be known as the age of faith in respect to its religion, says Yale philosopher John E. Smith, but it will be known as the age of experience (1973, xi). This suggestion resonates with my sensibilities and with those of many people I meet (especially colleagues and students). That perhaps only means that we are children of the twentieth century. This attitude reflects and is undoubtedly spawned by the empiricism that has been accruing in the human spirit for several centuries now. It remains for religion to ingest into our religious sensitivities whatever there is in the empirical tradition that can validly be appropriated. And there is a lot.

With an appeal to mystery and transcendence there has probably been more irresponsible discourse in the area of religious experience than in most areas of human endeavor. I want to make an appeal here for responsible religious discourse, that is, discourse rooted in experience. Language about experience not only relates experience; language also guides and creates experience.

It is difficult to achieve rooted-in-experience discourse about religious experience because mystery and transcendence are indeed real. In religious experience, as in any area of significant experience, there arrives a time when propositional statements and empirical descriptions have exhausted their power to articulate an experience. At that point the human impetus yields to poetry and song, as it should and must. But rooted-in-experience discourse ought not to yield to poetry and song until it has lost its power to elucidate and has begun to nod to modes better equipped for dancing with the music of the spheres. And there comes still another moment when poetry and song and even the motion of dance have had their say and know it. Experiential discourse had its day and performed responsibly. So the time comes for us to lay down our words, silence the music, and end our motion, out of respect for that muteness which the Unspeakable requires. But, responsible, rooted-in-experience discourse ought not to cease and desist one nanosecond before the ought of poetry impinges upon it.

The desire to keep religious discourse grounded in experience is a legitimate expression of the empirical bent that increasingly characterizes contemporary Western consciousness since the scientific revolution. The word "empirical" means different things to different people. The empirical sense that supports these reflections comes from process/relational modes of thought. I would like to invite the reader for a stroll through the process megastory that was told by Alfred North Whitehead.

The scientific interpretation of the world is conducted in terms of "event" and "becoming." In an imaginative application of this basic instinct, Whitehead describes all reality similarly. Our reality is our becoming. Whatever would stop becoming would stop being. Events rather than things are the building blocks of the cosmos. Whitehead calls them variously actual events, actual occasions, and actual entities, and sometimes he borrows a phrase from William James and calls them "drops of experience." "The actualities of the Universe are processes of experience, each process is an individual fact. The whole Universe is the advancing assemblage of these processes" (n.d., 199).

The word "experience" describes each event, for an event is created by gathering up the past to create the future. The "gathering up" is the experience, and the drop of experience is the reality. Again the imaginative leap: the word "experience" is extended beyond human meaning so that all becoming can be interpreted as all experiencing. Nothing is excluded from this megastory. "There is no going behind actual entities to find anything more real. They differ among themselves: God is an actual entity, and so is the most trivial puff of existence in far-off empty space" (Whitehead 1929, 27–28).

This is a giant step away from the megastory of classical theism with its Greek philosophical moorings. In this megastory rendition, God is not Being-itself, but a being, albeit a most extraordinary being, unique in the role played in the becoming of all experience everywhere. Any reference to God must be grounded in the role God plays, that is, in God's presence, in and to drops of experience.

The dogged empiricism of these modes of thought is in the axiom that any reason for any explanation for anything finally has recourse to drops of experience. "Actual entities are the only *reasons;* so that to search for a *reason* is to search for one or more actual entities" (Whitehead 1929, 37). Any God-talk must, therefore, finally refer speaker and listener to some actual, concrete experience of God. Reasonings about God are important, but they must be woven on the loom of concrete experience.

Experience names the coming together of an individual event. What we call "person" is a magnificently complex and sophisticated event. But, as Whitehead uses the word, there is the experience of becoming in an atom, or molecule, or sunflower. Whatever's influence is felt is experienced. The sunflower experiences the sun's movement and follows it. Only some part of the act of becoming is accessible to sense experience, a smaller part to cognitive experience, and a still smaller part can be articulated. Experiencing includes everything at all that impacts on what or who something or someone is.

When empiricism includes experience in such breadth and depth, it is a great ally, as James says, to religion. Sense experience alone, which is what empirical means to a lot of people, is not up to the task of religious discourse on its own.

Empirical process theologian Bernard Meland insists that all we ever have is our immediate lived experience (which includes our experience of the experience others have, of which tradition is an expression). If what is Ultimate is to be experienced, it can only be because the Ultimate has traffic with immediate lived experience at some juncture of event. Religious discourse depends upon that traffic. We can only know God if God is in the world with us, and we have read the traffic report accurately. Those worldly appearances of God are the ground for religious discourse, including that form of God-talk called theology.

In the *Kena Upanishad,* Indian wisdom tells us: "If you think you know well the truth of Brahman, know that you know little. . . . I cannot say that I know Brahman fully. Nor can I say I know Brahman not. The one among us who knows Brahman best is the one who understands the spirit of these words: 'Nor do I know that I know Brahman not.'" So, while we certainly cannot know God fully, neither can we say that we know God not. I will be suggesting four questions that are an attempt, within a particular interpretive framework, to say "something" at least. But first I will describe the larger interpretation that is the background for the four questions. (A fuller elaboration can be found in Lee 1979, 434–48.)

While we experience ourselves as individuals, we also reflect in popular language our experience of ourselves as composite. "She's got it all together." "Don't come unglued." "I am falling apart." "Someone's got a screw loose." "He's coming apart at the seams." Who we are is the outcome of incredible influences that have been absorbed into our personhood. The influence of God upon every drop of experience is the basis of God-talk.

As Whitehead has described it, God affects the world's outcome by luring it toward its own creative transformation. Creative transformation is a movement into a new future that implies novelty. Every creative transformation is a movement away from the sheer givenness of the past as it strives for some increment. In the biblical experience the prophet Micah names as well as anybody ever has the way God's lure is experienced: "This is what Yahweh asks of you, only this, that you act justly, love tenderly, and walk humbly with your God." We experience the lure through the invitation and sometimes the pressure to live as Micah indicated. God's lure is not above or beyond everyday's lived experience, but it confronts us precisely through experience.

We cannot only say Yes or No to what God invites; there is a wide range of responses: a hesitant No; a firm No; a resounding No; a little Yes; a medium Yes; or as passionate a Yes as was Molly Bloom's in James Joyce's *Ulysses*:

> and then I asked him with my eyes to ask again yes and then he asked me would
> I yes . . . and first I put my arms around him yes and drew him down to me so
> that he could feel my breasts all perfume yes and his heart was going like mad
> and yes I said yes I will Yes.

The presence of the Song of Songs in the canon of Scripture should remind us of the power of human eros to symbolize religious experience because it mediates religious experience (Lee 1976, 369–84).

Analogy

We are dealing with an understanding of reality that holds that God is available to us in every drop of experience. There are multiple components in every drop of experience. One way of describing the search for God is that it consists in taking drops of experience, cracking them open, identifying the component that is "of God," and embracing God in them. That can be how one witnesses to God.

This is the basis of a sacramental theology, one that nourishes, as David Tracy has developed so well, our analogical imagination. There are some elements of experience that are "of God." Equally, some are "of us." This is true because the creativity of each experience is touched by the lure of God and by the decisions we make. Something of the drop of experience is truly of me, because it is my experience. Something is also truly of God, because of God's creative efficacy. This is the basis for sacrament: something in human life can lead human life consciously into God because the same event is as truly of God as it is truly of the world.

Symbol

There is a dynamic operative in every human relationship. As I get to know you it will be through certain aspects of you. I can never know you or anyone else or anything else or even myself in every single detail. In our inter-action, certain things about you strike me, and those striking aspects become the "handles" by which I get a sense of who you are. The things about you that strike me have become components of my experience of you. The "handles" are parts of you that mediate your presence to me. They are incipient symbols: they tell the truth about you because they participate in you.

To understand this process we must give up on the expression "mere symbol," as if symbol were dispensable to my experience of you. Sometimes symbols do indeed help us communicate experience after the fact. But Paul Ricoeur also describes how symbol mediates experience in its very origination, and that is the sense here. There is no consciousness of another person or event that is not shaped in some way by symbols. Witnessing to God involves "cracking open" our experience to see what symbols tumble out that connected us with God and self and world as the experience came into being.

Presence

At first blush we usually take "presence" to name what is temporally and locally proximate. In this sense, all the people with me in the house now are present, but my friend in another city is absent. But a second sense gives a different reading. If I were to try to account for my identity I would be trying to let you know, as best as I can, what are the major events and who are the major persons who have shaped my life, and that includes my responses to them, both conscious and otherwise. My parents, neither of whom is living, have had far more do to with who I am than people I saw at work today. My parents, as with very important friends along the way of my life, are more constitutive of who I am than many who are temporally and locally near. On the long view, parents and friends maintain a larger presence to my reality than those others incidentally nearby.

In this second sense, presence names whatever has a hold on my becoming, what has effects on my reality, what shapes me, what contributes something of itself to myself. Presence does not primarily mean here rather than there, today rather than yesterday, close rather than far. It has more to do with whoever and whatever has played a large constitutive role in my experience.

Presence also has density in experience. In one sense, the whole world is totally present to itself. It is all there, all at once. It is only a question of how much one part affects another part. The more influence there is, the more density there is to the experience of presence. Thus the density of God's presence (this is an awesome thought!) is contingent upon my willingness to choose God largely, to let what God is up to extensively shape what I am up to.

When I break open my experience I may feel that there is very little in it that is "of God." It may be that my power of recognition is weak. It may also be that there is little of God there because there was not much Yes from me to God in the origination of my experience. It is at this point that I may rely on my past experience of God to transform the next drop of experience. I can take what I have already decided is of God in the past—one of those "handles" from past religious experience—and build it into the new moment so that what was not a component of experience when I cracked it open is now a component when I rebuild it for a new moment of creation.

One of the functions of tradition is that it is an active warehouse from which the presence of God gathered from the past can be assessed for the future. Tradition can, of course, be as inhibitive as constructive when "the warehouse manager" tries to control the architecture of the new moment, not recognizing that the wares therein, valuable as they are, can be transcended. The experienced good is often the severest enemy to the possible better. Tradition is full of thinkables. But God sometimes does the unthinkable, a presence different from any presence before.

The Ambiguity of "the Interpreted"

Chapter five will deal in more detail with the interpreted character of every fact. But we must address it briefly here. Let us say that with painstaking care I have cracked open a drop of experience. I have sorted out, as best I can, its many components. I know, of course, that my inventory is never perfect. Now the question is: on what basis do I name this component rather than that one to be "of God"? There is no identification bracelet. There are no footnotes. Every such identification involves an act of interpretation. And every act of interpretation involves some background understandings, some past experiences, some value judgments, some worldview. In short, every act of interpretation involves a hermeneutic.

If a hermeneutic says, as mine does, that it is God's character to call us always to be more, then if I crack open a drop of experience and find within it a pressure on myself to risk a new way of getting at life that seems to offer enrichment, I will probably want to call that component "of God." If I am a Franciscan friar and see within a drop of experience a suggestion about how I might better live in poverty as an instrument of sharing the gospel, then I will call that summons from an event the speech of God to me. If, as a Marianist, I uncover in an event a call to live community life more heroically, then with a Marianist hermeneutic I identify that challenge as an invitation from God.

The call of God, therefore, is not merely God's "speech" that is objectively the same for any participant in an event. Three persons witness an automobile accident. One is a physician, the second a weightlifter, the third a person of immense compassion. The first attends to injuries. The second uses his strength to force open a jammed door to remove another injured person. The third adds great calm and consolation from her own inner calm and compassion. Each responds to what the moment asks, based upon the personal strengths and the needs and possibilities present. None of them proves God. Each of them witnesses to God through their interpretive analysis of experience. Each grounds truth claims in the character of experience.

Putting Religious Questions to Experience

This language about "cracking open experience" is admittedly neither social scientific nor theological. It is a somewhat far-fetched play on Whitehead's natural theology. I intend it as a symbolic way of talking about experience that is open to interpretive witnessing to God's presence. It springs from pastoral concern in my experience as a spiritual director. I know from my own life as well as from interaction with others how easy it is to make

God say what we want to hear—we ventriloquize our own voices into divine providence. We know the expressions: "I know it is God's will that I. . . ." "I feel close to Christ." "God has been good to me." "The Spirit let me know that I must. . . ." "This is clearly a moment of grace." "God is not calling me at this moment to. . . ." If this language is to be reputable, more information is needed than what is supplied in the bald statements. I find the following kinds of questions useful in connecting God-talk to concrete lived experience.

1. From what experience did you derive this "information?" Whitehead's ontological principle requires that all explanations finally have recourse to real events (actual entities), or specific drops of experience. If God is available to your experience, it can only be because what is Ultimate is present in some way in the immediacies of lived experience. It is incumbent upon the religious speaker to ground religious speaking in those experiences that are claimed to be the bearer and discloser of God.

There are generalizations of experience, but there is no general experience. There is only particular experience. If you say you know God, however meagerly it may be, you should be able to point with some particularity to the drops of experience which are the sacrament of God.

2. How did you go about opening up your experience in order to sort out its components? Since experience is by nature complex and composed, some effort must be made to assess the components. No experience is entirely of God since our agency is also constitutive. In the process-relational megastory, God's presence is interpreted as embodied in all of the persuasions and pressures through which God promotes the world's creative transformation. Becoming more fully the reign of God is the Judeo-Christian metaphor for that transformation.

Moments or drops of conscious experience are, in the process-relational framework, immensely rich and full assemblages of influences pouring in upon us. There is such an organic welding together of an incredible welter of data that while experiences have temporal thickness, it is just not possible to make absolutely clear, unambiguous distinctions about how the various elements enter experience, get weighed and valued, receive a shaping role, and so on. But, having said all of that, we do yet have some ability to discern.

Ira Progoff's intensive journaling technique is a discernment process many have found useful. It is an analytical means of increasing one's groundedness in one's experience. It is not enough to record experiences in the journal. There are different sections in the journal, and a decision must be made about where some particular entry is to be made. I am not encouraging the Progoff journal (nor discouraging it), only offering it as an example of the procedure of cracking open drops of experience.

Not all prayer forms are discernment processes, but some are—and discernment is certainly one phase of the spiritual discipline of prayer. The traditional ascetical practice of "particular examen" is another prayer approach that sorts out lived experience. Nor is this practice necessarily a religious one, for a version of particular examen was a daily practice for Benjamin Franklin, without religious motivation.

3. Which of the components of experience do you call "of God"? Having sorted out and recognized at least some of the components of experience, which elements do you embrace as God's presence? Presence corresponds to whatever or whoever has a hold on one's becoming. Presence involves having effects. Trying to identify what is "of God" is trying to sense the hold that God has on the becoming of experience through God's effects on experience.

There is certainly some artificiality to the question, for God is not simply one causal agent among others whose specific effects can be clearly distinguished. Yet there is a real basis for the question, even if it is limited. For God does have effects in the world, and effects are particular and individual; and if they are that, then *something* can be said about them, and deserves to be said about them.

4. Why this and not that? This question returns us to issues of interpretation and is an invitation to make some hermeneutical identifications. Why do you identify this element rather than that element as an effect of God in your life? All of us always enter all experience biased, that is, with presuppositions, and rarely with much self-consciousness about our ideological convictions. It is not wrong to have them. It is natural. It is disastrous not to know we have them. Presuppositions normally hide themselves effectively. They surround what we take to be self-evident about reality. Self-evidence is their camouflage.

Some interpretative equipment is buried less deeply. We are often conscious, for example, of the biblical symbols and stories that guide experience. The image of God as father or mother might suggest to us that some nurturing component of experience is "of God." Pauline attention to reconciliation might command attention to open wounds in the web of relationality in which we live. Then the call to offer healing might well be understood as the lure of God, the effect of God, on that experience, or better yet, the presence of God *in* that experience.

The point is that components of experience do not come tagged. Interpretation of experience is always involved, and the omnipresence of interpretation means that we are never more than a footfall away from fallibility. There are times, of course, of moral certainty about what God is up to when our actions and commitments are less daunted by the shroud of fallibility that encompasses the human enterprise. On points of justice, mercy, and love our Judeo-Christian deep story is crystal clear.

Because our lives emerge from and are embedded in the lives of others, God would not intend anything for me that does not aver to my relational web. Therefore, discernment that takes place in the heart of community is a large help in cracking open and interpreting experience. Community is important for a second reason as well: our biblically grounded conviction that YHWH has plans for a People and not just for individuals one by one. People must therefore crack open experience together.

When sufficient clarity exists to compel our lives, we should be able to articulate some sense of the hermeneutics that guides our interpretation of experience and which opens our minds and hearts to the presence of the Ultimate within the immediacy of lived experience.

Limits on Religious Discourse

Although later generations referred to Whitehead's thought as "process philosophy," that was not his choice. He called it the philosophy of organism. Although his way of telling the story of experience does posit momentary drops of experience as the building blocks of reality, it is perhaps a deep sense of the pervasive, organic interrelatedness that better catches his basic mood. He understood that the whole world conspired in each new creation. Alan Watts catches the sense of this very well: "We do not 'come into' this world; we *come* out of it. As the ocean waves, the universe 'peoples.' Every individual is an expression of the whole realm of nature, a unique action of the total universe" (1972, 8).

Since the whole universe is implicated in each event, it is never possible to analyze it fully. The total experience always exceeds our limited perception of it. Our perception is always larger than our conscious, cognitive grasp of it. Our experience is so much wider and deeper than that of which we are conscious. Depth psychology warns us not to equate the ego with the contents of consciousness. Whitehead observed that "consciousness flickers; and even at its brightest, there is a small focal region of clear illumination, and a large penumbral region which tells of intense experience in dim apprehension" (1978, 267). Therefore, "insistence on hard-headed clarity issues from sentimental feeling, as it were a mist, cloaking the perplexities of fact. Insistence on clarity at all costs is based on sheer superstition as to the mode in which human intelligence functions. Our reasonings grasp at straws for premises and float on gossamers for deduction" (n.d., 79).

Few theologians have been as sensitive as empirical theologian Bernard Meland to the limitations upon rational discourse imposed by the very complexity and organicness of each drop of experience:

> The sheer event of existing, however, is deeper than consciousness, and deeper than anyone's sensory awareness of it. It opens into an on-going stream of interrelated events simultaneously enjoying and enduring the fact of existing.... The limits of our human structure preclude our having full understanding or steady awareness of this depth of mystery that has brought us into existence and, for a time, holds us in existence as humanly conscious being. Thus our existing as immediate occurrences takes place with but marginal awareness, and often with relative indifference, to the penumbral occurrences that carry and give intimation of the Ultimate Efficacy attending all existence. (Meland 1976, 45)

The final sense of limitations on God-talk could not be stated more poignantly than in these words of T. S. Eliot:

> So here I am ...
> Trying to use words, and every attempt
> Is a wholly new start, and a different kind of failure
> Because one has only learnt to get the better of words
> For the thing one no longer has to say, or the way in which
> One is no longer disposed to say it. And so each venture
> Is a new beginning, a raid on the inarticulate
> With shabby equipment always deteriorating
> In the general mess of imprecision of feeling,
> Undisciplined squads of emotion. (1971, 30–31)

Religious discourse will always be shabby when compared to the experience it names. My point is that it should not be any shabbier than it has to be. About any religious experience claim, therefore, it behooves us to ask: In what experience is the claim grounded? How did you sort out the complexities of your experience? What, in that welter of data, do you experience as "of God"? What symbolic world guided your interpretation? When those questions have been fielded, we still run headlong into the unmanageable, for the depth of experience never turns itself inside out. The mystery of God and history is of too great a size to be tamed fully into straight talk, though theology sometimes forgets that. Mystics regularly turn to poetry when straight talk brings them to the outer edges of intelligibility.

Mystery is not vagueness. Mystery is not abstract. The only genuine routing to mystery is through the labyrinth of concrete experience whose far reaches have been explored with deliberate care. We are, then, to make our best empirical effort to engage in straight talk about religious experience, not as a violation of mystery, but as a precondition for the deepest encounter with it.

Thick Empiricism

As the authority of past tradition tends more and more to crumble, men naturally turn a wistful ear to the authority of reason or to the evidence of present fact. They will assuredly not be disappointed if they open their minds to what the thicker and more radical empiricism has to say. I fully believe that such an empiricism is a more natural ally than dialectics ever were, or can be, of the religious spirit. (James 1967, 314–15)

We must, as this chapter closes, acknowledge the complexities of recourse to experience. Experience means different things to different people and different systems, and so do the methods of reading experience. Radical empiricism is thick, "an empiricism [that] must neither admit into its construction any element that is not directly experienced, nor exclude any element that is directly experienced" (James 1969, 42). Whitehead wrote that "the chief danger to philosophy is narrowness in the selection of evidence. . . . Philosophy may not neglect the multifariousness of the world— the fairies dance, and Christ is nailed to the cross" (1928, 512, 513). *Mutatis mutandis,* that is also the chief danger to religion and theology. For example, through layer upon symbolic layer our dreams reach deep into our unconscious experience in ways inaccessible indeed to sense experience or deliberate control. Five different dreams move the narrative of the first two chapters of the Gospel of Matthew.

Peter Berger and Lee Snook both have called upon empiricism, recourse to experience, as a response to pluralism. When new experience and faith seem to contradict each other, Snook sees these options: "(1) deny experience in order to save faith, (2) deny faith in order to save the facts, or (3) learn to think differently, which is to say, alter one's conception of God such that neither (1) nor (2) is required" (1980, 291). Snook notes a number of different uses of experience and theologians typical of each approach: Karl Rahner as an example of the use of experience to provide a rational base for faith; people in a somewhat process/relational mode like John Cobb and Langdon Gilkey; those who work dialectically, like Paul Tillich and Reinhold Niebuhr; the political theologians who engage social systems, like Jürgen Moltmann, Rosemary Reuther, and Gustavo Gutierrez; those theologians devoted to an integrative (of experience) approach include both Edward Schillebeeckx and David Tracy; concern for the deliverances of religious experience include Morton Kelsey, Thomas Merton, and Henri Nouwen. The pressure of experience upon their theologizing links all of these, as different as they may be in many other respects.

Berger begins *The Heretical Imperative* with a chapter entitled "Modernity as the Universalization of Heresy." The wide choice of worldviews and systems means that "modernity pluralizes both institutions and plausibility structures" (Berger 1979, 17). He examines the deductive and reductive possibilities as possible responses and then opts for the inductive option. He argues for "taking human experience as the starting point of religious reflection, and using the methods of the historian to uncover those human experiences that have become embodied in the various religious traditions" (Berger 1979, 127).

In his book *American Religious Empiricism*, William Dean does a tour de force journey through the American tradition. In his opening chapter he notes the affinity between contemporary empiricism and the ancient Hebrew instincts about God and history. "The ancient Hebrew community and its God lived in a relation of mutual interpretation. They lived in history, nothing more. There was no escape" (1986, 4). Like James and Meland, Dean recognizes not only our historicity but the bodiliness of our implantedness in history, again with affinity for Hebrew experience. "Like Hebrews in the wilderness, they [American empiricists] chose that unformed, uninterpreted, physical cacophony of emotional, valuational, largely nonconscious and in every sense ambiguous, objective experience, felt initially and blindly by the body" (20–21). Dean more than most theologians I know demands space for ambiguity as normative, not as temporary on the way to full clarity.

Donald Gelpi uses the work of Charles Sanders Peirce to provide a workable religious model in response to the turn to experience in contemporary theology (Gelpi 1994). He proposes a Peircean triadic model and then enters into a very useful dialogue with Schillebeeckx, praxis, process theology and transcendental Thomism.

In a chapter of *Empirical Theology* and in many parts of *Jesus and the Metaphors of God*, I have argued my own brand of experience-based theologizing (Lee, 1992, 1993). If you want to know what Spirit names, go to all of the passages in our earlier and later Scriptures that invoke the metaphor Spirit/*ruach* to interpret historical, religious experience. Then look for the common characteristics of those experiences that people connect with

Spirit (breath and wind are the literal meanings upon which the metaphor is drawn. What is happening in all of these passages in which action is attributed to YHWH? We are in the world and can only experience what is in the world with us. God may be more than our history-bound experience of God, but we can only approach the "more" through intimations from these worldly appearances of God.

Reprise

In this chapter I have grounded the empirical temperament of contemporary U.S. culture in the sixteenth century when science gave us a new systematic method (observationist inductive) and opened us to new knowledge and understanding through its use. The impact of the scientific revolutions is, of course, pervasive in Western culture; it is not just part of U.S. culture, though we have it in high definition. Lay experience that is educated in U.S. colleges and universities, whether religious or secular, is more deeply exposed to these currents than is seminary education. That is part of the reason why the social location of lay experience must be a valued resource in lessening the pile size of the piled-up revolutions.

I have also tried to say that while "experience" is a central cultural category, it eludes univocal meaning. Gelpi says it well, and I would like to end with his words:

> The term "experience" enjoys a certain pride of place among the weasel words of the English language. Weasel words twist and wiggle. No sooner does one think that one has pinned a weasel word down to a single meaning than one finds it signifying something totally different. (1994, 1–2)

IV

REVOLUTION TWO:
THE TRANSFORMATION OF POWER

Introduction

In his book *Power over Power,* David Nyberg says that Sigmund Freud's colleagues once chided him for his blunt language, especially the use of sexual imagery for psychological phenomena. They suggested that he would get a more ready hearing if he would change his language. Freud replied, "I like to avoid concessions to faintheartedness!" (Nyberg 1981, 18). Nygren suggests, and I agree, that we should talk about power issues straight on. Call them what they are. Without faintheartedness. In religious circles power talk is most often assiduously avoided, which always works to the advantage of those in power. This is not a chapter for the fainthearted.

I have addressed the French Revolution as a particularly vivid expression of a paradigm shift in Western culture's sense of how power should function among us. The American Revolution is no lesser expression of the same paradigm shift, but the social location of the new world situated the paradigm shift somewhat more benevolently, though indeed not without destructive fallout. I think it difficult for people in the United States to appreciate French skepticism about the relative "achievement" of the French Revolution, especially from a Catholic perspective. The social location of our experience is significantly different, since so many of those who came to the new world were getting away from the power arrangements of the old world. The ravages of the paradigm shift are still visible in Europe and the memories somewhat more palpable, though the European Economic Community is the larger power issue now.

In a small square in the old residential section of Bordeaux you can see today the entire exterior wall of a small Gothic church that was de-churched in the revolution. The Gothic windows have been bricked in, with residential quarters built into the church on two levels, except for a car repair service in one section. A large church entrance toward the rear has been retained as a door for bringing cars in for axle repair, and a large sign to that effect has been painted above the former church entrance.

In the Loire Valley, the abbey of Fontevraud was one of the church's most extraordinary experiments in how power might be structured in a religious setting. It was founded in the twelfth century by Robert d'Arbrissel (whose father was a Catholic priest) with five distinct components: one area for the hermits; the Grand Moutier for the virgins; the Madeleine for the other women; St. John for the Men; and St. Lazarre for lepers, who also formed a community there. Henry II, Eleanor of Aquitaine, and Richard the Lion Hearted are all buried there, a testimony to the abbey's prestige. Men and women alike in this abbey lived under the authority of the abbess, at a time when gender equality could hardly have occurred to anyone as an option. While the fortunes of the abbey waxed and waned, it remained a formidable presence until the French Revolution when, in 1792, it was closed down and sacked (statues broken, great bells melted down). In 1804 it became a prison and remained so until 1963.

My point in mentioning these items is to make certain that we do not miss the turmoil of the deep paradigm shift that we are looking at in regard to the transfer and transformation of power in Western culture. Alfred North Whitehead's comment upon profound change is indeed to the point:

> It is the first step in sociological wisdom, to recognize that the major advances in civilization are processes that all but wreck the societies in which they occur:—like unto an arrow in the hand of a child. The art of free society consists first in the maintenance of the symbolic code; and secondly in fearlessness of revision, to secure that the code serves those purposes which satisfy an enlightened reason. Those societies which cannot combine reverence to their symbols with freedom of revision, must ultimately decay either from anarchy, or from the slow atrophy of a life stifled by useless shadows. (1955, 88)

Given the changes incumbent on the church today, not only from contemporary transformations afoot this moment (Peter Drucker says the most radical societal change the world has ever known), but from the pile up of underaddressed revolutions over five centuries, Whitehead's words are newly precious (Drucker 1994, 53ff.).

As I indicated earlier, using the image of Simon Schama, the leitmotif of the paradigm shift from "subject" to "citizen" is participation. All people have a right to participate in the resources of the community necessary for a decent human life and a right to participate in decision making that affects their lives. The first is about resources; the second about power. The social teaching of the church has been attentive to issues of social justice in theory and in some places in practice. Therefore, I will focus more upon power issues and participation in the decision-making processes of our social existence. We will first visit the Christian Scriptures and early Christian history on issues around power. Then I will propose a contemporary resource for theological reflection on power (Bernard Loomer). Following this we will look at an option that was articulated already in the earlier history of Catholic experience in the United States, one that reappears today and is largely brought forward by those people upon whom I am focusing in this book. A new breed of educated Catholic laywomen and laymen is urging the U.S. Catholic church to reconsider more participative structures in the body politic of the church so that their experience shapes the decisions that in turn determine the shape of Catholic living. This is precisely what the Pharisees were able to accomplish within Judaism during the second century BCE.

Finally, I would like to offer a pastoral application of concerns from this chapter by presenting a model for assessing the healthiness of social systems and the power dynamics that must be addressed when social change is called for. This model has been developed in the context of developing small Christian communities in U.S. culture.

The Christian Scriptures on Power

In his lifetime on earth Jesus gave to his followers no particular way of organizing community. The New Testament proposes what we sometimes, in contemporary idiom, refer to as a "discipleship of equals." Jesus imposed no structures, suggested no ordering. He only provided metaphors for how power should function. *Only* metaphors. But to offer root metaphors is to shape a deep story, and, in the long run, to provide a template that is more sure and more flexible than a specific structure. Root metaphors admit of many implementations. The three important metaphors for power functions are shepherd, steward, and servant or slave. The latter two are close but not identical; they could perhaps be understood as two metaphors, except that in biblical texts they appear together.

These metaphors help tell the truth about the exercise of power in Christian community because, in each instance, there is something about steward or shepherd or servant that is really and truly like leadership. There is a cluster of possible meanings for steward, shepherd, and servant, but not every meaning is meant to be applied to leadership.

There is, and has always been, a symbiotic relationship between faith and culture. Even the language "faith and culture" is problematic. For religion is part of culture, and there is no religion that is not incarnated in culture. One can never truly disengage some religious notion from its cultural expression because it will then be expressed in another culturally influenced way. The metaphors for the exercise for power that come from Jesus take their literal meanings from his culture and have a second symbolic layer of meaning constructed upon and out of the literal meaning.

We will consider the discipleship of equals and then three metaphors that address power issues.

Discipleship of Equals

In Mark 5:21–43, we hear a story, and a story within a story. In the midst of a large crowd gathered around Jesus, a Capernaum synagogue chief, Jairus, falls at Jesus' feet and begs Jesus to go to his home and lay hands on his twelve-year-old daughter who is dying, that "she might become well and live." Jesus sets out with him to go to his home. At this point a woman who has had a flow of blood for twelve years and has exhausted all her resources on doctors who helped not at all (her condition grew worse) touches Jesus' clothing and is healed. Jesus stops the journey to Jairus's house and interacts with the woman. In the course of this delay, people arrive from Jairus's house saying that it is too late now, for his daughter has died. Jesus continues to Jairus's house, nonetheless, and raises the daughter to life.

To understand why Galilean Jews would probably have responded with amazement, and some perhaps even with chagrin, we must look at the cultural setting. The fact that we hear the stories within a patriarchal setting is already clear because the man is named and the woman is not. In the pecking order, Jairus has an honored position. First, he is male. Second, he holds a position of prestige. In this cultural setting, there is a rightful place in society for Jairus as male and as important because of a role. The woman does not merely happen not to have a public role. As a woman she is excluded from the possibility of having such a role. Even more notable to people of that time and place is the fact that she has had a flow of blood for twelve years, making her unclean and functionally a social outcast. Jesus delays going to Jairus's house in response to this woman, her need, and her faith. Jairus's request is desperate, but Jesus delays to be with the woman. In the meanwhile, Jairus's daughter dies. For Jesus, the unclean, nameless woman has no less honor as a human being than Jairus. Jesus not only ignores expected protocol but does not accept that the woman's touch has made him unclean, for he in turn touches the hand of Jairus's daughter, a forbidden act if he is unclean. Ched Myers observes:

> Jesus is portrayed in a way of social interaction that breaks the rules and expectations of the conduct that obtained in Palestinian honor culture, shocking those who heard the story and undermining their sense of social order and propriety. In the process of his symbolic construction of the new social order of the kingdom, Mark's Jesus was subverting the status quo in order to create new possibilities of human community. (1988, 199)

So what is the "logic" of Jesus behavior?

Like any good parent, God loves all God's children; and children of God, siblings, love each other nonjudgmentally in order to be holy in the same way that God is holy (Matt. 5:43–48). God sends sun and rain to the good and bad, just and unjust. God sets no bounds. God plays no favorites. Why?

The logic of this reconstruction of social order, as understood in the Matthean community, is presented later in Matthew 23:8–12. In our social relationships, no one takes ascendancy, and the reason is that radically we are, in fact, all siblings. We are siblings as a direct result of the fatherhood or parenthood of God. What God's fatherhood does is require that we forgo turning any sibling into a parental figure (father). "Call no human being 'father.'" Elisabeth Schüssler Fiorenza claims that the fatherhood of God does not legitimate patriarchal structures but rather disenfranchises them all:

> The saying of Jesus uses the "father" name of God not as a legitimatization for existing patriarchal power structures in society or church but as a critical subversion of all structures of domination. The "father" God of Jesus Christ makes possible "the sisterhood of men" (in the phrase of Mary Daly) by denying any father, and all patriarchy, its right to existence. Neither the "brothers" nor the "sisters" in the Christian community can claim the "authority of the father" because that would involve claiming authority and power reserved for God alone. (1983, 150)

Let us say, indeed, that there are benevolent, nurturing meanings of "mother" and "father." Sometimes it is appropriate for leaders to function out of these parental meanings. But the radical truth about our relationships as disciples of Jesus is that of siblinghood, and that is how the naming should go. To name the leadership role in a certain way is to engage in the social construction of reality, and to name the leader "father" is to set up behavioral expectations about both the leader and the community. We do not have to look far to know how "father" language has subverted "servant" language. In this same Matthean passage Jesus recommends "servant" as the naming we should embrace for the leader. A community is expected to look up to a father leader, whereas a servant leader is expected to look up to the community. This is no minor reversal, no minor social reconstruction of received dominant cultural reality, then or now.

The implications of the logic of our siblinghood are nowhere better expressed than by Paul in his letter to the Galatians:

> All of you are the children of God, through faith, in Christ Jesus, since everyone of you that has been baptized has been clothed in Christ. There can be neither Greek nor Jew, there can be neither slave nor free person, there can be neither male nor female—for all of you are one in Christ Jesus. (Gal. 3:25–28)

Privilege is neither to be given nor denied on the basis of race, socioeconomic situation, or gender. In the U.S. Catholic church, the feminist critique of patriarchy is one of the strongest challenges to church at all levels in respect to the discipleship of equals.

The Leader as Steward

The Greek word for steward is *oikonomos,* which is composed of two words. *Nomos* means "law" or "prescription," and *oikos* means home. The steward is the one who sees to it that the house is run the way it is supposed to be run. It is especially when the proprietor is absent that the steward has the greatest obligations.

In Luke 12:42–48, in response to Peter's question, "Are the things you are saying meant for us," Jesus described the function of the steward. The servant knows the proprietor's intentions (Luke 12:47), and the steward who performs well will soon be put in charge of everything. The steward is always accountable to the proprietor (Luke 16:2). Luke 19 has a parable about servants who are entrusted with the proprietor's wealth, and though the word "servant" is used, the function more nearly approximates that of the steward. Money is given to the servant/steward, and the expectation is that it will be put to use and grow. The most explicit reference to stewardship in reference to leadership is in the pastoral letter to Titus. The writer says that one chosen as presbyter or elder must be irreproachable, since such a one is God's steward.

The steward, then, is responsible for the house and its fruitful functioning. The steward is finally entrusted with major responsibility as a result of having proved trustworthy in lesser responsibilities. Stewards have worked their way through demonstrated household responsibility. The steward's function is especially important when the proprietor is absent. Let us draw some conclusions about power and Christian leadership.

The steward's power is there because the steward acts as Jesus did in exercising responsibility for the reign of God as it comes to be in the world. The steward does not own the house but is there for the house. The steward is to help the resources work for the growth of the house. In terms of community, this means identifying the gifts that exist within the community and calling them to fruitfulness within and for the community. James Whitehead, in his development of the stewardship model of Christian leadership, observes:

> A community of disciples is a place of mutual empowerment. Both gifted and wounded, we care for one another in a mood of mutuality. God's power finds tangible expression in the many strengths that appear in a community. These significant differences in ability and giftedness make us interdependent on each other, but do not afford any of us a privileged or superior status before God. The power we find in ourselves and the authority that our responsibilities call us to are rooted finally neither in us nor our role but in the Spirit who blows where the Spirit will. (1987, 69)

Whitehead speaks, in a wonderful phrase, of the "generous absence" of Jesus Christ, which creates the space for our stewardship in community (1987, 72).

I have a friend who works in a diocesan office. The bishop reminds those in the school office, in the office of religious education, and in the pastoral office, that "you work for me." I understand, especially in the current state of affairs in the Catholic church, where that remark comes from. But a steward leader would be more apt to say, "I work for God's reign, and because I do, I work for you, the household of God."

The Leader as Shepherd

The role of leader in the Christian community has been named often with the Latin words for shepherd and servant: "pastor" and "minister." "Minister" has been used often in the Reform tradition. It is only in the postconciliar church that "minister" has become part of Catholic vernacular as well.

In the Jewish Scriptures the shepherd is often an image of God's care. Psalm 23 is probably the Hebrew song most familiar to Christians and Jews alike. Because YHWH is our shepherd we lack nothing. We should never fear, no matter how bleak life looks, for YHWH the shepherd cares for us.

Jesus' long discussion of himself as a good shepherd in John 10 draws upon YHWH's self-description as a good shepherd in Ezekiel 34. What YHWH promises is exquisite care: the flock will rest in good grazing grounds and will browse in rich pastures. YHWH will watch over the fat and happy sheep but will have a special care for the lost ones, the wounded ones, and the sick ones. Jesus further stresses a kind of intimacy between shepherd and sheep: I know mine and mine know me. When Jesus discusses Peter's leadership in John 21 (a later addition to John's Gospel), he uses the shepherd image: feed my lambs, feed my sheep.

A leader and a leader's relation to the community is in some ways like that of a shepherd and a shepherd's relation to a flock. That is why the metaphor works. The shepherd cares for the flock; the shepherd leads and guides and cares for needs; and the shepherd has a special care for the needy members of the flock.

But there are ways in which a leader should not be like a shepherd. Shepherds certainly did not have a universally good reputation! Before YHWH uses shepherd as a self-image in Ezekiel 34, there is a long passage in which YHWH excoriates Israel's shepherds (leaders as well as shepherds) for their neglect of the fold. "My flock is astray on every mountain and on every high hill; my flock has been scattered all over the world; no one bothers about them, and no one looks after them" (Ezek. 34:6). In his analysis of the shepherd metaphor, David Miller reminds us that shepherds were denied civil rights in the ancient Jewish world and that people were not to buy wool, milk, or a kid from a shepherd, because it was presumed that these were stolen (1981, 12). That is why the adjective "good" in "the good shepherd" would have been an ear-catching, enigmatic metaphor.

When a leader is caring for all, with a special care for the lost and needy and wounded, the leader is being a good shepherd. When the leader has the kind of intimacy with a community that the leader truly knows the members of the community, and the community feels it has a personal relationship with the leader, the leader is being a good shepherd.

But people are people and not sheep and goats. The leader should not do things for a community that the community can do for itself. As Jung and others have noted, people should not be conditioned by a shepherd to behave like sheep. "However socially useful the image may be to civilization, the Good Shepherd's goodness can be devastating to the psyche, stealing liberty like a thief, killing the soul . . ." (Miller 1981, 12).

The shepherd metaphor always needs to be corrected by the image of a discipleship of equals. When one becomes a leader and *in some ways acts like a shepherd,* the leader does not stop being our sister or our brother. That is because leader and community are like shepherd and flock and also unlike shepherd and flock. When the shepherd image is used to elicit uncritical obedience to the leader, it is indeed damaging to the corporate community soul.

Shepherd, then, is an especially tricky metaphor. The special care and intimacy between leader and community are exactly right. Any form of shepherding that dishonors the intelligence and experience of the community is exactly wrong.

The complex of leadership metaphors needs to be entertained together. If shepherd is corrected by servant, for example, then the genuine tenderness and care for the community will be guaranteed. Servant, on the other hand, can be too laid back and stands to be corrected by the shepherd, whose job description calls for more proactive efforts to provide than does the servant's.

The Leader as Servant

In Mark 10:35–45, when Jesus and the disciples are on the road, James and John approach Jesus and ask him for places immediately at his right and his left when he comes into glory. The Gospels are often haunted by a Davidic messianic expectation that there will be one who will free Israel and sit as king. The two disciples are looking for privileged power positions in such a kingdom. It is a clear power play. Somehow the other ten hear what James and John are up to and are irritated with them. Jesus sits them all down and speaks about power, through a contrast. Secular rulers dominate those whom they rule, and they make certain that their power is felt. Among the followers of Jesus Christ there is a new and different kind of order, a stunning reversal of normal cultural expectations. The leader is to play the role of a servant—there to respond to need within the community. The community's agenda is the leader's agenda.

None of us has to reflect long to understand the depth of this reversal of leadership and power. Shortly after the publication of his book *The Anatomy of Power,* John Kenneth Galbraith was interviewed for an article in *USA Today* (Nov. 17, 1983, p. 11). Galbraith accepts Max Weber's familiar description of power as the ability of one person to win the submission to his or her purposes from another person. And he locates the ability to have this kind of control in three areas. First, there are personal abilities like physical stature, intelligence, convincing speech. Second, wealth, possessions, property, income, and the like, give a person clout. Finally, people with power are likely to have a strong organization behind them that inclines other people to submit to their purposes. I doubt that Fortune 500 corporations would advise junior executives to be leaders by behaving as the lowest member of the staff. The startling thing is that Jesus calls this strange behavior a redemptive approach to power. He uses his own life as an example: he comes not to be served but to serve.

When Matthew takes this narrative over from Mark, an interesting thing happens. The disciples in Mark's Gospel are generally portrayed as ever slow to catch on. Matthew rescues James and John by having the mother instead of the sons approach Jesus with the same power-grabbing question (Matt. 20:20–28). She does it in behalf of her sons. Their names are not given, but they are identified as Zebedee's sons. We are once again on the road to Jerusalem, and the mother of Zebedee's sons is apparently with the travelling group. She is not given a name, though present, while Zebedee is named, though absent. That in itself is a power device in a patriarchal society. The rest of the narrative unfolds the same way.

Luke's appropriation of this same material undergoes a very new development (22:24–27). James and John disappear by name. Neither is their mother given a presence. We only hear that an argument has broken out among the disciples about which of them should be counted as the greatest. The surprising development is that this discussion occurs at table at the final meal, only a few verses after the institution of the Eucharist. One can only surmise that power issues around the behavior of community leaders must have been pressing enough to relocate the discussion within the primary ritual of the early Christian community. In the earliest communities it is highly probable that whoever had leadership in the community's life also had leadership in the community's Eucharist, a central feature of its life. Two memoranda from Vatican II's Central Theological Commission recalled this to the bishops and theologians working on the *Dogmatic Constitution on the Church* (Legrand 1979, 413). Thus, the Lukan relocation of the power issue at the final meal and within verses of the account of the institution of the Eucharist suggests that the Christian reversal of normative cultural interpretations of power is so radical as to need constant reinforcement, already from the beginning.

In Mark and Matthew the two words used to describe leadership among the followers of Jesus are "servant" (*diakonos*) and "slave" (*doulos*). Luke introduces the notion of governing (*hegoumenos*), which makes it transparently clear that power in community is at stake. Luke also adds a new descriptor word for leader, namely, one who acts like a younger (*neoteros*) member of the community, one normally without power. In all of the Synoptics, Jesus applies the *diakonos* notion of servant to himself as an example to his followers.

In John's Gospel, as in Luke's, the setting is Jesus' last supper with his disciples before his death (13:1–15). This time there is no power play from disciples to frame the action. In John's Gospel, the conversation turns into drama when Jesus acts out the behavior of the leader. He removes his outer garment, girds himself with a towel as servants do when washing the feet of guests, and washes the disciples' feet. Peter registers the objection of dominant culture: "Leaders do not act like that." Jesus tells Peter that leaders acting like that is such a constitutive feature of his followers that if Peter cannot reverse his thinking, he cannot belong.

One could hardly think of a more compelling way to assert the reversal than having Jesus act it out. "You call me master," he says, "but look how I the master conduct myself in your regard. Now you conduct your power arrangements that way too."

Then as now, it is far easier to engage in the biblical exegesis of reversal than to engage in the biblical living of reversal! Peter felt our struggle for us. He puts his foot in his mouth, as is his wont. It is a reversal of still another kind that Jesus chooses Peter, the struggler and bumbler, for leadership so that his faith can be an example.

The more normal Greek word for servant is *diakonos.* In the New Testament, however, the word *doulos* occurs more frequently. Behind the word *doulos* probably stands the Hebrew word *ebed.* In one of the chapters in *The Pastor as Servant,* Paul Hanson explores the word *ebed* (1986, 3–19). If the word "servant" speaks of a leader's relationship with the community, behind the word *ebed* is a relationship with God that adds further definition.

While *ebed* can indeed simply mean "slave," this is a less likely metaphorical meaning when applied to leadership. In the context of treaty language, *ebed* sometimes carries the meaning of vassal. In the ancient world, vassalship meant that one owed all one's loyalty to the king. One served the king with all one's heart and mind and strength. An *ebed* leader, therefore, not only is servant to the community but is in covenant with YHWH. The *ebed* reminds the community of God's intentions for it and reminds God of the community's needs. Servanthood reaches in both directions.

Power

How the disciples of Jesus should handle power is starkly and clearly indicated in the contrast between the way pagan leaders lord it over their subjects and make their power felt and the leader who is a servant of the community, a steward of history in the "gracious absence" of Jesus on earth.

Not only is this "right" in the context of Christian community, but in whatever circumstances power functions in this way, history is redeemed. Few things could be as countercultural as believing that. Few of the reversals are as "foolish" as that—or as hopeful to a world, or to a church, in which men and women strive, usually against great odds, to be participating citizens and not subjects of lords.

To be sure, talk about power does not dominate public discourse today. But there are those who call for radical rethinking of the nature of power and possible modes of its exercise. In two recent books, Ched Myers offers a fierce biblical critique of public uses of power. He focuses readers upon Mark's Gospel in *Binding the Strong Man* and assesses the tensive nature of Christian interaction with the power of empire in Christianity's early days. In *Who Will Roll Away the Stone?* Myers details the many ways in which the public policy of the United States instances empire, and he is concerned to reaffirm the redemptive character of the Christian take on power.

I will gather some reflections based upon three voices articulating alternative interpretations of power, each of which stands a better chance of empowering citizens and not lords. In *Beyond Power,* Marilyn French speaks from a feminist perspective. Elizabeth Janeway, in her book *The Powers of the Weak,* is concerned with how those without power in the sense of domination may still be able to influence social situations.

Finally, and at more length, I will reflect upon Bernard Loomer's lecture "Two Kinds of Power." In the inaugural D. R. Sharpe Lecture in Social Ethics, in the Divinity School of the University of Chicago, process theologian Bernard Loomer addressed the issue of power in ways deeply consonant with the New Testament instincts we have been tracing. In this section I shall be calling upon his analysis of two kinds of power. In a slightly compressed form and with editorial changes that favor inclusive language, the text of this lecture appears in an appendix in this book. It has appeared only in *Criterion,* a publication of the University of Chicago Divinity School, and as an article in *Process Studies,* and deserves a wider public than the important but limited journal world.

Marilyn French

In her lengthy survey of Western experience, Marilyn French documents how power and control have been equated and how that equation has controlled relationships between individuals and social groups of every kind in a patriarchal culture. "There are only two ways to control living beings: eradication and domestication" (French 1986, 507). Eradication is murder.

Domestication is the use of intimidation and threat to bend people's wills. Foreign policy among nations is based upon the ability to go to war if that policy is threatened. This is a form of eradication, obviously. The death penalty belongs to that form of control. Sadly, the church has used this form of power in the crusades and in the auto-da-fé. There is no need to document the many instruments of domestication in most areas of public life, civil or ecclesial.

From the twentieth century, French points to the influential thought of philosopher Bertrand Russell, who said that power is the ability to compel obedience, and to sociologist Talcott Parsons, who described power as something like a possession that some people have which makes it possible to alter people's wills and make people conform to their own will instead (French 1985, 505). Michel Foucault says, "power contains a sort of fatality which weighs as pitilessly on those who command as on those who obey; nay more, it is in so far as it enslaves the former that, through their agency, it presses down on the latter" (French 1986, 509).

As the title of the book indicates, French does not seek an alternative interpretation of power. Power, which she sees as dominational, is so imbedded in and interchangeable with patriarchal structures that our best alternative is to move beyond power, that is, beyond patriarchal structure. Some of the strengths of her project are to remind us that the violent power systems that we have constructed are exactly that, *constructed*. We are able, should we choose, to undertake a social construction that is beyond power. To help realize that we do have other options, French reminds us that in some cultures, which our culture calls "primitive," alternative constructions that are beyond power do function effectively. As resources for thinking alternative constructions, French, for example, asks us to imagine arrangements in which right and left brain functions are equally valued and promoted. In the current arrangement in Western culture, rational behaviors get most of the rewards. She suggests that we might rehabilitate pleasure as noble, not as a hedonism that "is described as shallow and frivolous in a world of high-minded, serious purpose . . . [but as] a gratified response to quality—rooted in the senses, and for pleasure to be revalorized, the body and the senses must be revalorized" (358–59).

As avenue to a different sort of imagination about how things are, French cites Fritjof Capra's characterization of the subatomic world where "matter does not exist with certainty at definite places, but rather shows 'tendencies to exist,' and atomic events do not occur with certainty at definite times and in definite ways, but rather show 'tendencies to occur' " (498). French then suggests the potential for imaging human existence similarly, where "interconnection, interplay, is the cause of everything that exists. Power is neither substance nor force precisely, but the coming together of particular things in a certain way at a certain moment. . . . Nothing is dominant. Things work by attraction. . . . Even the detached observer is connected with what is observed. . . . No one can be an unmoved mover, a controller unaffected by what he or she controls" (499). French suggests applying that metaphor to social life among human beings.

In her recent book *Leadership and the New Science,* Margaret Wheatley does exactly what Marilyn French suggested: she applies an imagination derived from the new science to human organization. Werner Heisenberg and Niels Bohr are among her heroes. She takes seriously, for example, the relation of chaos theory to the functioning of an orderly universe. Barbara Fleischer, my colleague in the Institute for Ministry here at Loyola University, probes with students in pastoral administration the possible applications of Wheatley's proposal for ministry and leadership in the Christian community.

I have not done justice to a book as rich in historical, philosophical, and literary grounding as *Beyond Power.* The value of a book like this is that when it looks at how power has been exercised, it imagines that something else might be the case and funds the contemporary imagination in metaphors from science, anthropology, and so on. We will never get from A to B, from the power models of dominant culture to the reign of God, without (to quote my nieces and nephews) a "humongous" imagination.

Elizabeth Janeway

Elizabeth Janeway, like Marilyn French, is a novelist. Perhaps in literary imagination, as in prophetic imagination, there is the resource for believing that something else might be the case. Janeway's analysis of how power arrangements have been constructed by us is detailed and powerful, like French's. Janeway moves in a different direction, however, not looking for some arrangement that is beyond power but for rearrangements in the functions of power, especially those that empower the weak. What options do those out of power have? She names three. I want to focus briefly on the first two of these, because there are identifiable instances of their transformative operations in the Catholic church. The first power of the weak is disbelief; the second is organization, people gathering together; the third, in extreme conditions, is rebellion.

Janeway does not find those in power bad people and those without power good people. Neither is inherently better or worse than the other.

"What is 'better' is, first, that a relative balance should exist between the members of a power relationship, simply because one-sided relations are either unstable or else deeply oppressive and wasteful of human abilities" (1981, 158). The powers of the weak are, therefore, those possibilities at the disposal of the dispossessed so that power arrangements are two-sided, more stable, therefore, and more appreciative of each person's gifts.

One of the effective powers of the weak is disbelief, which is where Janeway says "an ordered use of the powers of the weak takes its start" (1981, 161). A vital part of the power of those in power is defining and interpreting experience. Disbelieving those definitions and interpretations calls the power of the powerful into question. The disbelief will be named disloyalty by those in power—treason is perhaps the most negative interpretation. But if those out of power continue to challenge the party-line interpretation, its hold weakens.

Here is where experience comes much into play. When the experience of those out of power leads them to different conclusions, their disbelief carries weight, because they are mustering counterevidence to the official position. The institutional church tends to look upon those who disagree with the official position on contraception as dissenters. Andrew Greeley's research indicates that those who disagree with the teaching and continue to function actively as Catholics form a larger group than the combined groups of those who dissent and left the church and those who agree and support the position against contraception. Those Catholics who disagree and stay are engaging in disbelief. They are saying, "Our experience does not allow us to believe in that way, and our interpretation of ecclesial reality does not obligate us to go elsewhere." My point is not that this group is either right or wrong but that they have kept open a closed question and have functionally kept the official interpretation from defining who is in and who is out. I believe that one of the powers of the laity as the out-of-power group is precisely disbelief. Many clerical interpretations on women's issues and celibacy are also among current issues that are up against disbelief, often as it registers in lay interpretations (though not exclusively there). For educated people, if the material authority of the issue (the weight its logic bears) does not lend credibility to formal authority, disbelief is a likely response. When formal authority is not confirmed by material authority, disbelief is a likely option. From the perspective of the institution, those behaviors undermine authority. From the perspective of those out of power, the same behaviors "adjust" power. Both claims tell some truth.

The second of the powers of the weak to which we shall attend is coming together, that is, organizing, finding public space and public presence. One of the responses that keeps the dispossessed on the margins and out of power is agoraphobia, literally, "fear of the marketplace." It is a fear of public space that keeps the disempowered homebound and "in their place." Janeway suggests that therapy for agoraphobia is instructive about the powers of the weak. The sufferers meet each other and find that they are not alone, and "out of the sharing comes an ability to trust those who have been caught in the same bind as oneself" (1981, 189–190).

Walter Brueggemann comes to a similar conclusion in his assessment of the dynamics of the exodus. He feels that the three component moments of the exodus are (1) ideology critique, when people identify the culprit and the ideology that drives the culprit; (2) a public processing of pain, which releases social energy; and, after these, (3) a collective exercise in social imagination, as people begin to ponder that something else might be the case. I would reverse the first and second of these. I believe that public processing of pain usually comes first, "an intentional and communal act of expressing grievance which is unheard of and risky under such an absolutist regime [the Pharaoh]. . . . As long as persons experience their pain privately and in isolation, no social power is generated. That is why every regime has a law against assembly" (Brueggemann 1987, 16). A first level of organization is to meet to name the pain. The second is to determine whose actions are responsible for the pain, and what kind of thinking (ideology) is responsible for behaviors like that. As soon as one can attribute agency, the pain and its causes begin to lose their anonymous elusiveness.

Naming painful experience, assessing its causes (agents and ideologies), and strategizing responses are all parts of an essential Christian act of discernment. One of the names for this operation is social analysis. In the pastoral-application section at the end of this chapter I will offer a format for engaging social analysis, of which critique of ideology is a central component.

Brueggemann calls social or religious imagination the third step on the way to changing a power arrangement. The public processing of pain and engaging in ideology critique can fund hope for a people, for we recognize that we are not alone and we know what causes the pain. Therefore, we begin to imagine that something else might be the case. Imagination is an essential component to hope. The civil-rights movement is a solid example of these dynamics. Once the pain and ignominy were named out loud and discriminatory laws and their defenders were identified, the time was ripe for Martin Luther King to say, "I have a dream." And millions of black people began to have a dream that something else could really and truly be the case. To claim that black is beautiful is more than a recovery of pride in

a heritage; it is an act of defining that begins to rearrange power interpretations in a social system. Equal opportunity legislation is one attempt to put
teeth in the dream.

In contemporary Catholic life in the United States there are new public
spaces for lay experience to process itself, to reflect upon itself theologically,
and in so doing to exercise the power to define. Examples are Call to Action,
the National Association for Lay Ministry, and the National Center for the
Laity. Both disbelief and organization empower the new lay hermeneutic.
The disbelief is more a form of deconstruction. The lay hermeneutic also
supports the construction of new meaning.

Before moving to Bernard Loomer's interpretation of power, let us note
the difference between the three theoreticians being considered here. Marilyn French assesses power in the way that patriarchal culture has defined it
and made it operational, and when power is invested with those meanings it
is not redeemable. We must move "beyond power" in the social reconstruction of our social systems. Elizabeth Janeway asks what powers the weak
have at their disposal in order to become effective power participants in
shared social life. Giving those without power a power base introduces
mutuality into social arrangements and redeems them. Bernard Loomer,
like Elizabeth Janeway, retains power as a working paradigm. He is not interested, however, in jockeying for power positions, using forms of power that
introduce the powerless into the power mix but are grounded in the similar
dynamics of asserting influence. Loomer's plea is for an interpretation of
power that is a radical alternative to the culturally dominant interpretation.
This interpretation asks all people to use relational rather than dominational power, not only because it redeems human history, but because the
relational nature of reality requires it. He grounds his claims ontologically,
not just sociologically or Christianly.

Bernard Loomer

Bernard Loomer's discussion in "Two Kinds of Power" is grounded in his
long creative work in the empirical wing of process theology. In his later
work Loomer consistently called this worldview "process/relational modes
of thought" rather than "process philosophy" or "process theology." His
treatment of power is primarily concerned with value theory: what constitutes the highest human fulfillment in a world that is fully processive and radically relational. When he received the Alumnus of the Year award from the
University of Chicago Divinity School, he was asked to comment on what he
thought mattered more than anything. He used the metaphor of "size":

By size I mean the stature of a person's soul, the range and depth of [a person's] love, [a person's] capacity for relationships. I mean the volume of life you can take into your being and still maintain your integrity and individuality, the intensity and variety of outlook you can entertain in the unity of your being without feeling defensive or insecure. I mean the strength of your spirit to encourage others to become freer in the development of their diversity and uniqueness. I mean the power to sustain more complex and enriching tensions. I mean the magnanimity of concern to provide conditions that enable others to increase in stature. (1976, 70)

Loomer is convinced that the dominant notion of power does not best foster the stature of the human soul. That is the backdrop for what follows.

The dominant notion of power is unilateral. The most powerful person is the one who has the largest influence on others and on the world, while sustaining the most minimal possible effects from those people or that world. This is a very nonmutual exercise of power. In fact, unilateral power tends to treat others as objects rather than honor them as subjects who also have claims upon events. When unilateral power is the ideal, we are not led to acknowledge our mutual interdependence, that is, acknowledge that we need each other and have gifts for each other. Independence is a value in the exercise of unilateral power. Our culture does not treat vulnerability as desirable but as weakness. "When power is defined in a unilateral or linear fashion as a capacity to influence another, it follows factually as well as logically that the gain in power by the other is experienced as a loss of one's own power and therefore of one's status and sense of worth" (see appendix below, 174).

Powerful people are measured by how effectively they can force their will—"anyone else be damned." When unilateral power dominates a social system, "the natural and inevitable inequalities among individuals and groups become the means whereby the estrangements in life become wider and deeper. The rich become richer, the poor become poorer. . . . From a deeply religious point of view . . . this manner of handling the inequalities of life results in an increasing impoverishment for both the strong and the weak" (see appendix, 175).

For Loomer there is no alternative to power, for "the presence of power is manifest whenever two or more people are gathered together and have any kind of relationship. . . . Power is co-extensive with life itself" (appendix, 169). If there is no alternative power, there is an alternative to unilateral power, and he calls it "relational power."

One particular understanding from classical philosophy and one contrast between classical thought and process/relational modes of thought set the stage for understanding relational power. Classical philosophers have distinguished between internal and external relationships. A relationship is internal if I am affected by that to which I am in relationship. A relationship is external if I have effects on something or someone but remain myself unaffected by the relationship. Unilateral power tends to stress external relationships between a leader and a group being led. This maintains the leader/subject texture of leader/group. When, as in religious life, the leader is called the superior, the corollary is that the one led is the inferior. By attributing "grace of state" to the leader and not mentioning it in respect to the members of the group being led, the cards are stacked against the subjects. They are not full citizens.

Relational power presumes that mutual, internal relationships are the proper way to understand the entire relational texture of human interaction.

> [Relational power] is the capacity to sustain mutually internal relationships. . . . This is a relationship of mutually influencing and being influenced, of mutually giving and receiving, of mutually making claims and permitting and enabling others to make their claims. This is a relationship of mutuality which embraces all the dimensions and kinds of inequality that the human spirit is heir to. The principle of equality most profoundly means that we are equally dependent on the constitutive relationships that create us, however unequal we are in our various strengths, including our ability to exemplify the fullness and concreteness of this kind of power. (appendix, 189)

The Pauline theology of the Body of Christ is a Christian text that calls for relational power, for we are all members of each other. Paul's word for community, *koinonia,* is rooted in the meaning "participation." We do not become internally related. We already are internally related. Relational power redeems our interrelatedness. The Judeo-Christian belief that God's Spirit is everyone's gift from God means that every human person has something to say and something to give to every other human person. Only in a system in which mutually internal relations are the norm can those gift-giving transactions enrich the whole social Body of Christ.

A contrast between classical and process/relational modes of thought on a similar issue helps further clarify the claims of relational power. In Aristotelian thought, substance is a category that indicates what something is. There are also some accidentals, which have effects on a substance but do not change the substance, for it is what it is. Relationship is a category among the accidentals. Loomer holds that relationships are constitutive. We do not first exist and then have relationships. Who we are is a gift from relationships from the very first. In the fine phrase of Michael Cowan, the relational web is the perpetual womb of our becoming. If our identity is an emergent from relationships, the logic of it would hold that the finer our relational world, the finer the identities that incubate within it. Relational power favors the incubation with grace, divine and human.

I believe that in the theoretical understandings of Loomer's "Two Kinds of Power" there are some very useful resources for the kind of leadership that Jesus says is normative for Christian community.

All three of these interpretations of power share the conviction that people should participate together in the way their worlds are shaped, that no one should lord it over the others and seek to make their power felt. Each of these interpretations is an expression of the paradigm shift that came to the fore in the eighteenth century and continues to evolve. Faith is always to find its expression within the cultural worlds in which it lives. Among the most serious challenges to the Roman Catholic church in our time is to renovate its power chambers in such wise that the People of God experience themselves as fully operative citizens in those chambers, in all ways that are consistent with the Good News of Jesus Christ. In the mutually critical conversation between faith and culture, culture is calling into question many aspects of the clerical hermeneutic that has fashioned ecclesial functions of power. There may, finally, be no more loaded issue than this, no more sensitive issue than this, no more fecund issue than this, in today's church.

Usable American Experience
on the Doorstep of Ecclesia

In Max Byrd's recent novelized biography of Thomas Jefferson's years in France, on several occasions the French show incredulity about the American experiment in democracy. One Frenchman suggests that it is only a matter of time before George Washington eases himself into the position of monarch. They are incredulous about the long-term viability of the new American commitment to participative structures in the style of a federal republic. The idea makes them smile at the American naïveté. The truth here is probably that Americans had a less monarchically damaged political psyche—there was great geographical distance between them and French, Spanish, Portuguese, and English monarchs. The Revolutionary War, to be sure, was no picnic, but it did not have the viciousness of the French Revolution, and religion did not suffer here as on the Continent. That may have left us overly sanguine about the possibilities of participative citizenship, but it also left us more deeply committed to the experiment in democracy.

I acknowledge my conviction that the American experiment in participative democracy embodies some understandings of power more congenial to the teaching of Jesus than many of the unilateral, monarchical structures that currently obtain in the institutional church. I am not suggesting that the particular model of democratic government that characterizes the body politic of the United States should be a model for church polity. But I am suggesting that there is a hankering deep down in the American spirit for participative power politics and some extensive experience with participative structures. I am also saying that there is some learning here that could fruitfully be appropriated by *ecclesia* without *ecclesia* losing its soul—probably, in fact, with a retrieval of some of its original New Testament soul. With reference to the medieval morality play, Carl Jung observed that any time people tell their own stories at a deep enough level, they tell the story of *Everyman*. In its most basic configuration, the American experiment is responsive to the paradigm shift in Western culture that exploded in the late eighteenth and early nineteenth centuries, though in the making for some while before those culminations.

It is my intention to indicate very briefly how the Catholic church in the United States has from the later years of the eighteenth century onward been attracted to democratic mores, and then to indicate some possible futures for the church of 140 BCE. There are already some fine studies that detail the effects and aspirations of the American spirit on the American Catholic church. There is no need to repeat those, though I will draw upon them. There are some very concrete proposals that have been brought forward, worth serious discussion. I will allude to some of them, but extending them is not the topic of this chapter. I am trying to get more of the cards out on the table so we can address the game.

The Interrupted American Experiment

"Taxation without representation" easily translates into "we are required to support a system and we have no participation in the power structures of that system." The system was the British monarchy, a system which in Great Britain experienced its own inner turmoil over the functions of power. We readily associate John Milton with "Paradise Lost" and "Paradise Regained." Not nearly as many know that he wrote a treatise entitled "The Readie and Easie Way to Establish a Free Commonwealth and the Excellence Thereof Compared with the Inconveniences and Dangers of Readmitting Kingship in this Nation." From the same period came James

Harrington's *Oceana,* with its case for private property and a kind of early free-market-enterprise position. Works like these, especially *Oceana,* influenced American thinkers. Americans had brought their revolution to completion, and their approval of their constitution coincided with the outbreak of the French Revolution in 1789. That is a good year with which to begin.

The Catholic church in the new United States now wanted a first episcopal see in this country and its own first bishop. In May 1789, clergy met in Whitemarsh, Maryland, to elect their bishop, in response to a favorable reply from Rome to their request to do this. They chose John Carroll as the bishop and Baltimore as the new see. The election was ratified by Pope Pius VI. When Bishop Carroll asked for the same process in the selection of coadjutor bishop for Baltimore, the request was not honored.

Americans, eager to participate in the selection of leaders, experimented with a lay trustee form of church life (Dolan in Bianchi 1992, 116–17). Trustees were elected by those parish members who paid pew rental. In some areas, clergy were *ex officio* members of the trustee board. In other areas the trustees were all lay. They chose the clergy, and the priests were accountable to the board. One or the other of these two trustee models operated in Baltimore, Boston, Buffalo, Detroit, New Orleans, New York, Norfolk, and Philadelphia. Catholics in New Orleans even attempted to have the state legislate that the bishop "govern the Catholic Church here in accordance with the spirit of our national customs and political institutions" (Dolan in Bianchi 1992, 118). Bishop Carroll supported the trustee system but held that final authority remained with the bishop. There were also many who disagreed with the trustee system, including John Carroll's own auxiliary bishop, Leonard Neale.

The most developed experiment of the trustee model took place under Bishop John England in Virginia and the Carolinas. A diocesan constitution provided for regular gatherings of clergy and laity to discuss the needs and challenges in their region. In this particular model, in the words of England, "the laity are empowered to cooperate but not to dominate" (Dolan in Bianchi 1992, 120). One of the easiest ideological ways to invalidate any position is to put an -ism on it. Often enough this experience is referred to as "trusteeism," an uncritical devaluation. The particular details of the trustee model may or may not be healthy for future ecclesial life, but its foundational instinct is accurate: every group deserves voice in the selection of its leadership. Early church history supports that praxis.

In the long run, none of these experiments finally became the parish model in the U.S. Catholic church. But we meet the American experience very early in this nation's history trying to incorporate participative structures into the life of the church. The desire to bring the American experience into dialogue with ecclesiastical experience is at least as old as Bishop John Carroll and the first American diocese of Baltimore.

The advantage of a trustee system or something akin to it is that it helps establish the more intimate connection between the parish and its leader. Some years ago, during a sabbatical at the University of Judaism, I heard an elderly rabbi instructing young rabbinate students in leading prayer. To lead a community in prayer, he urged, does not mean that you know where to find appropriate prayer texts, though that may be useful. It does not mean having a clear baritone voice or great rhetorical skills, though both may be useful. It does mean that you know a community so well, inside and out, that you can pray its prayers. And when it hears you pray, it recognizes them and says, "Yes, that is exactly right." Which is what the word "Amen" really means. The elderly rabbi then began to explore the relationship a rabbi must have with the community in order to be able to pray with a voice that is the community's voice, to pray in his words but with their voice. Only an insider can do that. That is what makes one a ritual elder, regardless of age. Elder (Greek *presbyter*) was in fact the early Christian community's name for its leader.

Every community leader within a large organization has a double duty. The leader helps interpret the *societas* and its concerns to the *communitas*. And the leader must, with equal insistence, interpret the experience of *communitas* to *societas*. In organizational terms, it is important that the leader, therefore, be accountable in both directions for accurate interpretation and representation. We know, indeed, that any leader feels most beholden to the one who does the hiring or appointing. Structures normally tilt one's accountability to the one who hires. The bishop assigns pastors, who, at ordination, placed their hands inside bishop's hands and promised obedience. There was, at ordination, no ritual that signified a community leader's accountability to the community led, nor any structures whereby such accountability could function. A priest's structured accountability is toward the bishop.

In the United States, bishops are appointed by the pope. They are required to go to Rome regularly to give an accounting to the pope. That is an accountability structure. There is no structure whereby the local church conducts a regular evaluation of the bishop who leads it.

In the years after Vatican II, Jean Jadot, the Apostolic Delegate, helped the church in the United States design a broad consultation process for the selection of bishops. The consultation process, to be conducted with the local church, was broad and inclusive. It has not functioned. It is well known that bishops were regularly elected by the local church and then confirmed by the pope. There remain some places today in which the choice of bishops is a local matter. Canon Law, in fact, still acknowledges election as one of the ways local leadership may be determined: the supreme pontiff freely appoints bishops or confirms those who have been legitimately elected (canon 377). The latter option, theologically, historically, and sociologically sound, is not the common practice. Saint Cyprian (210–258) wrote that "it comes from divine authority that a bishop be chosen in the presence of the people before the eyes of all and that he be approved as worthy and fit by public judgment and testimony." Similarly, Pope Leo the Great, two centuries later, observed that "he who presides over all must be elected by all." We did it before, and we could do it again.

Let us return to the interrupted experiment to introduce more participative structures into the U.S. Catholic church. By the middle of the nineteenth century not much was left of these early experiments with participative models of parish life. The next impetus came from Isaac Hecker, founder of the Paulist order. Hecker, a convert to Catholicism, had been in conversation with Emerson and Thoreau, but had finally found New England transcendentalism insufficient. The context of community and of the work of the Spirit within the total community appealed to his American sensibilities. If the Spirit works within the entire community and not just within the hierarchy, then American Catholics could propose a pneumatological ground for their desire to live a Catholicism more amenable to American culture. "I have the conviction," Hecker wrote, "that I can be all the better Catholic because I am an American, and all the better American because I am a Catholic" (cited in McCann 1987, 14).

What seems to have triggered Rome's concern with Hecker was some French fascination with the Hecker inculturation agenda, triggered by a translation into French of Walter Elliott's "enthusiastic" biography of Isaac Hecker. McCann suspects that for Rome this seemed to be Gallicanism rearing its head again at a time when Rome already felt its power under fire (McCann 1987, 10–11).

The result of Rome's discomfort was Pope Leo XIII's 1899 encyclical *Testem Benevolentiae.* When Leo XIII deplored "the Americanist heresy" in *Testem Benevolentiae,* he described a crass application of the American model to the church that American church people never proposed and did not espouse. James Cardinal Gibbons responded to the pope's allegations saying that what he had described had nothing in common with the views, aspirations, doctrine, and conduct of Americans.

The American experience is the oldest, most sustained response to the paradigm shift in Western culture when people chose not to define themselves as subjects any longer but as citizens who participate in making the world in which they live. Americans have tended not to see any essential conflict between participative structures and basic biblical instincts. New Testament metaphors around power and leadership and early church history are in fact supportive of participative structures. I think McCann is exactly right that the Americanism issue was not heresy at all "but an emerging style of religious praxis nurtured by the experience of Catholic people in America" (McCann 1987, 13). After this long a time, participative democratic instincts reside in our cultural genes and chromosomes, and we seek an inculturation of Catholic life that honors both the Christian and the American deep story.

More recent expressions of the participative impulse are the original Call to Action gathering, and the process used by United States bishops in addressing pastoral needs within our nation. The National Conference of Catholic Bishops instigated the Call-to-Action consultation as an observance of the United States bicentennial celebration. Two years of planning and consultation took place before the actual convocation in Detroit in 1976. The working papers bore the imprint of over 800,000 individual responses. The 1,340 delegates represented 152 of the nation's 167 dioceses. The recommendations themselves are indeed noteworthy (McCann 1987, 43–45). But the remarkable feature was the thoroughly participative process itself. McCann remarks:

> Call to Action was not a coup engineered by a tiny minority of professional activists intent upon usurping the public agenda of the church in this country. On the contrary, a committee of the American bishops consulted the faithful in a process so open and expansive that it could not be manipulated by any particular interest group, including the bishops themselves. . . . Alongside the Americanist heresy [Call to Action] stands as a dangerous memory precisely because it gives authentic witness to the hopes of ordinary American Catholics, unashamed of the knowledge that is theirs because of Vatican II. (45–46, 41)

The process used by the U.S. bishops in preparing the pastoral letters on economics and on peace is a stellar example of the effectiveness of the participative process. A first draft was made public, and there were widespread consultations to invite dialogue. Subsequent drafts, revised in response to dialogue, were handled similarly. Such a process not only adds wisdom to the final product but recruits the commitment of the many Catholics involved in the consultative process.

In sum, we have had some serious flirtations with more participative, democratic procedures in church life, but these have not been regularized. Further exploration is a must, and I reckon that the impetus will flow from the lay hermeneutic fashioned in the hearts and minds of a new, well-educated, theologically astute laity.

Evolution in the Deep Story
of the Catholic Ecclesia

First of all, Vatican II was not simply the wild idea of John XXIII. The pile up of revolutions described here in the second chapter left the church seriously out of touch with major currents in the world's daily life. The distanciation became more and more palpable in the years after World War II. Effective conversation between faith and culture was rare, and theologians who pushed that agenda were silenced. But their effect, nonetheless, was to prepare the Catholic mind for its urgent agenda— *aggiornamento*—or updating, which was John XXIII's image for the council's rationale.

Vatican II's People-of-God ecclesiology is a foundational move in self-interpretation that opened *ecclesia* to more participative structures. I would like to cite two aspects of this evolution, one the image of People of God as a root metaphor for church, and then the highly participative notion of collegiality. Following this, and as another evolving piece, I would like to note some changes in imagination around the idea of king and kingdom.

People of God

It has often been pointed out that treating the church as God's people before presenting it as a hierarchical structure involves a major ecclesiological shift. It must never be either–or. We are God's people first and foremost, called by Jesus Christ; and then, as they say, form follows function. The structure is what is appropriate for the People of God.

Of a piece with this valuing of the people is the council's emphasis upon the call of all God's people to the highest perfection. Marriage is a charism of perfection no less than religious life. Still of a piece is the clear affirmation that all of God's people share responsibility for the mission and life of the church. Once upon a time, it was said that the Catholic Action movement made it possible for lay people to participate in the apostolate of the hierarchy, a "borrowed" apostolate, therefore. But you cannot borrow what you already own. *Apostolicam Actuositatem* says that "by its very nature the Christian vocation is apostolic" and that the laity "exercise a genuine apostolate by their activity on behalf of bringing the gospel and holiness to people and by penetrating and perfecting the temporal sphere of things through the spirit of the Gospel" (§2). The redistribution of apostolic responsibility requires a declericalization of the previous pattern of distribution. I sometimes (most of the time, in fact) feel that the decline of priestly and religious vocations is a necessary precondition for a much needed declericalization. On the other side of the process, the meaning of cleric within the Catholic system of ministry and leadership will have undergone some far-reaching redefinition. As I indicated earlier, this involves both a transfer of power and the transformation of power, that is, how power functions. And that leads to the next point, collegiality, a concept that houses "participation."

Collegiality

The major focus of collegiality in chapter 3 of *Lumen Gentium* is upon the relationship that exists between bishops themselves as a college, and then the relationship between the college of bishops and the pope. This is a complex, technical issue, both pragmatically and theologically. There is much explication that remains regarding the nature of the local church and its relation to the universal church. The functional aspects began to evolve under Pope Paul VI.

Under Pope John Paul II the evolution has not continued. Vatican interaction with bishops and local churches has not been in a collegial mood. Most Catholics in the United States would interpret the bishops as appointees of the pope, with their authority delegated to them from the pope. *Lumen Gentium* affirms that bishops represent Christ (not the pope) to their local church and that their authority is proper to them personally as head of the local church. The authority is ordinary and immediate. It is, the document continues, regulated by the supreme authority in the church. Whatever "regulation" means, and that is one of the areas much in need of exploration, it must honor the reality of the authority of the local bishop, an authority that belongs properly to him as leader of a local church, and it is not there from delegation (*Lumen Gentium* §27).

I believe that one of the major effects of collegiality in the U.S. church is its symbolic power beyond its original usage. More recent books on ministry tend to presume that a collaborative approach to ministry best honors the gifts that people bring to ministry and best actualizes the responsibility for church that is theirs through baptism. The symbol of collegiality [which is different from the technical meaning in *Lumen Gentium*] and the American cultural desire for participative structures are colluding in the evolution of ministry in our church.

Playing with Metaphor: God's Federal Republic

I am using the title of William Johnson Everett's book, *God's Federal Republic*, not because I think it is the best possible option for rethinking a root metaphor—though it is an intriguing, creative, and very responsible proposal—but because it addresses the crucial issue of religious imagination.

Whenever we have had a profound religious experience we tend to ransack every idea and image at our disposal to mediate and communicate the experience. In fact, symbol was at work in the religious experience itself. In the ancient Near Eastern culture, there was no question about whether one would be under a king or not. The only question was, "under which king?" Those under a king lived out of their treaty or covenant with the king. The king's intentions were spelled out in the details of the covenant. To acknowledge God's power, the obvious symbol at hand was that of king, and then God's relationship with us would be mediated through the allied symbol of covenant. Jesus preached the kingdom of God, and under that rubric Jesus taught us the new covenant. The symbol of kingdom helped bridge daily life and religious life, private life and public life.

Any metaphor works because one thing is truly like another in some respect. There is a literal first meaning. A child is a "doll" because he or she is beautiful. The child is also not like a doll. Dolls do not grow up. The metaphor would not work at all in a culture that did not make dolls. Paul Ricoeur says that we have to live in the first literal meaning, that is, be thoroughly familiar with dolls, or the metaphor cannot lead us to the symbolic meaning.

We do not in our culture live in kingdoms with effective kings or queens. The few left in the first world are symbolic; they are not rulers. In fact, with the paradigm shift from subject to citizen, king tends to carry a negative valence. Few of us today would choose to live under a king. What Everett argues is that "this symbol utilizing kingship metaphors is no longer appropriate for bridging faith and public life" (1988, 8). Given the change in symbolism during the past two centuries from "kingship to republican images for ordering the life of faith and public action" (11), we must be about new metaphors for God's activity in the world and for the church as the sacrament of God in the world. "Kingdom has collapsed as a governing symbol" (Everett 1988, 17).

It was an easy move, especially from the late fourth century on, to make the kingdom of God on earth basically interchangeable with the church, in which case the monarchical metaphor structured church life as well. The pope was identified with the same title as that used for Julius Caesar and the emperors that followed him: *Pontifex Maximus*. Our religious imagination about God disposed us in that direction. The formal regalia (regal=kingly) of pope and cardinals does not signal the metaphor of servant or shepherd or steward. This is not a sniping remark. It is a serious question about the distance between New Testament images for leadership and current images. If king does not work well any more, elected president is not the alternative. The only conclusion that seems entirely valid is not about a specific alternative to how power functions in the church but that the issue of power must be addressed to give faith a maximal chance of being authentically inculturated into today's world. I think it highly likely that the pressure to address this issue will proceed from an evolving lay hermeneutic, knowledgeable in Scripture, history, and doctrine, and more responsive to the piled-up revolutions than to the institutional hermeneutic.

Reprise

I have tried in this chapter to address a paradigm shift in Western culture in how power is interpreted and how it functions in civil and ecclesial life. New Testament motifs for leadership and power functions were explored. We entertained questions about valid forms of faith's inculturation in post-paradigm-shift models of power, with particular attention to the United States' experiment of participative, republican, federal institutionalizations of power. We considered some contemporary analyses of power and recommended Bernard Loomer's reflection as a helpful dialogic partner in this discussion. Finally, we conclude that in the United States, a major contribution to this needed conversation will come from laywomen and laymen. We do not expect this development to be welcomed across the board. We need to engage it and to try to keep innocence intact.

A Pastoral Application: Social Analysis and Power

As I did in the previous chapter on experience, and as I will do in the following chapter on historicization, I want to offer a pastoral response to the topic discussed in this chapter, namely, how and where power functions.

Every true ecclesial community is both gathered and sent. Robert Wuthnow's recent research makes it clear how readily we Americans join small groups (Wuthnow 1994). One of every four Americans belongs to a small group. Few of these, however, have any commitment beyond their own needs as a group, however useful and good that might be.

In my work with small Christian communities over the years, I frequently meet people with solid social concern but without a clear sense about how to act it out. We are sent into the world with the Good News of Jesus Christ to collaborate with God in transforming history in keeping with God's intentions for the world. The transformation requires both works of mercy and works of justice. Transformative works of mercy are immediate responses to present need: food, clothing, housing, solace, loneliness, despondency, and so on. Transformative works of justice are a response to the way dysfunctional systems cause many of the problems that works of mercy address. If we attend well to the works of mercy but not to the works of justice, in effect we help dysfunctional systems continue because we keep picking up the pieces that they keep on creating. The works of justice belong to our character as people sent, and because they do, faith always has a public life.

In order to address our public life it is necessary to rehabilitate two important notions: power and politics. I hope this chapter has done so with power.

Politics, as I use it, means the strategies we use in public life to get things done that need to be done for the sake of the common good. Saint Thomas counts politics a virtue under the larger heading of prudence. Bernard Crick's *In Defence of Politics* makes a solid claim for the rehabilitation of politics:

> Politics deserves praising as—in Aristotle's words—"the master science," not excusing it as a necessary evil; for it is the only "science" or social activity which aims at the good of all other sciences or activities, destroying none, cultivating all, so far as they themselves allow. . . . Political activity is a type of moral activity. It is free activity, and it is inventive, flexible, enjoyable and human; it can create some sense of community, and yet is not, for instance, a slave to nationalism; it does not claim to make every heart glad, but it can help in some way in nearly everything and, where it is strong, it can prevent the vast cruelties and deceits of ideological rule. (1972, 145, 146)

In the pastoral education we offer at Loyola, especially in the program in Basic Christian Community Formation, we try to help students develop skills in social analysis. The following brief format benefits from *Social Analysis* by Peter Henriot and Joe Holland, from the approach of the Iona Community in Scotland as presented in Ian Fraser's *Reinventing Theology,* from the analysis of power conducted by the Industrial Areas Foundation in their national leadership training, and from the experience of my own small

Christian community here in New Orleans. The form of social analysis presented here is not the technical kind of social analysis used in sociological research. It is intended to be simple enough to be used by just about anyone, but still able to provide strategic insight. The schema is brief; but if the social situation is complex, it may take a long while to work through the process. There are three parts to the process.

Appropriating a Situation

1. Indicate clearly the social situation that is being interpreted: the city, the parish, a corporation, a school, a diocese, a board of trustees, and so on. Then ask those doing the analysis to name two or three features of the system that are most creative, supportive, satisfactory, life giving, positive. Then ask what are two or three features of the system that are negative, debilitating, disrespectful. It is as important to recognize and support the good things as to name and change the bad things.

2. For each item named, positive and negative, have those who did the naming now cite concrete, particular instances when that feature of the system was experienced. There are two reasons for this. The first is to keep the critique grounded in people's lived experience. The second is that when the time comes for supportive action or for change, an experience-based catalogue of items has more power than an abstract compliment or generalized critique.

Probing Presuppositions and Values—Ideology Critique

3. What policies support the features that are being named? What kind of thinking is the backdrop for what has been named as good or bad? Some interpretation of the human situation underlies the way every system behaves. What are some of the convictions that underlie how this system functions or dysfunctions? Try to be really fair here! It is very easy to caricature things we do not like or canonize too quickly what we happen to agree with. All of this is an exercise in ideology critique. All of us have ideological biases. It is not wrong to have them, but it is harmful to pretend that we do not. If our judgments are inaccurate here, the rest may go nowhere, or may even be quite damaging.

4. Who is doing the thinking just named? Who are the policy makers who support and reinforce operative policies? Whose convictions are getting enacted in the behaviors named above, good and bad? With these questions we are trying to locate agency. If we want to support good things or transform destructive things, we have to know where to go and to whom.

5. We need to be grounded in our own convictions. What is it in our faith tradition that leads us to judge that something is good or bad? We believe that God has intentions for the world. What do we think they are, and how did we come to that conclusion? How do our sacred texts, our community's story, fund the prophetic judgments we are making, if that is indeed what it is? We have to be *very* clear about our own interpretations.

Agenda and Strategies

6. Individuals are relatively powerless to affect systems by themselves. Systems are notoriously resistant to change. It takes a "we" to have much effect. We need to be networked with others who share our convictions. Organized people and organized money are the two most obvious instruments for either supporting behaviors in a system or putting a system under effective requirement to change. We must, therefore, be available to the formation of coalitions and networks in order to speak with a formidable voice.

7. Agenda and strategies are the most important and most difficult. We have to know how to get a system's attention. What must we do to insert ourselves effectively into the ongoing life of a system, or if we are already there in the system, who are the people who share our convictions? What kind of interventions in the life of a system stand a chance of leaving their mark? If we want change, we must be very concrete and specific. In fact, we need to be crystal clear on this. What we ask for must be feasible. When we undertake some initiative, we should have foreseen a range of likely responses within the system and have planned our own further interactions.

It is important not to overdo it (nor to underdo it!). The simplest, most respectful, and relational means are always preferred. But social change is often tough stuff, or "tough love" as the expression goes, because competing vested interests are involved.

8. Our safety net is our prayer life together. Abraham Heschel said that the prophets no doubt felt their own indignation toward institutions that clobbered the poor. No doubt their own sensitivities enabled them to feel the hurt and anguish of their sisters and brothers. But that is not finally what drove them. Their power came from their relationship with God. They were close enough to God to feel God's feelings, to feel God's tenderness, to feel God's rage. And when they experienced injustice they felt the world with the feelings of God.

> The fundamental experience of the prophet is a fellowship with the feelings of God, a sympathy with the divine pathos.... Prophets live not only their personal lives, but also the life of God. Prophets hear God's word and feel God's

heart.... As imparters, their souls overflow, speaking as they do out of the fullness of their sympathy. (Heschel 1962, 14, 26)

Christians who dare the difficult work of social change need a relationship with God that keeps us self-critical and close to God's heart. When
asked about prayer, Edward Schillebeeckx said:

What I always think is that prayer without social commitment becomes
reduced to mere sentimentality, and commitment to society without prayer
often becomes grim and even barbaric. I think what I would like to see most
of all is a unity between mysticism and commitment. (Schillebeeckx 1983,
124)

It is those strange, unimaginable connections between the individual and
the social, between the mystical and political, that we probably need to ponder a lot, because we care. Johannes Metz will have the final word in this
chapter:

Following Christ always has a twofold structure. It has a mystical element and
one that ... is practical and political. And in their radical nature the two do not
work against each other but proportionally in step with each other. The radical nature of following Christ is mystical and political at one and the same
time. . . . When the double mystical and political composition of following
Christ is ignored, what is eventually adopted is an understanding of following
Christ that ends up exemplifying only one half of what is involved. . . . What
happens is either the reduction of following Christ to a purely social and political dimension of behavior, or its reduction to private religious spirituality.
What is lost [in either case] is a continuation of the following of Christ in
which Jesus stands up for the glory of God in the midst of the individual and
social contradictions of the world. (Metz 1978, 42, 44)

The political dimension here refers to the voice of Christian community in
the larger world. But it may apply as well to the voice of Christians within the
ecclesial community where it is also sometimes required that one stand up
for the glory of God in the midst of individual and social contradictions
within the body politic of the Body of Christ.

V

REVOLUTION THREE:
A RENDEZVOUS WITH HISTORY

Introduction

In the Garden of Eden the serpent told a half-truth and a half-lie. The half-truth was that Eve and Adam were not like God because God knew both good and evil and they knew only good; so if they ate the apple they would know both because of their sin. The half-lie is that God's knowledge of evil was not the experiential knowledge that came from divine sin and that they could never be like God, for they were creatures and could never exit the condition of creaturehood. They became less like God by trying to be more like God. Their unwillingness to be like God *the way a creature is like God* was their downfall. They wanted to be like God in the way God is God. They could not tolerate their mere creaturehood.

In his Pulitzer prize winning book, *The Denial of Death*, Ernest Becker details, I think as well as anyone ever has, our dissatisfaction with our creatureliness and the ends to which we will go to avoid it or deny it. The dynamics of denial too often create the human character:

> The prison of one's character is painstakingly built to deny one thing and one thing only: one's creatureliness. The creatureliness is the terror. Once admit that you are a defecating creature and you invite the primeval ocean of creature anxiety to flood over you. . . . To see the world as it really is is devastating and terrifying. It achieves the very result that the child has painfully built [its] character over the years in order to avoid: it *makes routine, automatic, secure, self-confident activity impossible.* It makes thoughtless living in the world . . . an impossibility. It places the trembling animal at the mercy of the entire cosmos and the problem of the meaning of it. (Becker 1973, 87, 60)

When separated from our incurable temporality, we have given up the possibility of ecstasy.

In her splendid treatment of Anointing the Sick, Jennifer Glen suggests that this sacrament has the potential of helping a Christian soul and a Christian system (family, friends, community) learn how to make meaning before the realities of diminishment and death rather than discount the meaning of death by a preoccupation with heaven (1987, 33–63). It is a sacrament that allows us to say Yes to our finitude and thus to live the earthly truth of our creaturely relationship with God. The word "sickness" conjures up our expectation of a cure. We do not have much language that conjures up our taking ownership of our death, which—let it be said—is the same thing as taking ownership of our life and radically acknowledging our creaturehood before God. Dying and living are in fact coterminous. When either is completed so is the other.

Rainer Maria Rilke's "Ninth Duino Elegy" is a rhapsodic ownership of temporality and the ecstasy embedded in the ownership:

Oh, why *have* to be human and, shunning destiny,
long for destiny? . . .
Because being here is much, and because all this
that's here, so fleeting, seems to require us, and strangely
concerns us. Us the most fleeting of all. Just once,
everything, only for once. Once and no more.
And we, too,
once. And never again. But this
having been once, though only once,
having been once on earth—can it ever be cancelled? . . .
Here is the time for the Tellable, *here* is its home.
Speak and proclaim . . .
Praise this world to the Angel, not the untellable; you
can't impress him with the splendor you've felt; in the cosmos
where he more feelingly feels you're only a novice. So show him
some simple thing, refashioned age after age,
till it lives in our hands and eyes as part of ourselves.
Tell him *things* . . .
Show him how happy a thing can be, how guileless and how ours. . .
Earth, is it not just this that you want: to arise
invisibly in us? . . .
What is your urgent command, if not transformation?
Earth, you darling, I will . . . Supernumerous existence
Wells up in my heart.

The seriousness with which we take earth *now* is a commitment to do something significant, *now, here.* To be a history maker. To be a world maker. To be a dream maker. To be a kingdom maker on earth as it is in heaven.

Christians have often avoided the implications of creaturehood's temporality by focusing on heaven. Karl Marx was wrong about a lot of things. But his critique of religion for diminishing human responsibility for history is a founded position. As a small Catholic child I wanted to avoid sin so that I would go to heaven and not go to hell. Nothing in the Catholic culture in which I lived reminded me of the importance of my life's impact upon other lives. I was not catechized to know that my life had consequences for those around me. Of course, at some basic though vague level, I am sure I knew that. But that was never a motivation for a virtuous life. I know that my experience was not idiosyncratic. If there were those who knew the papal encyclical *Rerum Novarum,* it was not passed on to me and my peers. And when I did receive it, it came as a reasoned position and not a plan of action. I do not mean particular directives for specific interventions in economic systems. I mean that it was not accompanied by a process that engaged people in the conversation between their faith and their socioeconomic conditions, toward hopeful historical behavior. Some of our rational narrative's presumptions about *theory and practice* have not panned out, for example, the likelihood that true theory will lead to right practice. When I deal with Aristotle later in this chapter I will suggest a revision of our received understanding of Aristotle (frequently a distortion of Aristotle) that I recommend as a healthy responsiveness to the centrality of the human subject as a subject of history, that is, as a historical agent.

In the first part of this chapter, we will look at the paradigm shift, one of the revolutions largely stored still in the ecclesial basement, from understanding being human as being in the first place a rational animal who then acts out of that rationality to being an actor in history whose historical reality is guided and directed by reason, affect, and imagination—but whose destiny is to be a world maker.

The second part of the chapter speaks to what has become known as "the rise of historical consciousness." Friedrich Nietzsche's comment that there is no such thing as uninterpreted fact catches the sense of historical consciousness. No one can stand utterly outside of what is seen or heard or touched and experience it in such wise that one's own culture and language and personal history does not impinge upon it. Historically conditioned is the nature of all our knowing, including our faith knowing.

George Bernard Shaw once observed that there are two kinds of people, those who divide people into two kinds and those who do not. As slick as it is to divide people into two kinds, those of us who deal with faith issues, whether in education or in immediate pastoral interaction, recognize those who have a historicized sense of their faith and those who do not. In the document on biblical interpretation issued by the Pontifical Biblical Commission, a literalist reading of Scripture is called intellectual suicide. Without attributing bad motives (for most religious people are good intentioned), reading our tradition in an unconditioned way is damaging beyond measure.

It needs to be said at the outset that what I am calling historical consciousness is itself no less subject to being a conditioned position. How historical consciousness is interpreted varies greatly. In the ways that I address it I am very much influenced by Martin Heidegger, Paul Ricoeur, Hans-Georg Gadamer, and more recently by Jacques Derrida and Edmond Jabes. I take responsibility for how I have put them together.

The thesis for this book is that events in Jewish history a century and a half before Jesus can be a helpful metaphor for the church we might become. After the discussion of historical agency and again after the discussion of historical consciousness, I will draw the hidden revolution of the Pharisees into this conversation.

Finally, as in the two previous chapters, I will present a pastoral application of interpretation, namely, its role in the life of small Christian communities in breaking open God's Word.

Thought-Full Acting: John Macmurray

> We must not underestimate the difficulty of the enterprise to which we are committed. We have to shift the center of gravity in our philosophical tradition. . . . To change our standpoint is to transform our habits of thought. It is not to exchange one theory for another, but to change the basis of all theory. (Macmurray 1991, 84–85)

In his Gifford lectures in 1953, John Macmurray acknowledged how difficult it is to begin interpreting the human person primarily in terms of the splendor of human activity rather than in terms of the splendor of human thought and to interpret anew the relation between them. In the Hellenistic tradition, of which Western Christianity is a privileged child, the human being is defined as a rational animal. It is in our rationality that we find our nature and with our rational faculties that we enjoy the profoundest human happiness. The church's attention to belief systems is but one witness of this anthropology. More people have been declared anathema for their belief systems than for their behaviors. The presumption is that is we have our head on straight; we are equipped to behave virtuously, whether we actually do or not. One does not hear as a corollary that if we live right we will have an experiential resource for thinking straight, or that acting our lives is itself a way of knowing. Maurice Merleau-Ponty, the French phenomenologist, claimed that human behavior is the most primordial form of human. Acting itself is thought-full.

There is occurring a paradigm shift in Western culture that moves the central interpretive emphasis of the self from rational thinker to rational agent. This is about how we "imagine" our humanity. I do not mean that everyone everywhere has started interpreting in this new way, only that it appears to be a growing form of imagination. But the varied expressions of this development in human interpretation are considerable. G. W. F. Hegel imagines historical experience as being driven by the movement from a settled position (thesis) to some alternative position (antithesis), and their interaction toward a new position that incorporates the best of both the old and new (synthesis). The process is a *Bildung,* a constructing of human history, and the *Bildung* is the achievement of the Spirit. Being human and being Spirit driven is a relentless process. Immanuel Kant participates in this changing understanding in positing the primacy of practical reason. In the American tradition, Charles Sanders Peirce, William James, and John Dewey all establish an essential connection between what anything means and its consequences in some real or imagined world. Maurice Blondel and Maurice Merleau-Ponty are two French thinkers who focused, each in his own way, upon the self as agent: in the analysis of *L'Action* in the first case and in the *Phénomenologie du Comportement* in the second place. The French existentialist tradition sometimes stated its conclusion that *esse sequitur agere* (something is what it does) rather than *agere sequitur esse,* the classic starting point that activity is an expression of a nature. There are similar interpretations in Max Scheler, and Scheler's work was a major inspiration for Pope John Paul II's dissertation, *Person Acting.* Whitehead and others in the process tradition affirm in one way or another that the process is the reality: we do not first exist and then experience; our experiencing is our existing. Whitehead holds that consciousness and rational thought are woven upon our becoming. Human thought is reflective; it bends back upon and enhances our becoming. In section 31–32 of *Being and Time,* in passages that helped goad contemporary hermeneutics into many of its expressions, Martin Heidegger says that how we interpret always affects how the world gets spread out in front of us ("projection"). In much of this discussion I am indebted to Joseph Dunne's extraordinary analysis of this issue in *Back to the Rough Ground,* especially for his interpretation of Aristotle. His tracing of the primacy of historical agency includes analyses of John Henry Newman, R. G. Collingwood, Hannah Arendt, Hans-Georg Gadamer, and Jürgen Habermas. I am most indebted to Dunne's discussion of Aristotle (Dunne 1993, 237–74).

I will draw briefly upon two twentieth-century figures to flesh out this sense of the human person as a historical actor. The first is the Scottish philosopher John Macmurray, whose Gifford lectures in 1953 address the self as agent. The second is the German philosopher Hannah Arendt, especially in her book *The Human Condition.* Following the visit with John Macmurray and Hannah Arendt, we will knock on Aristotle's door.

John Macmurray

There are not two selves, one that acts and one that thinks, begins Macmurray's logic. Acting and thinking are different perspectives on the same self. When engaged in human activity we are all the while perceiving, feeling, thinking, analyzing, judging. Sometimes we pull away from activity in order to reflect upon activity, to imagine possible futures, to critique past activity. But even our thinking is, of course, a human activity. Sometimes, however, it is more or less removed from intentional acting in the world. The higher the level of generalization and abstraction, the more independent thought is of ongoing reception of data. "Action, then, is a full concrete activity of the self in which all our capacities are employed; while thought is constituted by the exclusion of some of our powers and a withdrawal into an activity which is less concrete and less complete" (Macmurray 1991, 86).

We are here to act out the human drama in history, and thought is part of that activity. We do not act for the sake of thinking. Our thinking, itself an activity, is for our acting out our lives. "Action is primary and concrete, thought is secondary, abstract and derivative. This must mean that the distinction between 'right' and 'wrong,' which is constitutive for action, is the primary standard of validity; while the distinction between 'true' and 'false' is secondary" (Macmurray 1991, 89). This way of naming priorities resonates with the contemporary discussion of the priority of orthopraxis over orthodoxy.

Whether one opts for a rational primacy or a praxis primacy, they are an essentially linked pair. But faith under the one rubric configures very differently from faith under the other rubric. At the level of instinct I believe that people in the United States are practical people who want to know what difference it makes to get at something one way rather than the other. Sometimes we are crassly practical and anti-intellectual when we discount how our acting can be enriched by meticulous thinking.

Vincent Wayer, one of my Marianist confreres in a parish in Helotes, Texas, has taken religious statements from several sources to provide a comparison between two kinds of language about God. He uses these in adult education and invites people to choose the language they prefer. I would like to cite them:

Language One

Faith in God leads us to turn to him alone as our first origin and ultimate goal, and neither to prefer anything to him nor to substitute anything for him.

The God of our faith has revealed himself as He who is; and he has made himself known as "abounding in steadfast love and faithfulness" (Exod. 34:6). God's very being is Truth and Love.

God is unique; there is only God. "The Christian faith confesses that God is one in nature, substance and essence."

God is the fullness of Being and of every perfection, without origin and without end. All creatures receive all that they are and have from him; but he alone is his very being, and he is of himself everything that he is.

In revealing the mysterious name YHWH ("I Am He Who Is," or "I Am Who Am," or "I Am Who I Am"), God says who he is and by what name he is to be called. It is at once a name revealed and something like the refusal of a name, and hence it better expresses God as what he is—infinitely above everything that we can understand or say: he is the "hidden God," his name is ineffable, and he is the God who makes himself close to men.

God transcends all creatures. We must therefore continually purify our language of everything in it that is limited, imagebound, or imperfect, if we are not to confuse our image of God—"the inexpressible, the incomprehensible, the invisible, the ungraspable"—with our human representations. Our human words always fall short of the mystery of God.

By natural reason man can know God with certainty, on the basis of his works. But there is another order of knowledge, which man cannot possibly arrive at with his own powers: the order of divine Revelation. Through an utterly free decision God has revealed himself and given himself to man.

God, who "dwells in unapproachable light," wants to communicate his own divine life to the men he freely created, in order to adopt them as his sons in his only-begotten Son. By revealing himself God wishes to make them capable of responding to him, and of knowing him, and of loving him beyond their own natural capacity.

The apostle entrusted the "Sacred deposit" of the faith (the *depositum fidei*), contained in Sacred Scripture and Tradition, to the whole of the church.

The task of giving an authentic interpretation of the Word of God, whether in its written form or in the form of Tradition, has been entrusted to the living, teaching office of the church alone.

Mindful of Christ's words to his apostles: "He who hears you, hears me," the faithful receive with docility the teachings and directives that their pastors give them in different forms.

Language Two

Family life is holy ground. In fact, it is the place where we meet God most frequently, most intensely, and most differently. This is the first and most basic belief expressed in "Follow the Way of Love." It's also one of the hardest to hold on to, especially in the messiness of everyday living.

"What?" you might say, "My family holy? You've got to be kidding! Yes, we love each other in a way, but we fight, some members are estranged, others are divorced. We've had problems with alcohol and drugs. We're stretched thin worrying about jobs and money." Does any of this sound familiar?

But listen to the Good News found in the pastoral message. "Baptism brings all Christians into union with God. Your family life is sacred because family relationships confirm and deepen this union and allow the Lord to work through you. The profound and ordinary moments of daily life: mealtimes, workdays, vacations, expressions of love and intimacy, household chores, caring for a sick child or elderly parents, and even conflicts—over how to celebrate holidays, discipline children, or spend money—all are the threads from which you can weave a pattern of holiness."

God's grace is never limited by our notions of what is acceptable or correct. "Grace is everywhere" was the revelation given to the dying pastor in that classic novel *Diary of a Country Priest.* And in case we did not get the point, the bishops put it another way: "Remember, a family is holy not because it is perfect but because God's grace is at work within it, helping it to set out every day on the way of love. Wherever a family exists and love still moves through its members, grace is present. Nothing—not even divorce or death—can place limits on God's gracious love."

This is our starting point: There is a homemade holiness in family life. This is true for single-parent families and two-parent families, for families in a religiously mixed marriage and families in a second marriage. Consequently, we find in the pastoral message a valuing of diversity in family life.

* * * * * * * * * * * * *

Our pilgrimage with God's people has made us more conscious that often we encounter God in what we would have considered thirty years ago an unlikely place: in the world. Like the Samaritan woman, we have encountered the Source of Living Water in the midst of our daily life and activities. Our encounter has been a deeply personal one, nourished by prayer, which has led us to interpersonal encounters as well at times with those judged as "outsiders."

In our following of Jesus and the Gospel, women religious have struggled to be at the side of the poor and the marginalized and have discovered there the face of God. As women, we have been sensitive to the life of "God's little ones," caring especially for life that is just beginning or fragile, which is wounded or abused. We have done this by direct service as well as by addressing the causes of injustice and abuse. We have likewise been aware of the source of water within each person, particularly with women who are at times unaware of their own dignity.

The effects of local and global injustice and violence have deeply affected us. We have accompanied and shared the pain and sorrow of our companions on the journey—the sick and the weary, prisoners and children, the elderly and lonely, those seeking education and empowerment. The poor of the world, in ever increasing number, have been a special revelation of Jesus to us and we wish to manifest his preferential love for them in all that we do. All our encounters with the needy have, we trust, made us more faithful disciples of Jesus who gave his life for the life of the world.

When adults were asked which of the two "languages" stirred their religious aspirations, it was Language Two across the board. Language One is mostly about how we should think about God. Language Two is mostly about how we should act in the world because of who God is.

In fairness, these different texts come from very different kinds of documents. All of the Language One texts are from the *Catechism for the Catholic Church.* The first group of Language Two texts is from an article by H. Richard McCord in *Origins,* "Viewing Families from Three Perspectives" (McCord 1994, 291–96). The second group of Language Two texts is from an article in *America,* "Women Religious and The World Synod of Bishops," by Janise Farnham and Mary Milligan (Farnham and Milligan 1994, 22–23). The text was prepared by the Religious Sisters Task Force for the international meeting in Rome concerning religious life. They are not parallel statements about the same thing. People are more moved by articulations that connect who God is with the immediacies of historical experience. They appreciate speech in which they find themselves called forth as historical agents in the drama of redemption.

In the 60s "relevant" became a buzz word. If it was not relevant, it was too bad. I think it important not to write relevance off as superficial, even if those who say the word go mute when asked for better information. The instinct at the untutored gut level expresses a historical being's care that we attend to lived experience. It is my thesis that the religious appetite for relevance is funded by the paradigm shift to human self-understanding in terms of historical agency. I likewise posit that the continuing decrease in Roman Catholic church attendance is related to a lay hermeneutic that has made many of these adjustments and a clerical hermeneutic that has not. To be sure, some lay People of God have not caught the historical fever, and some ordained People of God have. I am talking typologies.

Thought-Full Acting: Hannah Arendt

For Hannah Arendt, the active life (*vita activa*) flows necessarily from the human condition. To the active life belong three major activities: labor, work, and action. I will focus on action.

Plurality is a feature of the human situation. It means, "we are all the same, that is, human, in such a way that nobody is ever the same as anyone else who ever lived, lives, or will live" (Arendt 1958, 8). Action names all that transpires between people without the intermediary of things or matter (Arendt 1958, 7). Action is about how we manage to be together. The place where people work out their destinies together is the city or village or tribe, in Greek, the *polis*. Whatever pertains to making the *polis* work is *politikos*, "political." "Action needs for its full appearance the shining brightness we once called glory, and which is possible only in the public realm" (Arendt 1958, 180).

In his analysis of culture, Clifford Geertz says that animals have instinctual guidance about the particular world they will make, a dog world or a bird world or a fish world. But, he says, human genes are "silent on the building trades" (1973, 93). Culture is what allows us to pass on the know-how, since the genes do not do it. We interact and organize through speech and symbol and ritual. Culture houses our memory. Arendt speaks of this activity in terms of a relational web and the stories we enact within it.

There is a frailty about the arena of human action. We act with a certain intention, but once we have acted we have lost control over the effects of our action, and that is equally true whether the effects are good or bad or mixed.

The effects spread out, sometimes where we intended, other times where we never imagined, and very often, where we shall never exactly know. This is one example of the arena of human activity: the future is unpredictable. The human activity that gives most promise is exactly that: the making and keeping of a promise:

> Without being bound to the fulfilment of promises, we would never be able to keep our identities; we would be condemned to wander helplessly and without direction in the darkness of each [person's] lonely heart, caught in the contradictions and equivocalities—a darkness which only the light shed over the public realm through the presence of others, who confirm the identity between the one who promises and the one who fulfils, can dispel. (Arendt 1958, 237)

When our action has damaged the relational web, what are we to do? If the future is unpredictable, the past is irreversible. Arendt says that our sins hang like the sword of Damocles over generations to come (1958, 237). We need not only the faculty to make and keep promises but the faculty to forgive broken promises:

> Without being forgiven, released from the consequences of what we have done, our capacity to act would, as it were, be confined to one single deed from which we could never recover; we would remain the victims of its consequences forever, not unlike the sorcerer's apprentice who lacked the magic formula to break the spell. (Arendt 1958, 237)

Let us recall in respect to the Hebrew experience, where our role as actor is so clear, that the binding mortar for that world is covenant. Covenant is none other than mutual promising. And the ritual high point of Jewish religious life is Yom Kippur, which comes immediately after Rosh Hashannah. Rosh Hashannah is the new year, and there can only truly be a new year if forgiveness of what has gone before makes it possible. What insight into the human condition to juxtapose promising and forgiving!

In Jeremiah 31, one of the tenderest passages in the Prophets, YHWH offers a new covenant. A new covenant means new promises, starting over in a new way. YHWH wants YHWH's people to commit to the new promises but recognizes that these chosen daughters and sons need to know they are forgiven so that they *are able* to make new promises. YHWH asks Jeremiah to tell the people that YHWH will not remember their sins, which I take to mean not that YHWH forgets, but that the new relationship will not be conditioned by the old sins.

In recent Catholic experience, I wager that the near abandonment of the Sacrament of Reconciliation does not mean that we have lost our need for forgiveness, but that this ritual as it stands does not accomplish it. The form of Reconciliation that draws people is the communal experience followed by general absolution—we together who sin and infect each other's world are forgiven together. How sad that the church who promulgated it keeps it out of circulation. I wonder whether the Catholic soul has not made its own ritual arrangement by coming to Ash Wednesday in unheard of numbers to acknowledge its creaturehood and the need for repentance. The other ritual to which the Catholic soul is responding is the Easter Vigil, not just as a vigil but as the moment when new members of the church are admitted through Baptism, after a long period in which the faithful have played a key role in the transmission of Catholic Christian identity. We who have long since been baptized renew our promises just after the new members have made their first baptismal covenant. It is a powerful moment. The beginning and end of Lent are about forgiveness for brokenness in our action and promises for hope in our action. This is how historical agents, united with God in covenant, get on with it.

The Pharisees and Historical Agency

There is a simplicity I want to avoid, which is that one should choose between thinking and acting, or that acting and thinking somehow interfere with each other. It is a matter, rather, of how a root metaphor functions in a community's narrative structure and how all other features of a story take their clues from the root metaphor and arrange themselves accordingly.

Moses' dialogue with God is an identity-creating piece of the Jewish narrative. When Moses asks God for a name, God's reply is "I am who am"—a poor English translation of the Hebrew sentence. There are no tenses in classical Hebrew comparable to those in English. Two points of reference work together in Hebrew and they cannot be separated: whether an action is portrayed as *finished or not*. In selecting the verb form, the issue is not whether the action has in fact been completed, but whether the statement uses a completed verb form, for we can imagine an action as completed in the future. Thus, "I saw," "I had seen" and "I *shall* have seen" are stated as completed, even though the *shall* reference would for us sound future and thus incomplete. These would all be the same verb, and one would understand its precise meaning from the larger context of narrative. Using a designation from our language system that does not neatly apply to Hebrew, grammars often call these perfect (completed) or imperfect (not completed). This grammatical distinction omits reference to the manner of portrayal.

In the Hebrew of God's reply to Moses, the two verbs are imperfect or unfinished. This fits into the larger picture of a culture in whose storied tradition God is most often spoken of in connection with historical people and historical actions: the God of Abraham [and Sarah], Isaac [and Rebecca], Jacob [and Rachel]; the God who led us out of Egypt, who took us across the Red Sea, who fed us in the desert, who gave us a land according to a promise. In the prophetic tradition God neither hankers for, nor is especially pleased by, our songs and our incense, but is primarily concerned for social systems that function justly, for people who deal with each other mercifully and compassionately, and for those who walk humbly for they know that God's presence in history is redemptively necessary—they cannot do it alone.

Within that narrative, when God uses "imperfect" verbs in self-description, perhaps we should better understand God to be saying something like this: "You have always known who I am by experiencing how I have been with you in your history. And since our history together is still unfolding, you need to continue consulting how I am being experienced in your history in order to do a better and better job of understanding my name and its content. You will forever be adding content and therefore new clauses to the sentence that begins, "YHWH who. . . ."

Organized Hebrew concern for orthodoxy was expressed in its legislation against idols, that is, images that are not accurate tellers of YHWH's historical presences to the Hebrew story. Idol worship is a behavior that does not tell the truth about history and therefore cannot be trusted as a guide to moral behavior.

People and God acting in history are the centerpiece for the Jewish imagination about our reality and our destiny. There does not exist in the classical Hebrew experience explicit philosophy or explicit theology. These are attempts to use human reason to systematize our thinking about the natures of reality and the nature of God. This is not a comment upon the value of reason, only upon its relative absence in classical Hebrew culture. The reasons for that lie in the nature of the Hebrew imagination that has the historical agent on center stage and interprets God equally in the categories of God's historical agency.

Every narrative's bright side has an underside that is dark. The shadow side is always the flip side of the gifts. We have learned from Carl Jung that you cannot diminish the shadow side without debilitating the strengths of the gift side. The challenge, rather, is to come to terms with the darkness: to compensate for it when feasible, to befriend it as much as possible, and to embrace the irreducible ambiguity of the human condition.

David Tracy observes that we need to remain aware that even our classic texts have a dark side, and he makes the same generalization about events:

> No classic text comes to us without the plural and ambiguous history of effects of its own production and all its former receptions. Nor does any classic event, be it the Renaissance, the Reformation, or the Enlightenment. "Every great work of civilization" as Walter Benjamin insisted, "is at the same time a work of barbarism." (1987, 69)

The Pharisees intervened in Jewish history in the painful aftermath of the Maccabean revolt against the imposition of alien cultures and foreign gods. They focused upon the Jewish behaviors that were, in their experience, appropriate historical responses to their religious and political situation. What we have called "law" in English is closer to "helpful directives" in the intentionality of the Hebrew mind. This movement is the beginning of the codifications that will find embodiment in the Mishnah in 200 CE and in the Jerusalem and Babylonian Talmuds another four centuries later. If the grace of this narrative structure is its meticulous attention to the character of historical agency, a "natural" shadow side is to become preoccupied with the letter of the directives or law and forget their original character as behavioral guides (the spirit of the law). In the Christian tradition (look it up in your dictionary!), pharisaic is understood to mean legalistic. We have named a brilliant movement by its shadow side and not by its grace and have consequently severed ourselves from its wisdom. Concomitantly, we have prided ourselves in the remarkable accomplishments of the rational mind and have named the grace side of our human narrative by defining the human person as a rational animal. But we have no cultural name for the shadow side as it has expressed itself in the large number of people excluded from communion because of their ideas in comparison with those excluded because of their conduct.

Praxis: A Rare Question Comes Home, Maybe

That really rare question goes something like this: what kind of a world do we want to make for ourselves and our progeny? It is a long-term question.

During the year in which I am working on this text there has been quite an uproar about the proposed display of the Enola Gay at the Smithsonian, marking the fiftieth anniversary of the bombing of Hiroshima. The logic often invoked to support the American decision to use the atomic bomb is that it brought the war to an end more quickly, and that in so doing many American lives were saved.

The theoretical mind of Albert Einstein brought into the world a knowledge that made the development of atomic weapons a possibility. Not only Americans but others Western nations were also trying to "get there first." If Germany had gotten there first, it would probably have been a different World War II. Einstein anguished over how this knowledge was used. He said that concern for humankind and the fate of humanity should be the centerpiece of human thought.

Suppose, therefore, that the United States had announced that it knew well how to produce and use an atomic bomb, but that it chose not to produce it and not to use it because it wanted to forgo the terror of a world in possession of fifty thousand nuclear warheads. There is no guarantee that the world in fact would have become different. But this nation would have had the moral authority to stand for that kind of a world. And just maybe the world would be a different place today because someone asked the rare question: "In the long term, what kind of a world shall we choose for ourselves and our children?" In the best sense of the word, that is a truly political question for it is about how people elect to organize the life they share.

Jesus spoke Aramaic and not Greek, but all our earliest records of what Jesus is remembered to have said are in Greek. I want to refer to a Greek word in the mouth of Jesus in Mark's Gospel that reflects the rare question. The noun form of the word is *phronesis*; the verb form is *phronein*.

The eighth chapter of Mark is a turning point in the Gospel. The first half of Mark deals largely with the figure of Jesus as one who heals and reconciles. The second half is about the road to Calvary and about how the followers of Christ as well as Christ must be ready to suffer to bring a new world (the kingdom of God) into being. A short exchange between Jesus and Peter is the turning point. Jesus indicates clearly that the cross is part of the picture. Peter scolds Jesus for talking this way. Jesus said to Peter, "You *think* things out in the easy way that the world *thinks* them out, but not the way God *thinks* them out. Therefore, you actually do the work of Satan by subverting God's *thinking* as a way of making meaning in the world" (Mark 8:29–33).

The Greek verb here is *phronein*. Another Greek verb, *gignosko*, means "thinking" in the common English understanding of the word. *Phronein* means not just to think, but to think about the larger question concerning the kind of world we hope to make by how we act.

My concern is not with interesting Greek vocabulary but with how to give this rare question a privileged new place in our living together in our larger world and in our church. Those of us who sense ourselves as historical agents do not want to get caught up in the kind of instrumental activism that sociologists say is a characteristic of American culture: "What kinds of things can we make, and let's make them. Once we make them, let's sell them. Let's encourage people to want these things, and then let's help their wanting get turned into needing." These are the dynamics of consumerism, as presented in Eric Clark's *The Want Makers* (1988).

Instrumentalism is a kind of activity that goes from "able to do it" to actually doing it without passing through the *phronesis* question: is this good for the kind of world we want long term to be making? When I speak of the turn to the subject as historical agent, I want to stress how essential *phronesis* becomes. The relative absence of the rare question registers in the ease with which we juxtapose the categories of theory and practice, without the middle piece concerning the human world we bring into existence by practice.

If lay Catholics are to help the church into conversation with the paradigm shift from primary emphasis upon subject as thinker to subject as actor, it is because they are more susceptible to this cultural shift from their daily immersion in it. I am suggesting further that the many Catholic laypeople who are studying ministry at the graduate level in some of the member schools of the Association of Graduate Programs in Ministry are likely to be critically equipped by practical theology to add the rare question into the mix. I would like, therefore, to show how practical theology, as both a theological and an educational method, does this. To begin with, we shall make a visit to Aristotle.

In the *Nicomachean Ethics,* Aristotle speaks of three ways of knowing, each way of knowing has a name for the activity that carries it out:

1. *Theoria/Episteme*   Theoretical Knowledge
2. *Praxis/Phronesis*   Practical, Political Knowledge
3. *Techne/Poiesis*   Instrumental Knowledge about Production

What Aristotle means by *theoria* is a superb clue to his sense of the human subject as a rational subject who finds ultimate bliss in contemplation. His sense of the word does not correspond closely with what we tend to mean by theory. Human satisfaction, *eudaimonia,* is experienced in the wonder that comes from knowing, and for this we were made.

> Through theory we do not acquire a knowledge-content which can then be exploited in the practical business of life; the spheres of theory and practice are incommensurable. Through theory we are made receptive to being—which is beyond time—and to an order and harmony which are quite beyond our own powers of construction or interference. (Dunne 1993, 238)

But we do have to get on in the world. Getting on in the world can make it possible to have the time and space to ponder the good, the true, and the beautiful, and to be filled with wonder. For Aristotle, *praxis* and *techne* are simply necessary, but inferior to the possession of *theoria*. There is a Christian version of this.

When St. Thomas appropriated and baptized Aristotle, the centrality of contemplation to human fulfillment was retained, and our final happiness was called the beatific *vision*, a final fulfillment interpreted as contemplative. There has been a tendency in Christian spirituality to find "living here on earth" little more than a temporary and provisional activity, albeit necessary. It has not had much glory about it. Some of the liturgical prayers from the ordinary used to ask God to help us look down (*despicere*) on things of earth and only look up (*aspicere*) to things of heaven. The sounder strata of spirituality affirm the continuity of personhood from "now to eternity." Whatever we have made of ourselves, in fidelity to God's intentions for the world, those are the selves and the only selves that endure in our relationship with God.

ARISTOTLE

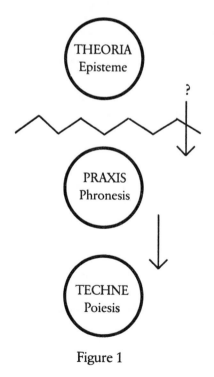

Figure 1

Figure 1. *Theoria* is a kind of knowledge, and *epistemé* the way it functions. It is our way of knowing truth about the nature of reality. It fulfills the essential highest human desire to contemplate truth, and as such is its own complete reason for being. It has pride of place among the ways of knowing, because it fulfills our nature. Whether, or to what extent, *theoria* informs the tasks of daily human living is at best ambiguous in Aristotle's sense of things. What we mean in popular usage by "theory" is more closely related but not simply identical to the kind of knowledge called praxis, and to *phronesis* as the actual functioning of *praxis*. *Praxis* informs our sense of what kind of world we ought to be making. It's about how we function together with others in a world that is good for us individually and together. Once we understand the kind of world we want to bring into being, *techné* is knowledge of the actual ways to make it happen, and *poiesis* is the informed, effective activity of building it. This structure presumes that rationality is what most essentially defines humanness and that human happiness is experienced in the fullest contemplative functioning of our rationality. Making the kind of world that maximizes the contemplative experience is the human vocation.

PRACTICAL THEOLOGY

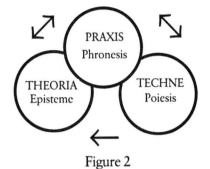

Figure 2

Figure 2. Practical theology is based upon a sense of the human person as an actor/agent in human history. It is in making the right kind of world that we experience fulfillment. For a Christian, God's intentions for the world clarify the history-making to which we are called. In this context, *praxis* is the kind of knowing that holds pride of place, and *phronesis* the activity that enables us to discover and understand what our world-making needs to be like. The experience and appreciation of beauty and truth and goodness is no less fulfilling in this framework, but they are features of our world-making. *Praxis* values the knowing that accrues from intercourse with the world through agency. There is a reciprocity between *theoria* and *praxis:* their learnings inform each other. What this framework forbids is going from theoretical understanding of anything to an implementation of what we know is possible, without passing the implementation through *praxis.* It is a dangerously technicized world that does what can be done for an immediate result (*poiesis*), without validating the making by its contribution to the kind of world we want to help forge.

No small part of the power of Aristotle's analysis of human knowledge is the genius of *praxis* as a kind of knowledge about the kind of life we ought to be about together—*phronesis* is the activity of *praxis*. *Techne* is instrumental knowledge about production or fabrication. The use of that knowledge in actually making things is *poiesis*. Most of the time when we use the word "practical" in English, we mean knowing how to produce, how to get particular things done expediently and effectively. But this technical know-how is instrumental good sense, and not *phronesis*. The pairs of words that are common to our assessments—theory and practice, or science and technology—omit reference to the rare question: "Yes, we know how, but should we?"

One way of understanding what practical theology does is to see how it rearranges Aristotle's three ways of knowing, redefining theoretical knowledge in so doing.

For Aristotle, *theoria* is the finest, most profoundly and humanly fulfilling kind of knowing. It is about the very nature of being. No doubt theoretical knowledge seeps through to inform *praxis* and *techne*, but that is not its primary reason for being. What I believe is implied in practical theology, in which the person as historical agent is foremost, is that *praxis* plays the central role. This is not a chronological priority in the way knowing happens but a functional priority about where the executive voice should originate. I take *theoria* to have several expressions. It can be the generalization we make from particulars. It can be intuition and imagination woven upon experience (e.g., Einstein's theories of relativity). It is nourished by human engagement in the world, whether through *praxis* or *techne*.

Praxis knowledge is central to people whose fundamental human vocation is to engage together in making the worlds in which they live. *Phronesis* is the process of doing that thinking. When practical theology is called by that name, what is being named is precisely the central importance of *praxis*. The language, however, is by and large not helpful because most people connect the English word practical with *techne*, which is instrumental know-how about production or fabrication, and not about how to live. In fact, a consumerist culture like ours comes very close to substituting *techne* for *praxis*.

The Western European version of theology as responsible to people as history makers is often called political theology. Johannes Metz is a spokesperson for this take on theological *praxis*. "Political" would be a proper description, for this word names what is important to the *polis*, that is, all the social systems within which we live. The word "political," however, also suffers from the fate of popular meaning, for it so often carries with it a sense of "dirty" and "unsavory." In Latin America the *praxis* model is often called "liberation theology," because for most inhabitants of many of those countries it is not possible to live the way the children of God should live until they are free from poverty, marginalization, often sheer desperation. Any intervention in the systems that are responsible for injustice is by its nature political. It is not possible to stand for God's intentions in social systems and be apolitical.

The punch in practical theology comes in two places. The first is in the methodological conversation between interpretations of our faith and interpretations of our sociocultural and socioeconomic situation, which is indebted to David Tracy's discussion of practical theology as a revised correlational method (Tracy in Mudge 1987, 139–54). Second, the conversation is sustained until the agenda becomes clear, until faith in dialogue with lived experience levies claims and we know the claims.

Most of the fifty member-institutions in the Association of Graduate Programs in Ministry (AGPIM) subscribe to some form of practical theology. There are over six thousand students in forty-two of these institutions. I surmise there are an additional twenty-five hundred students in eight other

AGPIM schools, in Catholic institutions who do not belong to AGPIM, in non-Catholic divinity schools, and in public universities where Catholics are enrolled in graduate ministry or theology programs. I believe that Catholic lay people in this country, educated in AGPIM schools, and elsewhere to be sure, are finding words for the historical turn that wells up inside them as denizens of Western culture where the historical revolution transpires.

Historical Consciousness and Life at Sea

The search for foundations has been an insistent part of the intellectual tradition of the West, especially notable in philosophy and religion. We want whatever we build to be on *terra firma*. Who among us was not reared to yearn for perfect certainty! Friederich Nietzsche named the essential character of historical consciousness in a single sentence: there is no such thing as uninterpreted fact. There is no understanding of anything that does not bear the conditioning marks of language, place, time, culture, mood, bias, and so on. No one can stand outside of conditions and provide an unconditioned station of adjudication. At some level we have always understood something about conditioning. The ancient story of the ten blind men who touch an elephant each in a different place and then described it very differently is witness to our sense of perspective. But not until recently has the nontranscendable pervasiveness of perspective and bias registered. It has roots longer ago than our century, but only in our time has it begun to work its way into the structure of consciousness.

For us human beings who hanker for *terra firma*, the truth of historical consciousness can cause motion sickness. Our feet do not stand still. But when the human organism is for a long time at sea, it adjusts to the incessant motion beneath it until that base in water becomes normative and not nauseating. The ever-moving water does become a base that supports. Learning to be at sea in history is a metaphor for the radical nature of historical consciousness. Jean-François Lyotard describes postmodern consciousness as giving up on the possibility of a metanarrative, that is, on the possibility of a metahistorical, metacultural perspective that is not itself conditioned (Lyotard 1984, xxiii–xxiv).

During the years that the U.S. involvement in Viet Nam was building I was a student living in an international house of studies in Fribourg, Switzerland. Because of its character, we regularly had newspapers and news magazines in English, French, German, and Spanish. I would sometimes read an account of an event in Viet Nam in an American publication and then read the same event recounted in a French publication, and almost wonder whether they started with the same "facts." Each of these countries interpreted events from the perspective of their own deep involvement in that country, the French earlier, the United States later. The interpretation in the German paper would usually have quite a different emotional tone, because that nation did not have the involved history with Viet Nam that the Americans and French had. However, Germany had its own historical war memories of World Wars I and II, and was certainly not free from bias. No one is ever bias free.

When I returned to the United States in 1967, after fours years away, I hardly recognized the mood of the nation. I recall the frequent painful awkwardness at the prayer of the faithful when some would pray for their brothers or husbands or friends in Viet Nam and ask for a quick victory and end to the war, while others would pray for forgiveness for the U.S. presence there at all, and ask for the national courage to withdraw. These people praying these prayers were good people, holy people, who presumed they were basing their judgments on the "facts."

There is the same profoundly painful relationship today between those whose primary agenda is the restoration of the Catholic church and those for whom the issue is refounding. I confess that I am more in the latter arena, for that is the thesis of this book. I do not expect either of us "to get the light" so that we can then largely agree.

I never perfectly, without omission, fully know anyone, anything, or any event, not even my closest friend, and not even myself. There is a sameness that makes conversation possible, and there is an otherness that makes total mutual comprehension impossible. It is the otherness—the distanciation—that makes interpretation possible and necessary.

Distanciation is one reason why interpretation is necessary. Another has to do with the historical conditioning of everyone who interprets. Biblical studies have brought this home. Jesus was a Jew who lived his whole life within Judaism. But all of the earliest recorded memories of Jesus are in Greek. There are Aramaic words that do not have counterparts in Greek and vice versa. So every translation is in fact an interpretation that partly transmits and partly falsifies. Thus the ancient rabbis said that every translator is a traitor. In a splendid book called *The Church the Apostles Left Behind* Raymond Brown shows how life within particular communities shaped how they remembered Jesus. What we remember is internally and causally related to what we do not remember, or do not even notice in the first place. How can Paul say that faith saves us, not good works, while James says that faith without good works gets us no place?

My concerns here are about how laypeople interpret differently than clerics, about how Americans interpret differently than other cultures, and about how people educated in practical theology interpret differently than those who have not grappled with historical consciousness. For, as David Tracy has reminded us, we have not just a conversation between faith and culture, but between *interpretations* of our faith and *interpretations* of our social worlds.

I would like to schematize the dynamics of interpretation that are responsive to historical consciousness. In the final chapter, where consideration of a community of interpretation is suggested as matter for ecclesiology, I will reflect further upon the development of a lay hermeneutic under several rubrics: the hermeneutics of suspicion, the hermeneutics of retrieval, marginal hermeneutics, and the hermeneutics of tears.

Historical Consciousness and Interpretation

It has been my thesis throughout this book that lay people educated in the sacred sciences and in the theology and skills of ministry, critically sensitive to both their faith and their culture, are an insistent, articulate new presence in the Catholic church in the United States. AGPIM member institutions are one of the places where they are receiving graduate education, and they are practitioners of practical theology, some more and some less. Since interpretive skills are central to anyone's dialogue between *interpretations* of faith and *interpretations* of one's social situation, hermeneutics is part of ministry education. I have adapted the sections that follow from texts that are used in the educational system of the Institute for Ministry at Loyola, New Orleans. I do not know if any other institution's introduction to hermeneutics is exactly like this, but I do know from the annual AGPIM conventions that developing a strong historical sense of Catholic Christian faith is a commitment across the board.

The material in this following section on interpretation is deeply indebted to experts in hermeneutics like Martin Heidegger, Hans-Georg Gadamer, Paul Ricoeur, David Tracy, and Jürgen Habermas.

Pre-Understanding

We always bring to the task of interpreting, whether a text or a person or an event, a lot of ideas and convictions long in the making in ourselves. Consider how the expression "manifest destiny" has supported U.S. policy in respect to other nations of North and South America, for example, our unilateral interventions in Nicaragua and Panama. Consider Christian attitudes toward Jews after having named the Christ-event a "new" testament, presuming that the "old" is thereby superseded and hence inoperative. What do we do with the whole history of supersessionist Christology now that the Catholic church has affirmed with conciliar voice that God never abrogated God's covenant with the Jewish people, who indeed are properly called God's chosen people? (*Nostra Aetate* §4)? That startling conciliar confession brings to awareness a pre-understanding we thought was "fact," one that has funded nearly twenty centuries of Christian prejudice.

Our pre-understandings bear the marks of our culture, our personal lives, our location in the power arrangements of our social systems, and most of all, the language we speak. The effect of gender on interpretation is increasingly being brought to consciousness in U.S. culture.

Language is the chief carrier of the effects of history and culture into our present moment of experiencing. Heidegger rightly calls language the "house of being," for how we speak about experience shapes experience (1977, 213). The use of "man" to indicate "all people," and the use of "he," "his," and "him" to do the same generic duty are a patriarchically linguistic "house of being," and only those marginalized by the language (out of power) are likely to demand linguistic renovation of the house of being.

Similarly, English has no at-hand word that corresponds to *praxis* or *phronesis*. That makes it less likely that it will occur to us to utter that rare question embedded in it.

All of this "stuff" that we have inside as we start interpreting anything constitutes our pre-understandings—our unaware presuppositions. We are not conscious of these biases until we get caught short in trying to understand something very other and very puzzling. When some strangeness stands between us and what we are trying to understand, we become aware of our need to interpret if we are to know.

Initial Understanding

Initial understanding is whatever meaning something has for us at first blush, where all our presuppositions are already at work. This is our unanalyzed, instinctive first understanding. Initial understanding is regularly revised with further experience. But the most radical revision occurs when in dialogue with others we have become aware of the pre-understandings that shaped our initial understanding and recognize that revision is called for at that level—then much else in our interpretation is likely to appear different.

One of the best ways to identify pre-understandings is to share initial understandings in a group and then ponder why we heard such different things. Communities too have their own biases, but interpreting in the context of live community interaction is a healthy way of identifying pre-understandings and initial understandings and being opened to the relentless activity of interpretation.

Free Construction

I will begin with an example of what I consider to be free construction. This originates in a period before historical consciousness had developed and when historical-critical methods of biblical interpretation were unheard of.

The Catholic church felt its reality under serious attack in the Reformation; its very structure was under siege. One of the issues was how many sacraments there were; Catholicism defended its seven, and other new traditions, for example, claimed three. The Council of Trent laid out the logic of its counterattack, which contained the claim that Jesus directly instituted each one of the seven sacraments. I think a pre-understanding animating this claim is first of all the church's experience of the life-giving centrality of its sacramental system, and second, the underlying sense that the authenticity of the sacraments requires institution by Jesus. Therefore, we must begin looking for the places where each sacrament was instituted.

If Eucharist was instituted at the Last Supper, and if Eucharist is understood to be essentially dependent upon priesthood, then clearly Jesus also ordained at the Last Supper, especially in the directive to "Do this in memory of me"—at least that has been an operative logic.

It would be a rare Catholic theologian or exegete today who would claim that sacramental authenticity requires direct institution by Jesus Christ. Moreover, no apostle or disciple in the New Testament is called a priest. The earliest titles that lay behind a later development of priestly identity are *presbyter* (elder) and *episcopos* (bishop). There is simply no material, textual indication whatever that Jesus instituted a priesthood or ordained anybody. Christian community, in fact, does not have an identity separate from Judaism until the last decades of the first century. The word "priest" does not become a common designation for the leader of Christian communities until the third century.

Further, although women are not given explicit presence at the Last Supper, the absence of mention is no indicator of the absence of women. In the texts that come from a patriarchal culture, women are usually not named unless something truly notable occurred that involved them. Mary and Martha are named because they are explicitly involved in a narrative that makes a substantial point. But at the feeding of the crowds by Jesus, we are told there were five thousand men, "not counting women and children." In the narrative within the narrative of two healings, Jairus the synagogue official is named, but the woman with the flow of blood is not. The Passover meal was and is a family ritual. It is historically very unlikely that a group of only men would do a family ritual, especially since we know that women accompanied Jesus on the trip from Galilee to Jerusalem. A pre-understanding in the consciousness of men in a patriarchal culture would be that women are ordinarily not counted and mentioned, unless something extraordinary calls for it.

I would hold, therefore, that an interpretation that Jesus ordained men at the Last Supper is a matter of free construction added on to what is there, not as a deliberate ruse, but as an honest response to some "obvious" logic.

Free construction is a normal element in interpretation. Since there is no such thing as an uninterpreted fact, we are always interpreting and always biased by our histories. It is impossible not to be biased, that is, not to have a perspective. We could know nothing without a starting perspective. It is not bad to be biased, but natural. However, it is dangerous not to know we are biased, and to interpret anything as though we are not biased. We can never entirely eliminate our own contribution to every interpretation, and we have a hard time identifying what we ourselves contributed to the interpreted fact.

In other words, there is always some "free construction" from the interpreter that penetrates into the inside of every "fact," and it is hard to isolate it and name it because it looks exactly like "fact." This phenomenon is not a failing against "objectivity." It belongs to the nature of human knowing and has a lot to do with how we make meaning in the world.

Hearing a Text on Its Own Horizon

Because it is such hard work, we must really intend to hear a text speak from its own world, on its own horizon. If we do it consistently enough, it can even become a learned disposition to otherness so that the intention need not be remade each time. We must presume that no other voice speaks with a set of meanings identical in every respect to our own meanings. A text provokes our closer attention by its otherness, its strangeness, its remoteness. Otherness makes us suspect that we do not really know exactly what it means.

Consider, for example, the Gospel account of the woman cured from a flow of blood which she has endured for twelve years. She exhausted all her money on doctors and grew worse, not better. In an act of final desperation as well as an act of faith she touched Jesus' garment and was healed. Jesus said, "I felt power go out of me." All of us are moved by the healing, by the compassion of Jesus, and by his gentle words to the woman. We are glad that she is healed.

Few of us in our culture would immediately feel what any Jewish woman at that time would have felt. Purity legislation from Leviticus 15 says that a woman with a flow of blood beyond her menstrual period is subject to the same law as applies during her period. She may touch no one. No one may touch her. No one may touch anything she has touched. No one can sit on the same chair or bench with her or at the same table. Anyone who violates those regulations in respect to her in turn becomes "unclean." For twelve years this woman had lived as a total social outcast, untouchable to another human being. Her cure was not just a healing of one person's body, but the reintegration of that person into the social body. When saying "what does this mean for us," a community would come to one conclusion if the narrative is interpreted as tending the sick, and a different conclusion if the narrative is interpreted as an action of Jesus toward a social outcast and the reintegration of that person into normal social life.

Any Jewish person of the time would have noted that Jesus knew he had been touched by a woman with a flow of blood and that made him ritually unclean. It would have been unlawful for Jesus to touch someone else. But from the healing of this unnamed woman, he goes to Jairus's house and takes Jairus's daughter by the hand and says, "get up, little girl," an act of religious disobedience.

When interpreting anything or anyone, we have to make every effort to allow it to speak from its original setting. When I hear another person, if I want to understand, I must let the words mean what that person makes them mean and not what they mean to me. I need not agree, but I will not accurately interpret if I do not let the other have her or his otherness.

I have a long-time interest in how theology has made use of philosophy in trying to add intelligibility and plausibility to the experience of faith. A word like "identity" has a different meaning in Aristotelian/Scholastic philosophy than it does in process philosophy. Sometimes just a single word needs to speak from its larger systemic setting if we are to interpret accurately another's single sentence.

Self-motivation toward one's goal in business is a virtue in Western thought and a path to unhappiness in Theravada Buddhism. Striving to be successful is a noble Western aspiration and a destructive resolve in Hinduism.

In the framework of historical consciousness, you cannot canonize any human articulation unless you canonize the worldview in which its words and grammar are embedded. The fact that in Western culture "person" normally means an individual center of consciousness makes it difficult if not impossible to understand what the Greek word that we now translate as "person" meant in the Nicene confession of trinitarian faith or the Chalcedonian confession of christological faith. We do not live in the categories of argument out of which those ancient controversies arose. Interpretation can help broach the distance but cannot overcome it.

Interpretation as Conversation

Interpretation has the character of a conversation. As we struggle to understand some text or person or event, there is a back-and-forth movement. We begin with initial understanding. We sense soon that the other is somewhat different than our first take on it and that it is situated on a horizon not at all exactly like our own horizon. We the interpreters make an adjustment and the other is different than before, and the conversation begins all over as we once again find some new otherness. A conversation ensues between the text on its own horizon and me on mine.

The conversation has the to-and-fro movement of question and answer, and sometimes of agreement and disagreement. The to-and-fro movement is like a game; it has some rules, but we cannot be good players if we are always thinking about the rules. Sooner or later the game must play us. These reflections on the dynamics of conversation are like some of the rules of the game of conversation.

The kind of conversation described is often powerful, because listening openly to otherness never leaves us untouched by the encounter. If we are really to listen, therefore, we must grant that the other point of view is worthy of consideration and must attempt to enter sympathetically into the inside of the otherness. We may not change our position, but even so we will understand it better and hold it more deeply. Or, we may be changed a lot. The encounter with something truly other will relativize some of the understandings with which we began the conversation. Thus, true conversation always puts the interlocutor at risk. It is not a timid act. We never emerge from any true conversation exactly the same as when we entered it.

Arguing

There is a mutually critical correlation between us and a text. We interpret it, and it interprets us (sacred texts especially must be allowed to interpret us). This is true whether what is being interpreted is a text, or another person, or, in the context of this book, the church. When interpretive critique is mutually critical, this may not mean that both are finding mistakes in each other, but perhaps naming incompleteness, or imbalance. No interpreter is free of critique.

One of the key factors that makes perspectives different is the social location of the interpreter. The poor will not interpret the economy the same as the wealthy. Women are making it clear that they interpret history differently than most of the men whose interpretations have controlled our culture's sense of its own history. Black Americans do not interpret U.S. history the same as white Americans. The position of this book is that the dominant understanding of Catholic Christian identity has for basically all of the church's history been interpreted almost entirely by men, and more specifically, by men who are part of the power structure. This does not of itself make the interpretation wrong, but it does of itself make it incomplete and tilted in the direction of one set of vested interests.

Sometimes, therefore, there is "a rub" between us and the other which honorable argument addresses. It is possible to disagree with some part of a text, and even to have placed a part of the text under permanent suspicion, without the text losing its status as a true classic (e.g., anti-Judaism passages in the New Testament). Argument is not a time-out from conversation;

> [it is] a vital moment within conversation if the conversation itself is to move forward. . . . All argument assumes the following conditions: respect for the sincerity of the other; that all conversation partners are, in principle, equals; saying what one means and meaning what one says; a willingness to weigh all relevant evidence, including one's warrants and backings; a willingness to abide by the rules of validity, coherence, and especially possible contradictions between my theories and my actual performance. (Tracy 1987, 23, 26)

In the best of all interpretive worlds, argument has the character of what Karl Jaspers calls "loving struggle." Both arguers "show themselves without reserve and allow themselves to be thrown into question. If I know something that will bolster your argument against my argument, I must give it to you, even if it questions me. Authentic living, not winning, is the issue" (Jaspers 1970, 59–60).

Societies need space for such conversation and, when necessary, a chamber for argument. The only fair space is that under joint ownership. The only safe chamber that which is neutral. The church no less so. The Spirit is in every social location.

"Something Else Might Be the Case!"

Martin Heidegger says about human beings, "we are always already ahead of ourselves," for we are always "projecting" the possible lives we might live (1962, 182–88). Every encounter we ever have with otherness affects in some way, large or very small, the meanings out of which we live. We look at our present moment, and our encounters often tell us that something else might be the case. The something else that might be the case is often not some specific, immediately practical option; it is often just a different way of being in the world, a different way of relating, a different way of understanding important things, a deeper and therefore different way of continuing to do the same thing.

It is important not to instrumentalize projection. The projection that belongs to interpretation does not first and foremost mean a precise strategic plan. It means that we make meaning differently out there in front of us as a result of what we come to understand. Making meaning is the structure of understanding. Sometimes, of course, these differences do finally express themselves behaviorally in quite specific ways. "Texts," says Paul Ricoeur, "speak of possible worlds and of possible ways of orienting oneself in these worlds.... Interpretation becomes the grasping of the world-propositions opened up" (1978, 144).

All those projections about the possible worlds in which we might live are intrinsic to a text's meaning. To understand what something means we must know what difference it *might* make. The American pragmatic tradition has been one of the most explicit philosophical responses to the paradigm shift from rational subject to historical agent, albeit often in need of nuance. Charles Sanders Peirce and William James give vivid expression to the connection between meaning and actual or possible effects:

> To attain ... clearness in our thoughts about a [text] we need only consider what conceivable effects of a practical kind [it] may involve. ... All realities influence our practice, and that influence is their meaning for us.... There can be no difference anywhere that does not make a difference somewhere else.... In what respect would the world be different if this alternative or that were true? If I can find nothing that would be different, then the alternative has no sense. (James 1969, 43–45, passim)

The business of making possible worlds stand up in front of us is especially important in our interpretation of our Scriptures. Jesus proclaims that the reign of God is breaking into our histories. His teaching is mostly about what a new world out in front of us might look like, and about the claims which those potential transformations make upon our present historical experience. The possible new worlds in front of us are constitutive of the intrinsic meaning of our texts. Texts are performative as well as informative.

The Pharisees as the Grand Interpreters

There is debate among Jewish and Christian scholars alike whether the rabbis of the Midrash, Mishnah, and Talmuds are direct descendants of the Pharisees. I do not claim the necessary scholarship in this area to stake out a clear position on the direct descendency issue. But I do at least claim some continuity in essential spirit, especially as the normative role of interpretation becomes increasingly and visibly insistent.

First of all, the experience of reinterpretation does not begin with the Pharisees. In his history-of-ideas study of covenant, Delbert Hillers demonstrates how the experience of covenant undergoes development and reinterpretation, and how the reinterpretations reflect changes in practice in the function of treaty in Near Eastern political life (1969). As appropriate, religious self-understanding makes critical use of (or should) many of the categories of cultural self-understanding, or else religion begins to feel irrelevant. In a comparative study of the American and Hebrew legal traditions, William Dean notes both the profound historical sense of the lawyers [Pharisees] as well as their role as interpreters:

> Hebrews [made] efforts to found themselves on historical actions rather than on transhistorical ideals. Americans, like Hebrews, are a nation of wandering emigrants who continue to reinterpret their covenant with God as they restlessly cross space and time, and who, in that series of reinterpretations create their religious reality.... [They] create their religious truth from actions—present actions reinterpreting earlier actions, thereby becoming new actions, over and over again. (1987, 1)

For reasons of social location, these historical adaptations and reinterpretations are far less likely to come from priestly interpretation, which tends to be conservative of tradition, and rightly so. The impetus for reinterpretation is more likely to come from those in frontline contact with developments in culture—*communitas* rather than *societas,* and rightly so. This tends to be the social location of lay experience. The more knowledgeable of the tradition the lay members of *communitas* are, the more impact they have upon the institutional life of faith as they propose contemporary reinterpretation. The genius of Jewish religion in the second century BCE was that it opened itself, not without painful contention, to a dialectic between interpretations.

The storytelling of Jesus is midrashic in form and is the setting for his own pattern of reinterpretation: "You have heard it said ... but I say. ..." Midrash is a narrative form of interpretation rather than a rational, propositional form, whose intent is to bring faith and daily lived experience into life-giving encounter. It is not so much a method of interpretation as it is a whole way of life. Gerald Bruns, in his study entitled *Hermeneutics Ancient & Modern,* says that "midrash is concerned with practice and action as well as with the form and meaning of texts" (1992, 105). He cites a midrashic text that proclaims, "Let the Torah never be for you an antiquated decree, but rather like a decree freshly issued, no more than two or three days old. . . . Indeed, Ben Azzar said: not even so old as a decree issued two or three days ago, but as a decree issued this very day" (cited in Bruns 1992, 106). I believe the same can be said of practical theology—it is not just a method, though it is that too, but most of all it is a spiritually charged way of living a Christian life.

Bruns notes how contrary this approach is to the long-nurtured Christian desire for unassailable foundations. Our instincts resist accepting "the finite, situated, dialogical, indeed political character of human understanding. . . . Our ideal is an uncontested grasp of the text. We want to say: 'All interpretation aside, what does the text really mean?' But," Bruns adds, "this transcendental desire is unsatisfiable with respect to the historicality and social heterogeneity of understanding" (1992, 112). In a sentence, historical consciousness is a new human situation and needs a new approach to interpretive authority in the Catholic church. Our own roots in the Jewishness of Jesus and the Jewishness of our origins should open us to metaphors in that tradition that might help us process our new situation today.

A Pastoral Application:
Interpreting the Scriptures That Interpret Us

Again, I shall speak from my local situation. In some form or another, we give all of our students a solid introduction to hermeneutics, not just as an interpretive method for Scripture, but as a norm of experience, no matter what the text or event or person or social system. What I offer here is a model for small Christian communities who are committed to lectionary-based Scripture as part of their regular life together. This is a process used in the Basic Christian Community Formation Program in the Institute for Ministry at Loyola. It is also part of the regular programming of the Center for Lay Marianist Communities and Lay Spirituality, of which I am co-director along with Richard and Faith Pinter in St. Louis. Frankly, most dialogue homilies rarely get much beyond free associating, where we who are gathered do our interpreting. It takes a more disciplined approach if we are to allow our sacred texts to interpret us and help create for us a reign-of-God agenda that wells up out of the conversation between interpretations of faith and interpretations of culture. This kind of process goes hand in hand with the social-analysis process present at the close of the previous chapter.

I will outline the process, with a Markan text in mind. References to the Markan pericope reflect the kinds of reflections that are frequently offered when a group goes through this process with a facilitator. What I shall outline are basically directives to a facilitator who would guide the process for a community. It takes an hour and a half or two hours to do justice to this process. Early in a community's use of such a process, attention to the various steps and questions is more self-consciousness. It soon becomes second nature.

We Interpret the Text

1. Listen to the passage as it is proclaimed (the proclaimer preferably tells the story by heart). Just absorb the narrative. Do not try to be analytical. Let the story wash over your sensibilities.

> Jesus was teaching in the temple as follows. He said to those gathered, "Beware of the scribes. They love to go about in their long robes. They relish the titles with which people address them in the marketplace. When they go to the synagogue, they take the front seats. When they attend banquets, they try for the best places. They devour the widows' resources in exchange for the long prayers they promise. These people will receive the severer judgment." Then Jesus sat down facing the treasury, and watched as people put their money in. Many of the rich gave sizeable contributions. Then a poor widow came forward and dropped in two tiny coins. Then Jesus called his disciples to him and said to them, "I tell you truly, this woman made a larger contribution than all the rest, for they gave from their surplus, but she gave from her substance." (Mark 12:38–44)

What stands out for you: an image? a feeling? a mood? some words? Take a few quiet moments to get in touch with how the story affected you. Now, please share your experience with members of your small group (not more than five or six in a group). As you do, stay with what *you* experienced as *you* heard the story, even though you may feel and think additional things as you listen to others?

Here we are asking for initial understanding. Some people focus upon Jesus' critique of the scribes for wanting to be the center of attention. More frequently people focus upon the generosity of the poor widow. Popularly, this Markan narrative is known as the story of "the widow's mite," and that fact—someone else's interpretation—often influences how people have focused.

2. There may be similarities, but no two people heard the story in exactly the same way. Spend a little time trying to identify what made you hear it the way you heard. What experience recent or old shaped your hearing of the story? The mood you were in? Something precious to you at stake? Some vested interests?

We are asking here that participants name some of their pre-understand-ings, things inside them that had an effect on how they heard. We are rarely aware of the biases within us that affect how we hear each other, or hear a text or an event. Only in an exercise like this do we usually become aware of our starting place. An important feature of this part of the process for a small community is that community members, when they answer this question, are sharing their own stories. When this happens week after week, we learn a lot about both ourselves and each other. The disclosures nurture commu-nity bonding.

3. For Christians our sacred texts are not just tales of long ago. They are no less the instigators of today's stories. They are as if the decree were issued this very day. God speaks to us now through Scripture, and the sacred words become the Word when they make a claim on us, when our lives have been accosted by what we heard. The meaning of Scripture is not behind the text but out in front of the text and us.

Against that background, do either of these two things. Have some moments of quiet while each of you goes back to the original way you heard the story, and based upon that particular way it was heard, what does it ask of you now? Or as a group, focus together on one of the ways that someone in the group heard the story, and ask together what that hearing could ask of the community. Only by allowing the words to levy practical claims do they become true Word.

The Text Interprets Itself

4. Sometimes the text is so clear, direct, and uncomplicated that no back-ground briefing is needed. But because these texts come from another time and another culture, we often need some help to get back to the original voice. In the base communities of Latin America it is usually the catechist that offers some remarks here. Often in communities in the United States, the leader will have consulted helpful commentaries. This should not be a Scripture lesson—only as much as will help us with the immediate text.

In the Markan text given above, Jesus scolds the scribes for taking advan-tage of widows' resources, promising in return some public prayer. One of the functions of scribes was comparable to what we might today call an executor of a will. Widows were not allowed to do this for themselves. Scribes took huge cuts, and part of the payback was their promise to offer prayers for the widows (Myers 1994, 320–22). Since there was no distinc-tion between civil and religious law, it was both a civil and religious system that kept widows poor and scribes rich. No wonder they could put much more in the treasury. Jesus in fact is leveling a biting social critique against the system that disempowers the already disadvantaged. This should not be called the story of the widow's mite but perhaps the social criticism of scribal behaviors vis-à-vis widows in that culture.

The Text Interprets Us

5. Back in your small groups, see whether you can identify situations in our world today where the system takes advantage of those who are already likely to be disempowered and marginalized. When we can make a connection like this, we are on level ground with the original situation.

At this point we are trying to hear the story with fresh ears and to make connections between the horizon of the original story and the horizon of our current stories. We could, of course, have begun with the background before the gospel was first proclaimed, or right afterward. But we would not have come to experience our need for the interpretive process because of the historicality of all human life all of the time.

6. In the light of our rehearing of the narrative, how does that story now impact upon us today? What are some of the ways we can respond to the claims the text makes on us so that the reign of God in our world can take hold and transform and save?

At this juncture, the dialogue between faith and culture is especially important and explicit. It is here also that the fruits of social analysis as laid out in the previous chapter might be introduced as a critical conversation partner.

* * * * * * * * * * * *

What I have outlined here is really a long-term process, a way of life with our sacred texts. It is helpful often to experience the process step by step. Sometime the entire process is drawn out over weeks or months.

With obvious modifications, we can use similar processes in a critical retrieval of doctrine, of events in church history, of theological tracts, of last Sunday's homily, and so on. Interpretation is not just something we must do when meaning is unclear. Interpretation is a feature of all experience. Even when meaning is patently clear, it is still interpreted meaning.

I conclude with an observation of Gerald Bruns, replacing Bruns's "midrash" with "community of interpretation":

> Community of interpretation presupposes not ultimate ground (*Letzbegrundung*) but common ground; it presupposes belonging and participation rather than logical foundation. Community of interpretation is not method but form of life. (1992, 114)

VI

THE FUTURE CHURCH

OF 140 BCE

The fundamental shape, the social structure of a community, is its interpretative authority writ large. The location of interpretive authority... patterns the shape of community. A community lives out a pattern of interpretative authority, and recreates that pattern at level after level of its own life. ... The shape of a community is the direct result of who has say in the interpretation of its central texts and its situation, and who has no say, and how that is decided—how the conflict of interpretation is adjudicated, and what happens to the voices of those whose interpretations are not granted authority.

The broader the community of interpretation, the more complex and difficult it will be to define its identity. But its identity will also be more fully formed. It will be more fully formed because it will more nearly reflect the actual breadth of the community's life. A process that is more open, plural, social and dialogical, changes a community.

To open the process of interpretation, therefore, beyond the guild of interpreters who have accepted (or taken) the authority to say what meaning is, is revolutionary. (Edgerton 1992, 62–63, passim)

The Pattern of Interpretive Authority

The thesis of this book is that the pattern of interpretive authority in the Catholic church in the United States (elsewhere, as well, to be sure) is undergoing critical transformation with the introduction of an educated, articulate Catholic laity into public discourse—a lay hermeneutic, if you will—especially as this occurs in the mix of ministry and leadership in ecclesial community. This is not a mere development but, potentially and needfully, a profound development of a People-of-God ecclesiology, one consistent with Christian origins.

By claiming that such a development can find support in Christian origins, I do not mean that the unfolding of a new dialogic relationship between a lay and clerical hermeneutic is the inexorable logic of Christian origins. For the driving energy of this possible development comes equally from developments within Western culture in the last four centuries. What I do mean is that there are working instincts within the ancient Jewish soul, including certainly the Jewish soul of Jesus, that offer historical support from 140 BCE for a future Catholic church. We have too long cut ourselves off from the riches of Jewish experience and spirituality.

I have also indicated my judgment that the teachings of Jesus are disposed to a different interpretation of power and its functions than have tended to be embodied in the life of ecclesial communities. Contemporary biblical scholarship, for example, is skeptical about strict genetic claims between priesthood as we know it today and instituting activity on the part of Jesus, or with overly tight connections between priesthood and the historical lives of the apostles, or between the college of bishops and the college of apostles. Anachronisms abound in the kinds of historical connections that have been posited. Continuities are one thing, and they surely exist.

Above all, the possibilities for a more dialogical ecclesiology find support in pneumatology, our understanding of the presence of God's Spirit. At Pentecost, the tongues of fire come to rest upon the group that had gathered in the upper room (Acts 2:1–4). The membership of the group includes the eleven apostles, some women, and Mary and Jesus' brothers (Acts 1:12–14). When Peter addresses the crowd that has gathered, he begins by telling them of the pouring out of the Spirit on all people: old and young, men and women, slaves. Paul teaches the Corinthian community about the large pool of gifts that it holds within its community for the sake of the community, "but at work in all of these is the same Spirit" (1 Cor. 12:11).

Clearly, ordained Christians have long had a towering interpretive edge, and from their social location they have been the principal architects of Catholic Christian identity. From early on, ordained Christians have been male, and for most of the last thousands years, they have been celibate males. This is not an indictment of their interpretation, but an acknowledgment of its incompleteness and one-sidedness. Our culture has been and remains patriarchal, and since we live in culture the way fish live in the sea, we have not been aware until recent times of the pervasive maleness of Western cultural biases. But that is one of the obvious reasons why the clerical interpretation has had the place of honor in the interpretive structure of the Catholic community.

People with knowledge are always in a position of power to influence others. In Western culture, education has largely been the provenance of males, and more affluent ones at that. Until recently, lay Catholics have been less educated in the sacred sciences than have clerics. In affirming the need for a much more dialogic ecclesiology in the U.S. Catholic church, no small part of the urgency comes from the education of Catholics in the 238 Catholic colleges and universities in the country, and especially from the education of Catholic women and men in graduate ministry programs in over 50 of these institutions. There are more laypeople receiving graduate education in ministry and pastoral theology than there are celibate men in the four years of theology leading to ordination. And 70 percent of the lay-people are women. The combination of lay learning, the lay social location of lay interpretation, and the further social location of women's interpreta-tion are gathering cogency as they formulate their insights into Catholic Christian identity. With church attendance in this country down to 26.2 per-cent, it is certainly a fair guess that lay Catholics are not hearing their story named.

I want to say again as I move into this final chapter that the categories of lay hermeneutic and clerical hermeneutic are a typology that stresses the importance of social location to interpretation. The concerns of daily fam-ily life and the concerns of daily parish life or daily diocesan life are quite dif-ferent—not antithetical, but very different. There are ordained members of the church who are profoundly sensitive to and supportive of lay interpreta-tion, and lay members of the church who are equally sensitive to and sup-portive of clerical interpretation. Further, and obviously, laypeople do not all think alike, nor do clerics. But there is a difference, and within the right kind of dialogic structure, the truth of both can shape community.

Sociologists understand how authorized speakers control the meanings out of which a community lives. Communal reality is produced and buttressed by the talkers. In the Catholic church only clerics may interpret the meaning of Scripture for community in a homily set within Eucharist. Clerics "talk" at Mass. There are some provisions in Canon Law for lay-people to reflect on Scripture, but not within Eucharist. Books on church, theology, and religion were always required to be approved by the censor of books (*censor librorum*); when nothing was found to stand in the way of its being published (*nihil obstat*) then the church allowed the book to be printed (*imprimatur*). Each of these permissorial judgments was made by a cleric. No book by any Catholic, lay or cleric, was to be published without the *imprimatur.* Once again, a lay Catholic could not talk in print without clerical approval. No layperson belongs to the Congregation for Defense of the Faith, where Catholic "talk" is adjudicated as admissible or not admissible into the authentic conversation of Catholic culture. It is patently clear that the structure of authorized interpretation, the guild, is fundamentally clerical.

In the long tradition of self-understanding, *Lumen Gentium* §31 affirms that the laity, by their very vocation, seek the kingdom of God by engaging in temporal affairs, while the ordained are primarily concerned with sacred ministry. The irony is that those whose social location is engagement in temporal affairs do not have a normal, structured voice in that official conversation of the church. Educated laity in the U.S. Catholic church are this church's best bet against a further pile up of revolutions, and in favor of addressing the still-existing pile up. The need for dialogic ecclesial interpretative structures is pressing and poignant.

In every society, necessarily and redemptively, there is also life in the margins. There are talkers there too. Their voices do not easily penetrate the official auditorium, but somehow, sometimes, they are overheard. However, this does not occur often enough for their sagacious foolishness to freshen the dialogue. I want to attend, therefore, to the important voices of those who live in the margins, often found in grassroots, small Christian communities. For this I will be indebted to my colleague and friend Terry Veling. I shall reflect upon the lay voices also under the rubrics of a hermeneutic of exile and a hermeneutic of tears. For these perspectives I am indebted to W. Dow Edgerton's splendid work, *The Passion of Interpretation,* from which the citation at the beginning of this chapter is taken.

In these final pages we will look at the interpretative voices of those who live in the margins. Then I will offer a summary of the reasons for which the Pharisees from around 140 BCE are a useful metaphor for the self-understanding of the U.S. Catholic church as it ponders alternative futures for itself in conjunction with its sister churches throughout the world. Finally, I will address the ecclesiological potential for dialogic community as a space for ecclesial praxis.

Living and Speaking from the Margins

The play of writing in the margins represents an area of freedom where an interpretive community is partially released from the burden of prescribed meanings and weighty, dominant receptions of a text. It is relieved of taken-for-granted conventions and established readings of texts that have become ensnared in familiar and set patterns of interpretive construal. Play releases a community into what Roland Barthes calls the "pleasure of the text," the pleasure of interpretive activity that runs freely across the wild and fertile field of the text. Writing in the margins is excessive and indulgent writing that scribbles madly anything and everything that wells up and wants to be written (Veling 1994, 203).

Before speaking about that dimension of the lay hermeneutic that is a marginal hermeneutic, three terms need to be clarified: the word "lay"; the meaning of the pages of a "text"; and textual "margins."

Lay

When the social sciences are invoked to elucidate history and theology there is often the fear (and the possibility) of reductionism, that is, of allowing explanatory insights to become the total explanation. On the other hand, the Spirit of God works through our humanity, individually and socially—in no other way, in fact, because there is no other way. Whatever sheds light on how we are individually and socially human, therefore, will shed light on the shape of grace. It is in that context that we need to recall from Alexandre Faivre's study, *The Emergence of the Laity in the Early Church,* that "there is no question of 'lay' in the New Testament. There is no trace of that term! There is not even a trace of any reality that could be transposed and put in parallel with our contemporary phenomenon of the 'laity'" (Faivre 1990, 3).

When the Greek word *kleros* and its cognates occur in the New Testament, they refer to all Christian people and not specifically to ministers. The word for laity, *laikos,* occurs for the first time in the *First Letter of Clement.* This letter is addressed to the church at Corinth, which is beset by dispute. Clement asks that people in that church respect each other's function in the life of the church. In that context he names those who have specific designated ministries and the other members of Christ who do not have such designated tasks—the latter person is an *anthropos laikos,* a layperson.

When I use the expression "lay hermeneutic" I want to signal the importance of social location. Those who interpret Christian life primarily from their position as designated leaders and ministers in the community are closer to what has become known as clerical in their perspective. Those whose interpretation is primarily from the position of family and so-called secular life offer a lay interpretation. I am not using lay and clerical in the meanings that developed later, affirming a difference in kind, not just degree, between lay and clerical. I am stressing the difference that social location makes in how anyone interprets the church.

We may soon be faced with the need for a new name for a new state in the church. Laypeople who maintain their place in family and secular careers are also assuming positions in ministry and leadership in the church. Business people and lawyers are often on parish councils and financial councils, for example. Arrangements like these are expressions of the transformation afoot in the patterns of interpretative authority. These are functional changes, and in the future church of 140 BCE it is to be hoped that formal transformations will also have occurred, that is, that form will have followed function.

Text

Hermeneutics, to be sure, has been primarily concerned with texts and language, and especially with written materials. Since all experience is interpreted experience, we can, by extension, talk about the "text" of our lives, the "text" which the church is, and so on. Each time I have spoken about a lay hermeneutic or a clerical hermeneutic, my concern has been with how being "lay" or "cleric" influences one's interpretation of Catholic Christian identity. My discussion of marginal hermeneutics below has the church as "text."

The Margins

Pages have margins. When students read their textbooks they often write notes in the margins. Those of us who love books write a lot of notes in the books we love most (or hate most!). We note what is important or what is omitted; what we agree with; where we dissent. In the Middle Ages scribes would occasionally incorporate an interesting marginal note into the main text (whether intentionally or not, who knows). In any case, new ideas have a way of hanging around the edges of conventional ideas, trying themselves out as marginal comments. From there they occasionally make their way into the text. What is important about the metaphor of margin is that while the margin is not the text, it is still on the page; and what is written there influences how the text is read. Who has not experienced reading a borrowed book with someone else's yellow highlighting (a modern form of marginal comment), and recognizing how someone else's marginal reflections influence our reading of the text?

The second and wider sense of margins is found in the work of Edmond Jabes, whose influence on my thought I have amply noted in the foreword and afterword to *Jesus and the Metaphors of God* (Lee 1993). For Jabes, the margin is not just the white space around the edges of the text, but "the whiter one that separates the word strewn page from the transparent, the written page from the one to be written" (1993, xii–xiii). In his foreword to Jabes's book *Margins,* Mark Taylor says that "the margin is the limited space separating the written page from the page that always remains to be written" (Jabes 1993, xiii).

There is a clue to Jabes in Taylor's words about a page that always remains to be written. Jabes is under the full sway of historical consciousness, in many of the ways that deconstruction has processed it—but he is there in the way that only a rabbinic Jewish soul can be there, certain about the unremitting interpretability of every text. Our logocentric Western tendency has been to end discussion with a definitive statement, an unambiguous text. For a Jew, the Mishnah interprets Jewish reality; the Talmud interprets those interpretations of Jewish reality; and throughout the centuries rabbinic students have interpreted those Talmudic interpretations of the Mishnaic interpretation. Interrogating Jewishness belongs to Jewish identity because its meaning is inexhaustible. The Jewish mystical tradition from the Middle Ages, the *Kabbalah,* is also a strong influence on Jabes. The mystery of being permeates his thought and deepens his sense of both the necessity of the books we write and of their immediate inadequacy. That is why the margins are constitutive of the tradition. They are the constant reminder of the book that remains to be written. And then, when that book is written, it too will be beset by margins.

For us Christians who acknowledge the mystery of the church, its relentless interpretability needs to become a normative part of Catholic consciousness. The fact that the reign of God is larger than any institution, including the ecclesial institution, is a further reason why the margins of the text called "church" are as precious as they are obnoxious—they are a constant reminder of our orientation to God's reign and not to ourselves. We are too preoccupied with ourselves as church.

It is helpful to remember that the voice of Jesus was a marginal voice in the religious institution that was his context from beginning to end, as even the title of John Meier's recent and acclaimed book proclaims: *A Marginal Jew: Rethinking the Historical Jesus* (1991). Jesus never spoke other than as a Jew within Judaism. The early Christian communities continued to be marginal, first of all within Judaism, and then beginning in the final decades of the first century within the Greco-Roman Mediterranean world as well. This remained the case until the overassimilation of the church into the Roman empire following the conversion of Constantine.

Let us look, then, at the marginal hermeneutic.

A Marginal Hermeneutic

Among those whom I consider marginal, I have encountered some resistance to being tagged as marginal, and I understand that resistance. Popularly, marginality often means "of no or little consequence," more "out" than "in." Some of that feeling, at least, is a response to not being counted "in" by the mainstream, official hermeneutic. No one enjoys being counted out.

While my focus in this book is upon the emergence of a lay hermeneutic into a real voice, I want to note that there has certainly also been a marginal clerical hermeneutic. In our own century we can name Pierre Teilhard de Chardin, Yves Congar, Henri de Lubac, Karl Rahner, and Hans Küng. From another century there is Thomas Aquinas. Many of these were marginal because they brought the "text" into dialogue with new learning that challenged the received tradition and reshaped it.

The thing about margins, whether the border of the text page, or the space between the text written and the text waiting to be written, is that the margin exists only because there is a text and for the sake of the text. Veling writes:

> Marginal hermeneutics is what happens when the twin events of belonging and non-belonging, faith and doubt, trust and suspicion, the written and unwritten, presence and absence—when these "unresolved two" burst into life in the thin, interpretive edge that both joins and separates them. (1994, 199)

What I am naming as a developing lay hermeneutic are laywomen and laymen who critique the "text" as insiders. But they are at the same time outside critics because they critique the story that does not substantially include their own story. They, therefore, place part of the "text" under suspicion. When a current version is under suspicion, the interpreters begin to hanker for an alternative reading. Edgerton calls this a hermeneutics of desire, people who are hungry for a different future. "If interpretation is founded upon desire, then that desire, or the dynamic of desire itself, informs everything that follows" (Edgerton 1992, 41). The search for alternative futures readily involves the search for alternative pasts with which to fund it. This is a hermeneutics of retrieval.

Many women have become profoundly conscious of the patriarchal structures that have been the fabric of most human culture. They hear women discounted. They notice with pain that Jesus is reported to have fed five thousand men, "not counting the women and children," and with no less pain that Paul says women must not speak when the community assembles. Is that Jesus' intention? Or is it that "free construction" from culture that weasels its way into interpreted "fact"? The hermeneutic of suspicion quickly gives way to desire for interpretation that opens itself to the gifts of women. Moved by both suspicion and desire, the early "texts" are being reread and reconstructed; things really there in the text are retrieved for the sake of a different future.

Suspicion, desire, and retrieval conspire to rebuild and transform a living "text"—it is in the margins that these grace-full instincts are incubated and from which they are born.

An overwhelming number of canonized saints are men who are ordained and/or religious. Most canonized women saints are virgins, often members of religious orders. In the "text," priestly life and religious life have often been called the way of perfection. Laypeople who are married hear themselves very largely excluded from the "text" about perfection. Today that puts a lot of the "text" about holiness under suspicion and creates a desire for "text" that acknowledges lay life, single and married, as charisms of a perfection to which all are called. All the bits and pieces of the received "text" that honestly support a different future "text" are retrieved and elaborated, sometimes discovered for the first time. New "text" is needed. Once again suspicion, desire, and retrieval conspire to rebuild and transform a living "text"—and once more it is in the margins that these grace-full instincts are incubated and from which they are born.

Laymen and laywomen have not belonged to the guild of authorized interpreters in the church. They still do not belong officially. But, as we have noted along the way, there are now some regular places where their voice is heard. One of the most obvious and most significant is parish life, where twenty thousand paid professional ministers assist in parish ministry and parish leadership, most of them women.

A particularly important interpretive point of insertion is the position of parish life coordinator. These pastoral agents are not admitted into the guild of official interpreters, but their social location in the life of a community is one of great influence.

Small Christian communities are another social location for the development of a lay and sometimes marginal hermeneutic—this is not the case with all small Christian communities, but with some. We will look at both of these experiences, the parish life coordinator and the marginal communities.

Parish Life Coordinator: Interpretive Space

"Parish life coordinator" (PLC) seems to have become the most acceptable description for the person who functions as the primary pastoral agent in a parish in which there is no resident priest-pastor. The PLC is usually a very seasoned pastoral practitioner, comfortable with her or his position in church life. These people are not marginal in the way that some grassroots communities are. But they are marginal in that this new position is not a juridical position in church structure. Canon Law provides for the possibility of such a role but does not locate juridical power in the person who functions in it. What is crucial is simply that the parish life coordinator is a "space" in the church where non-ordained Catholic leaders offer a community an interpretation of the Good News and of the community's own life.

It is not uncommon to hear priests talk about the priest shortage as a description of the present ministry crisis. I do that sometimes myself when initial instincts have not yielded to another perspective. The other perspective is the one I am more likely to take when I come away from conversation with laywomen and laymen in the graduate ministry program at Loyola (and about anywhere else). Sometimes they almost feel a ministry "glut," because not all of the many lay students who want to offer their gifts to ministry are able to find a position.

Personally, I do not agree with the judgment I often hear, that if we are more faithful and prayed better, God will send us the vocations we need. Vocations to ministry are, in fact, abundant: they just do not look like what we are used to seeing them look like. They often look like laywomen and laymen. We are neither much worse than we used to be nor much better than we used to be. We are the same old beautiful, grungy souls we always were. My intuition is that God is doing a new thing with us, and that includes declericalizing an overly clericalized *ecclesia*. Knowing how power functions in all human institutions, and knowing that the church is a human as well as a divine institution, it is most unlikely that we clerics would declericalize. "Cleric" will not disappear, and should not, but will look very different on the other side of all of this change. Lay will also look very different on the other side of the transformations afoot—it already does.

A shorter way of saying all of this is simply that the system of leadership and ministry in the Catholic church is undergoing far-reaching change under the power of its new root metaphor: the People of God.

The role of the parish life coordinator in a parish without a resident priest-pastor is a current emergency adjustment, but one that is on the way to some place that we cannot yet see clearly. It will be a while before that clear day "when you can see forever."

These people, the parish life coordinators, most of them women, have great impact upon the shape of parish ministry, prayer life, and liturgy. They often lead Scripture services and communion service when there is no

Eucharist, and in that context they frequently offer reflections on the Scriptures. In this latter capacity, they interpret the text of Scripture and the "text" of church.

The fact that three major studies have examined the parish life coordinator is itself an indicator of the growing importance of this position. The first of these, *The Emerging Pastor,* by Peter Gilmour, studied the phenomenon in five regions of the upper Midwest, largely villages and rural areas. At the time of the book (1986), Gilmour counted about thirty dioceses with non-ordained pastoral agents in parishes. As he indicates, Canon Law does not allow non-ordained persons to be designated as pastor, but in fact they function in many of the typical pastoral roles of the priest-pastor, no matter how they are named (Gilmour 1986, 4). Canon 517.2 does, however, allow for "a deacon or some other person who is not a priest, or a community of persons, to be entrusted with a share in the exercise of the pastoral care of a parish," although this is to be under the direction of a parish priest.

Ruth Wallace's study, *They Call Her Pastor: A New Role for Catholic Women,* looks at twenty women who have pastoral responsibility for a parish. All of them have had some college education. Thirteen have first degrees, and twelve of the thirteen have masters degrees. Some are better educated than the parish's sacramental ministers. In sixteen of the parishes the women preach with some regularity, and in the other four they preach only rarely or on special occasions.

Many of the women in these key parish positions are members of religious orders. There is ambiguity about whether members of religious orders are laypeople or not. *Lumen Gentium* §44 says that religious life does not belong to the hierarchical structure of the church (a religious priest would, by dint of ordination). As such, then, it does not participate in the structure of authorized interpretation. Religious life has, in fact, often been a prophetic presence. Religious life shares with lay life a social location outside of the power structure. I raise this because I believe that while religious women have a different social location than single or married laywomen, they have shared the struggles of American women, and very often bring that perspective to bear in their ministry and leadership.

All indications are that the number of priests will continue to decrease and that the pastoral leadership of non-ordained Catholics will become more and more prevalent just within the current decade. Already in many areas there are no longer replacements for the priests who die, retire, or resign.

The research conducted by Gary Burkart and reported upon in the book *The Parish Life Coordinator* is the most comprehensive research to date on this position. In his 1986 book, Peter Gilmour noted about thirty dioceses with parish life coordinators. In his 1992 book, Gary Burkart has fifty-six dioceses represented in his study of PLCs and notes that an additional thirty dioceses indicate they may accept PLCs in the next five years. These figures in themselves do not give a count of the number of dioceses who have parishes without a resident pastor, because other solutions have been used—compressing parishes into a super-parish, or giving one priest responsibility for several parishes.

In conversations with younger priests whom I taught in the seminary, there is a kind of pain, if not angst, that I am beginning to hear. It comes from some of those who are responsible for several parishes. Each parish has its own history, its own relational web, its own local culture. In the best of circumstances it takes a new priest some years to begin existentially to belong to the community whose life he celebrates. The pain I hear is that of "not knowing to whom I belong." One of the legitimate satisfactions of priesthood has been that of an identity-forming tie with a community. To be without that fundamental relationship is deeply disorienting. I do not know how widespread this experience is—I am not relying on studies, but on limited interactions. I think it may not be untypical. Priests cannot indefinitely add on more parishes.

We have no certainties only pointers, and we should use them as intelligently as we can. If we are looking at a lasting systemic change rather than serious but temporary inconvenience, then the patterns of interpretative authority are being reformulated and perhaps the lay hermeneutic, as it shares pastoral agency in the communities of Jesus Christ, will at last find a formal place to be. This, as Edgerton pointed out in the citation with which the chapter began, would qualify as a revolution affecting an entire system. And it would resonate with another revolution from 140 BCE.

Small Christian Communities: Interpretive Space

The small Christian community movement is world-wide. I will focus upon those in the church in the United States and will pay more attention to those which are more marginal (and less visible). I will, however, highlight a characteristic that most of them share wherever they are, a characteristic that pertains to the development of the lay hermeneutic. The appropriation of the small Christian community (SCC) model varies from continent to continent, region to region. In Latin America most members of SCCs are from the poorer classes, where the power for change lies. There is no large middle class. Many of the SCCs among Hispanics in southern Texas and southern Mexico are similar to the Latin American model. The study undertaken by the Woodstock Center in the early 1980s characterized SCCs in the United States as middle class, better educated, and left of center ideologically. The Woodstock study was very limited and did not include data from Hispanic SCCs.

We do not, in fact, have any accurate data at the present time on the number, character, and location of SCCs in the U.S. Catholic church, though research planning has been initiated and is well underway at this writing. There are seven large networking efforts, and these provide us with some real information and real stories. There are two additional offices that service needs and interests of SCCs, and these too have gathered some information. Two Catholic universities have made SCCs a special focus of the pastoral ministry programs. In 1993 three organizations cosponsored a First National Meeting of Small Christian Communities. A second such meeting will take place in 1997 under a broadened cosponsorship.

Parish life in the U.S. Catholic church has a long history of vigorous activity, often including an excellent grade school and sometimes also a high school. Often the cohesiveness of the parish community came from its ethnic origins, less often a feature today as ethnic groups are integrated into broader American culture. SCCs in parishes are making two important contributions to parish life. The first is through the support for people's faith life that SCC membership brings with it. The second is through the restructuring of parish life itself, when SCCs are not simply among the numerous activities of the parish but are integral to parish structure, parish leadership, and parish ministry.

Many religious orders have had third-order members. Many orders have had different forms of associate or affiliate membership. Today, as membership in orders declines, many orders are developing profound collaboration between laypeople imbued with the order's charism. They will continue together making a gift of that charism to the world. SCCs are sometimes a way in which these lay and religious men and women gather. I would draw an analogy here. Once laypeople understand from the ecclesiology of Vatican II that baptism gives them the right and duty to participate in the apostolate, they do this on their own, not needing to wait for someone else's ecclesial initiative. Laypeople are similarly beginning to acknowledge that the charisms of religious orders are susceptible to lay appropriation and are undertaking the appropriation on their own initiative.

I am seeing this from close up. A congregation of Marianist sisters and a congregation of Marianist brothers and priests were founded respectively in

1816 and 1817, out of a movement of lay communities in southwestern France that was fifteen years old. These two congregations are autonomous in their structures but interdependent in their mission. Both have a history of easy and effective collaboration with lay members of the Marianist family. Lay Marianists throughout the world have now organized themselves internationally and nationally. They convoked a gathering of lay Marianists from five continents in Santiago, Chile, in 1992. They have an international leadership team and regional structures. Lay Marianists in North America, including Mexico and Canada, have had four continental assemblies. It was something of a surprise—a development that came from what many religious Marianists would have considered the margins—that we now have a third Marianist branch, autonomous in structure, and interdependent with the other two branches in mission. Lay members outnumber religious members three to one! There have been some similar lay developments with the Maryknoll charism.

The third kind of SCC in the U.S. church is the grassroots community, where more of the marginal energy is at work. Some of the members also participate in their parishes, but they want more than is available there. Other people have more or less given up on the institutional church at the present time, consider themselves Catholic at core, and are creating options. Some of the grassroots SCCs are women's groups, angry at the absence of juridical inclusion of women in church leadership. Most of these grassroots SCCs break open the Scriptures together and work together in some form of mission. Many gather for some kind of simple meal in connection with their gatherings and break bread and share a cup without using the formula of Eucharist, but they feel that this connects them with the wider eucharistic tradition. They experiment with forms of collaborative leadership and minister to needs within community and beyond community. They welcome prayer leadership from women and men alike.

Marginal SCCs dream about futures, sensing that their experience may well help nourish the future. They do not receive much respectful attention from mainline church groups. What is important is that they are reinterpreting what it means to be community, to be Christian, and to be Catholic. They may not use those words, but they are exploring meanings by the very nature of their gatherings and the reasons for the gatherings. They are writing the hitherto unwritten in the margins of the "text" called church. You can "play" in the margins in ways that you cannot "play" in the "text." Veling writes:

> The play of writing in the margins represents an area of freedom where an interpretive community is partially released from the burden of prescribed

meanings and weighty, dominant receptions of a text. It is writing relieved of taken-for-granted conventions and established readings of texts that have become ensnared in familiar and set patterns of interpretive construal, Play releases a community into what Roland Barthes calls the "pleasure of the text," the pleasure of interpretive activity that runs freely across the wild and fertile field of the text. (1994, 203)

Generally, SCCs are a place where the lay hermeneutic often gets practiced, especially in the interpretation of the sacred texts. But it is above all in the grassroots communities that the marginal hermeneutic is most developed and practiced, for reasons that are obvious.

Metaphorical Connection with 140 BCE: Perhaps Two Real Presences

For a metaphor to tell the truth, one thing must truly be like another. But they are not identical, or there would be no metaphor. Alike and not alike. Synagogue and basic Christian community. Whatever their many differences, they are alike in the central role of Word.

I believe there may be another shift afoot in Catholic cult, tectonic in dimension, that relates to the topic of this book. There is enough evidence to warrant playing the possibility out loud. The possibility is that Catholic cult is being systemically reshaped by the retrieval of Scripture in the post-conciliar church.

When I was growing up, going to Mass on Sunday, not eating meat on Friday, and thinking Mary was very special, were things that distinguished the Catholic kids from the other kids in our neighborhood. Of the three, it was surely Mass more than anything. Eucharist was the absolute center.

To fulfill the Sunday obligation, it was necessary to be present for all three principal parts of the Mass: offertory, consecration, and communion (you did not have to receive communion, but you had to be there). If you missed the offertory, you could catch the offertory of the next Mass and leave. But if you missed two parts, you had to do the whole thing at the next Mass.

The liturgy of the Word was not included. The basic message was that missing Scripture and sermon was not missing anything essential. In the religion classes I took in sixteen years of Catholic schooling in San Antonio—grade school, high school, and university—we never read the Old or the New Testament. Catholics were not encouraged to read Scripture on their own. No one told me I could not and no one suggested that I should. My experience was not unusual for that time, and for centuries before that time.

The absolute specialness of Mass was signalled by what the tradition has called Real Presence. Now presence is either real or it is not presence. Unreal presence is absence. What "real" has named for Catholics is the utter centrality of Christ's presence in the Eucharist.

Two things happened together after Vatican II. First, Mass was returned to the community in its own language, often with the musical idiom of the people. It became available in ways we had not known. I was a high school chaplain in the late 60s when the football team had Mass in the gym and the drama club had Mass on stage. There was Mass at home and Mass in the park. Many of the other devotions receded: the novenas, benediction, and so on. The return of Mass to the celebrating community—different from attending or hearing Mass in a foreign language— was a systemic change in Catholic cult.

The second change has been the retrieval of Scripture. The Catholic church opened itself to historical biblical criticism, hermeneutics, literary criticism, and the like. In many of the basic Christian communities in Latin American, Scripture became the centerpiece of community gatherings, because there were few priests and Eucharist might be possible once every few months at best. But.Scripture has not turned out to be a mere substitute for Eucharist. It is developing a new hold and a new presence.

Unlike the congregation hearing the priest's short homily as Mass, an SCC spends an hour or two, or longer, connecting Word and world, in many of the ways that I described in chapter five. Communities stay with the text until it becomes God's living Word, active and powerful in their midst, that is, until their living has been accosted by God's Word. When that happens, a community knows that it has experienced, through Word, the effective presence of the living God.

What happens here is not merely a matter of taking more time with Scriptures, though that counts for a lot. The difference between hearing a homily and engaging in a dialogic process is huge. Jürgen Habermas has helped us understand better that there is an interactive character to knowing, some of which he learned from the psychoanalytic process. Dunne describes the issue well:

> Psychoanalytic knowledge is generated in the first instance by the analyst, but he cannot simply "apply" it to the analysand and "make" him well-adjusted. Rather it is confirmed only when it is communicated to the latter in such a way that he appropriates it into a process of self-reflection—which will be released in him only if the communication manages to outwit his resistances. (1993, 181)

A homily has tended to function as if it were able to *apply* Scripture to Christian listeners who would then be *made* into better Christians. Sometimes a homily helps do that, but it is, finally, not a dialogic event. The hearer is not brought into the conversation, and certainly the community does not hear together as a community and process as a community. God speaks not only to individuals but to nations and cities and communities. In SCCs it is more likely to be the case that a community engages in a process of self-reflection, and I can say from experience that this kind of dialogic appropriation also helps us outwit our resistances, for we are not alone and we know we are not alone.

SCCs, therefore, that are deprived of regular Eucharist often do not feel deprived of the active, real presence of God. This a new experience in Catholic culture, for Word has never played that role. The real presence of God in Word is not interchangeable with the real presence of Christ in the Eucharist. Communities do not want to substitute one for another. But they are richer for having access to two real presences. For those who have not experienced Word in this way, language about *two* real presences might sound exorbitant. If Eucharist does not have to bear the major role of cult alone, it is released to become once again a community's celebration of its own experience of the death and resurrection of Jesus Christ. In those situations in which Eucharist is a daily experience, it easily becomes more of a daily devotion than an active, participative celebration of the entire community's life.

There is something remarkable about the new experience of God's real presence in Word, and that is the integral role of community interpretation in the process. This new and heightened experience of God's real presence in Word is facilitated by a new arrangement in the interpretive pattern of the community. The lay contribution does not replace the clerical interpretation but works in a dialogic relationship with it. Lay hearts, lay minds, lay ears, and lay tongues are effectively and collaboratively contributors to Word's great presence. Marginal SCCs are the place where this second kind of presence is being felt and named. The lay hermeneutic is a constitutive feature of this second real presence.

So what might this have in common with Jewish life in 140 BCE? Something, but not everything. The Temple was at the center of Jewish worship, where sacrifices were offered by the priests. Jews in Galilee and Judea were expected to be present in Jerusalem for the great feasts, at least some of the time. The Temple sacrifices were not central in the same way as the sacrifice of the Mass has been central to Catholic life, but it was an experience of cultic sacrifice and was a priestly rite.

The Greek word *synagogue,* like the Hebrew word *knesset,* like the Greek word *ecclesia,* and like the English word *church,* did not first of all name a place, but rather the gathered people. But the gathered people soon lent its name to the gathering space. There is debate among scholars about the time and nature of the synagogue's origins, but its presence is well attested in the last centuries of the Second Temple period (and plays an increasingly larger role after the destruction of the Temple). "In contrast with the Temple, which was in the hands of the priesthood, especially the high priests, the synagogue was run by the congregation and the community in general. . . . Indeed, the whole institution was based on public participation, and it was this communal character which gave it its special status" (Safrai and Stern 1976, 914, 915). Men, women and children came to the synagogue, but only men would have read and interpreted the Scriptures.

The reading and interpretation of Scripture were the central activities of the synagogue. The Scripture text was read first in Hebrew, and then a translation was provided in the people's vernacular tongue. But it was not a literal translation, it was an interpretation. We are familiar with Jesus reading from Isaiah (Luke 4:16ff.), then laying the scroll aside to interpret its meaning. Safrai comments:

> One should not think that a translation was provided merely for the sake of the uneducated or the women and children who understood Hebrew not at all or at best imperfectly. But there were other reasons for it, since it was a sort of commentary, and ensured that the transmission of the Bible was done in accord with oral tradition. Hence the saying: "Anyone who translates a verse literally is a traitor." Translation was also justified on other grounds. "Since the Scripture was given through a mediator, we too must deal with it through a mediator." The gift of Scripture was being made anew, as it were, when it was read. (1976, 930–31)

The phenomenon of small Christian communities does not, at least at this time, have the official status that the synagogue had. But many of the SCCs have in common a central commitment to God's Word, read and commented upon, being made anew in the process of grasping the lives of those assembled. SCC and synagogue are alike in this.

SCCs, then, are creating a space where laypeople are interpreting the sacred texts of the community, and their interpretation authorizes their decisions about how they will live out their faith. SCCs are an interpretive space. This is the case for both mainstream, parish-based SCCs, and the more grassroots SCCs where the marginal hermeneutic is more active.

This interpretive space is sometimes also a space of dialogue for both lay and clerical interpretations, since priests as well as religious sisters and brothers are often members of SCCs. In SCCs it is usually the case that all there are "citizens," that is, co-equal participants in a place of serene mutual hearing, speaking, and acting.

I have also suggested that Word might be gaining a preeminent place alongside Sacrament in the cult of the Roman Catholic community, a second privileged experience, as it were, of God's real presence. The Catholic retrieval of Scripture is certainly one of the most enlivening developments in the postconciliar church. Whether this will develop institutionally and structurally into something like a second real presence, different and equally precious, only time will tell. But it is a possibility that deserves naming, and one that is grounded in some new lived experience of the People of God. And, after all, *lex orandi lex credendi:* How we pray is, in fact, how we believe.

Back to the Metaphor, Our Own Metaphor

I want to avoid the melodramatic yet not flinch before what appears to have the dimensions of revolution as educated Catholic laity in this country find voice, courage, and confidence. Laypeople have spoken out at different times in the church. But the lay experience has not helped define Catholic faith and Catholic identity. The vast literature of doctrine, dogma, and law has been created by ordained men. The agenda of the church has been shaped by their interpretation of priorities. Only men have juridical space in the power structure.

My reflections throughout this speculative book are indeed unbalanced. I have paid major attention to an emerging lay hermeneutic and minor attention to a long historical clerical hermeneutic. The splendor of the church owes much to the clerical interpretation. Truth and beauty abound. The historical interpretation has it greatness and has its dark side. If a lay hermeneutic finds a patterned place, it will show both greatness and darkness too. If it does not find a patterned place, it will be a tragedy.

I have also noted the pile up of revolutions, the great paradigm shifts, in Western culture. They have not been adequately addressed, in great part because a church that felt itself deluged did not have enough energy left over from its self-preoccupation. Many of the things it attended to, the Counterreformation, for example, had to be attended to. Most of the educated Catholics were clerics so that lay learning was not in a position to open itself to new paradigms, sift them, and welcome them into Catholic culture.

I have named three of these great paradigm shifts and the need to integrate them critically and positively. There is room for different methodologies responding to the evolution of inductive approaches, need for attention to the deliverances of experience in the interpretation of norms and faith's self-understanding, and need for formal authority to be conjoined to material authority. These are partial interactions with the scientific revolution. There is great need to rethink models of power and to devise participative structures so the People of God can be citizens in the church and not subjects of the church. There are partial interactions with the French Revolution and the shifts in Western self-understanding which that revolution instances. The most far reaching of all of the three revolutions is historical consciousness, which claims the conditioned and partial nature of all human experience and understanding and discourages the quest for metasystems and unassailable foundations. This revolution reminds us that all experience is interpreted experience, and all "fact" is interpreted fact. Because every interpreter interprets from vested interests (it is not possible to do otherwise), a healthy community is one that is enriched by a wide dialogue of interpretations.

What is unique to the U.S. Catholic church at this point in its life is that never before in the entire history of the church has there ever been a Catholic laity as generally well educated as the U.S. Catholic laity; nor has any nation ever had as many lay Catholics with graduate degrees in theology, ministry, and religion—and this number grows; nor has any church ever taken so many laywomen and laymen into active church ministry and active church leadership. All of these educated and committed laywomen and laymen work and live outside of the juridical corridors of power. When the great churchmen meet, laypeople may be invited to observe and for consultation, but never to vote on how Catholic faith will be interpreted.

Whenever we are faced with great challenge and can find historical precedents to guide the way, we are blessed. That is why the transformation of Jewish religious life in the second century BCE occurs to me as a metaphor. This was the interpretive tradition in which Jesus lived, the tradition that allowed Jesus as a lay Jew to interpret Scripture in the synagogue. In the early church the prophets, some of whom were women, probably none of whom had hands laid upon them, had places of honor in the pattern of interpretive authority. The *Didache,* a first-century Christian document, says that when an itinerant prophet comes through a community, the prophet presides at Eucharist rather than the resident leader.

If the Jewish tradition, as it was refashioned a century and half before Jesus, was in fact the context for Jesus' preaching and teaching and was the context for the earliest Christian communities, then we should not look upon that period as theirs (the Jews') and not ours. Anthony Saldarini's new study, *Matthew's Christian-Jewish Community,* holds that the community of Matthew's Gospel was still a community of disciples of Jesus who understood themselves as operating within Jewish life (1994). Both the Christian community of Matthew and the larger Jewish community of which it is a part (I agree with Saldarini's thesis) are on the cusp of separating and reinterpreting their institutional reality, but there is no decisive break yet.

Hayim Perlmutter, developing earlier Jewish proposals to the same effect, suggests that the Judaism and Christianity we know are more like siblings (1989). Each of them refashions their self-interpretation following the destruction of the Temple in 70 CE, and each of them creates a trajectory that is a substantially a novel recreation of an already remarkable tradition. The rabbinic tradition created out of Ushna in Galilee is as different from its predecessor as the doctrinal tradition created (largely) out of Alexandria is from the original setting and forms of the Jesus-event. As I have developed elsewhere, the distance is not, as Tertullian would have it, between Jerusalem and Athens, but between Ushna and Alexandria (Lee 1991, esp. 106–8).

I recall these early historical pieces because I want to make the point strongly that if we use the events of Judaism in the second century BCE as a metaphor, we should understand that *we are borrowing from our own tradition.*

I would like to return briefly to the Pharisees.

Pharisees: Lay Interpreters Remaking a Tradition

I have addressed much of the historical background and cultural context for the emergence of the Pharisees. I have tried not only to rehabilitate the reputation of the Pharisees but to claim them as a part of Christian inheritance. I have never doubted the workings of a legalist dark side of the Pharisaic spirit, but Christian ignorance of the extraordinary achievement of these people has been a historical distortion of tragic dimensions. Very often in recent years when I have observed that Pharisees can help us see a possible future church, some of my hearers presume this is a dim forecast rather than an opening to creative transformation in God's Spirit. In a brief reprise, I want to evoke the Pharisees as a metaphor that might offer wisdom to a valiant and struggling Catholic church in the United States. I know the issues are larger than the U.S. Catholic church. My hope is that if we tell our story accurately and at a deep enough level, others will find their story there too.

The hidden revolution of 140 BCE was hidden because, as far as we can tell, it was not the result of anyone's conscious plan. The hidden revolution for the future church is similar. The new roles for a Catholic laity were not planned ahead of time by anyone, unless perhaps by the Spirit. The revolution of 140 BCE was indeed a revolution, because it restructured the pattern of authorized interpretation in the community. The church that is coming into being *may* be a revolution, for it remains to be seen whether we can open our ancient guild of authoritative interpretation to embrace lay experience and a lay voice as no less a medium of God's speech to us than the familiar clerical voices of the centuries.

The 140 BCE revolution, to review, has these characteristics. First, there is the rather sudden appearance of a group of (mostly) lay Jews with a considerable influence in religious and civil affairs. Lay life is their social location, and it reflects their vested interests as influential interactors on the community. Because of their influence, and their perspectives as lay Jews, they celebrate and ritualize the holiness of family life. They confer a Temple-like sacredness on the home and transfer some of the cleanliness rites of the Temple to the equally sacred home. They observe the distinction between lay and priest but they disallow a clear line of demarcation between a mundane life and a sacred life.

Second, the major source of their influence is their learning. They are as educated as the Temple leaders, the priests, and they are more numerous than the priests. Learning is not an automatic ticket to power. The issue is that people with learning speak with an authority that is recognized by others. They know the tradition and speak knowingly from it for legitimate vested interests.

Third, the Pharisees become the grand interpreters. They introduce what comes to be know as the oral Torah. They recognize a truth outside of Scripture that has the same authority as Scripture, the written Torah. If God always acts in our history, then normative revelation always goes on. The ongoingness of revelation implies an ongoing serious dialogue with one's historical situatedness, and that means a dialogue with culture.

Fourth and finally, and this may be the cornerstone of what was built into Judaism by the Pharisees, they introduce dialectic into the structure of interpretive authority. The dialectic has several dimensions. It is able to insure a steady interaction between the lay and priestly interpretations of what it means to be a good religious Jew. Neither the lay nor the clerical interpretation alone sets the agenda. The dialogue does. This arrangement is not free of tension, but it is rich in the inclusion of insight and multiple interests.

Because of the Pharisees' lay dialogue with culture, conversation with culture is now endemic to the Jewish life institutionally. This conversation maintains a critical edge. It comes to terms with but does not capitulate to culture. This is a second dimension of dialectic.

The Pharisaic dialectic does not just exist *between* (*between* laity and priests, between religion and culture), it also exists *within* (the Pharisees). For a considerable period of time, leadership among the Pharisees was exercised by two people, representing varying opinions. We are probably most familiar with the school of Shammai and the school of Hillel, because they are near the time of Jesus and because their debates haunt later rabbinic literature. This arrangement makes the dialogic process normative, rather than any specific position. Position is not only not dismissed, but gains in importance. Argument and debate are cherished because in dialectic community it becomes more important, not less important, to have truth claims and to be able to substantiate them to show the material authority they carry.

Catholics in the United States: Lay Interpreters Remaking a Tradition

I want to summarize the parallels I have been noting throughout the book, and then, in the final pages of this "text," I will recommend what I judge to be an urgent ecclesial agenda. Not solutions, but agenda.

Lay influence in the U.S. Catholic church is growing remarkably. Part of the reason is because of the number of laypeople in key positions is growing: in chanceries, in parishes, in universities and colleges, in seminaries, in small Christian communities, in publications in theology and spirituality, and so on. Another part of the reason is a voice with a different ring, one that comes from the marginal life of institutionally disaffected Catholics. The feminist critique of patriarchy is a good example. People in the margins often know more clearly than anyone else what is working and what is not working.

The lay influence is commanding attention because the knowledge and commitment of laywomen and laymen are palpable. They understand the tradition, and they speak out of it in behalf of their experience.

Lay Catholics, because of what lay life usually looks like, are generally more exposed to the currents of contemporary culture through their education and through the contacts of daily living and working than those of us educated for a clerical life. They do not always know the technical vocabulary I have sometimes used to talk about the revolutions that have piled up. They may not have the language of inductive method, but they know their experience teaches well. They may not have the political language of power, but they know it is right to want to participate in decision making, in the selection of community leadership, and the like. They may not know the language of historical consciousness and dialectic community, but they are reasonably comfortable with pluralism and tolerant of ambiguity.

Some of them, however, do have the conceptual equipment and language to press these points. Many of these are the laypeople who have been educated in the theology, religion, and ministry programs in Catholic colleges and universities. Because of their education and their perspective as laypeople of God, they have a contribution to the dialogue that the church needs very much.

Interpretation is about understanding, of course. But interpretation is never innocent in the sense that it is disinterested and pure. The social location of interpretation is always connected with vested interests. That is not a negative comment. It is just the normal situation. So interpretation is also always about power. Because it is, the pattern of interpretive authority is very difficult to break into. Any serious transformation of patterns of interpretive authority is tantamount to a revolution in the life of a community. And that is what this final section of the book is about: a serious and brief commendation of the model of dialogic or dialectic community to the U.S. Catholic church.

Church as Community

The New Jerusalem Bible translates Matthew 16:18 in an entirely appropriate and unaccustomed way. Jesus says, "You are Peter, and upon this rock I will build my community." We are accustomed to hear Jesus say, "I will build my church." Many Catholics, for obvious reasons, think of Jesus founding a church much the same then as it is now. But the community of Matthew was likely to have been a community, or communities, of disciples of Jesus who understood themselves to be within Jewish religious life. Whether within Jewish life, or soon outside it, the formation of communities was and is an immediate response to the Good News. Each community and all communities together are the Body of Christ. The church is about community. *Societas* is for *communitas*, not the other way around.

There is no more central question than what kind of community the church needs to be today, faithful to its origins and interdependently interactive with the worlds in which it lives. In U.S. culture, community is equally urgent. How can we survive as a nation without a retrieval of commonwealth as a working value? Free enterprise tends to make the right to private property the fundamental right, rather than the right of all members of a community to a decent life. What versions of human community are incompatible with the early communities in which Christian life originated? If the hunger for community in this country is so deep that four out of every ten Americans belong to some kind of small group, why is not community at the top of the agenda for the U.S. Catholic church?

There is a quest for community at the level of nations for, as *Lumen Gentium* pointed out, nations can no longer have separate destinies. We are so interconnected and interdependent that our destinies are of a piece. The very nature of national community is called into question. The church as a community of communities is taxed to become a world church, which is not possible without surrendering a Eurocentric Christianity. Can you honestly ask a Chinese or African community to profess its faith with a Nicene Creed when it has never trafficked with the worldview that this creed presupposes for its intelligibility?

Once acknowledge the conditioned status of all experience, knowledge, and speech; once admit that all metasystems for adjudicating truth claims are under suspicion because you can never stand outside of all systems; once address the futile desire for an indisputable Archimedian foundation—then how can people live together in community? Dialogic community deserves attention.

I shall address dialogic community from the perspective of historical consciousness. Then its rationale will be looked at from the perspective of the human reality as essentially dialogic. We will then see the reemerging importance of *praxis/phronesis* in human community. Then we will consider the grounding of dialogical community in pneumatology. All of these pieces together support the fruitfulness of dialogic community as an ecclesiological self-understanding.

Finally, I will be suggesting that dialogic community be integrated slowly and reflectively into the praxis of Christian living and that this evolving praxis become grist for the theological mill in the future church of 140 BCE in the U.S. Catholic experience (and beyond, if we tell our story at a deep enough level).

Dialogic Community and Historical Consciousness

For many of us reared in traditional Catholic thought, we feel a disorientation after giving up on the possibility of an utterly "objective" hold on the world of experience; and at the same time, we are unwilling to capitulate to the kind of relativism the makes communication and community impossible between five billion discrete human beings, or between five members of the parish council. How can people be together in these circumstances? Not merely be together, but be together in rich and supportive human community?

In his book *Beyond Objectivism and Relativism,* Richard Bernstein characterizes the dilemma clearly and searches for a different kind of solidarity upon which to make community. He offers the image of dialogic community (Bernstein 1983). I would like to name some functional characteristics of dialogic community and then some preconditions for its development.

Dialogic community is a form of public life. What gathers participants is not common agreement about content but about an intersubjective process. Participants in dialogic community agree to something like the following:

1. We agree that when we speak we will so speak as to give others their best chance possible to know exactly what our positions are and why we hold them. The purpose of this communication is not to convince another of the truth of our position but to help them know what the position is, and why an intelligent person of good will might actually reach such a conclusion. At this point our speaking must never be contaminated by the motive of convincing the other to "come over to our side." We communicate to make ourselves more intelligible, not to convert the other.

2. When we listen to others our first motive must be to understand as best we can what another believes and why the other believes in that way. We fail against dialogic community if we listen in order to find the flaws and prepare our disputation. We listen because we believe that others, like ourselves, care about how the world is interpreted. And we want to grant them the dignity of having room to search. An underlying love for the power of questioning makes this kind of listening not just durable but delightful.

3. We promise that we will not go away from the conversation. If the kind of respect required for the first two conditions actually obtains, then it will be easier to commit to being there, no matter what.

4. How we understand something always influences how we live. There is meaning out in front of every interpretation. One of the most fruitful ways of continuing an exploration of different understandings is to focus upon what kind of world we want to make, and how our different understandings create different worlds, or perhaps how each understanding would differently affect the same world we care to make together. In this context, the way we make our truth claims becomes important. Within the context of his-

torical consciousness, our obligations to offer substantiation in as much detail as we know becomes even more crucial.

Any reader knows immediately how much easier it is to lay out a few functional guidelines for dialogical community than to do them! Sometimes people speak of dialectic community rather than dialogic community, because it better sounds the note of the tensive relationship given, in Bernstein's words, "the irreducibility of conflict grounded in human plurality" (1983, 223). We are not practiced in this form of public life together, partly because it is so difficult, and partly because this is the first age that has seemed to require it.

Let us entertain a concrete example. Most of us in Catholic colleges and universities understand the concerns for Catholic faith and culture expressed in *Ex Corde Ecclesiae,* which affirms the accountability of Catholic higher education to the bishops as magisterium and asks for implementations that can enforce that accountability. I would have to say that for the most part, in my long experience within the Catholic university system, the relationship between theologians and bishops has been very cordial and mutually respectful. Both are what they are because they care deeply about a shared life of faith. Bishops have a profound concern for the unity of the faith community. Because of their social location as pastors to a large and complex Catholic community, they normally feel more deeply the issue of unity within the community. Theologians care about unity as well, and recognize that one of the functions of the theological community is apologetic: to help all of us make our faith plausible and intelligible through adequate interpretation. Theologians who are not pastors will not experience the same urgency for the same reasons.

A few bishops are or have also been professional theologians, but most of them are not, even though in differing degrees they share a background in theology. Many of them are very effective administrators. One of the functions of the professional theologian is to engage in speculative theology, to try new formulations to interpret new Christian praxis (e.g., liberation theology) or to reinterpret Christian praxis within a new system of thought and symbolization (e.g., process theology). This is not a social location out of which bishops ordinarily think through the daily work of leading a local church.

Practitioners of pastoral ministry, at whatever level, are probably more effective if their theology is as solid and up to date as their pastoral skills. If there were more accountability of pastoral practice to informed theology, it would be a plus.

Because pastors sometimes experience the community in ways that theologians do not and because they are nearer Christian praxis, the more accountability theologians have to pastoral practitioners, the nearer they stay to the praxis of the community. The relationship is mutually critical.

I would recommend, therefore, that dialogic community might be a very fruitful model to entertain in respect to the relationship between Catholic colleges and universities and the bishops of the local churches in which they are located, for each knows and interprets in ways that are important to the other, and each lacks perspectives which the other has. There is room for mutual accountability. It is full of respect. There is room for dialectic and for the fierceness of conviction. Most of all, commitment to being there and staying there together in community is the best long term guarantee for truthfulness to obtain in the praxis of Christian life.

Dialogic Community and Human Experience as Dialogic

Before the onset of historical consciousness, truth tended to mean a correspondence between what is in the mind and what is out there in reality, outside the mind (*adaequatio rei et mentis*). A retrieval of the Greek meaning of truth offers a different perspective. In ancient mythology if one ever left Hades, the underworld, to return to the earth and human habitation, it was necessary to cross the river Lethe. Whatever one experienced in Hades was forgotten when the river was crossed. What was left behind was hidden. The prefix in Greek that negates what comes after it is the letter *a-*. If *lethe* is "hiddenness," then *a-lethe* is "unhiddenness." The Greek word for "truth" is *aletheia*. Whatever is brought out of hiddenness and makes its appearance in the light is what we call, as best as we can describe it from what has appeared, the nature of what we experience. The verb for coming into the light is *phyo*, and the word for nature, that is, for what has appeared, is *physis*. Now nothing is ever fully disclosed once and for all, turned inside out without remainder. The world is relentlessly disclosing itself in *our* interaction with it. The *our* is crucial. The disclosure of the world to *us* is dialogic. Language itself is dialogic, and the disclosing brings what is experienced to language. We are in the world only and always as dialogical beings and we make truth together in response to the world's self-disclosing that never ends.

Another take on our dialogic nature comes from the narrative theological tradition. To be human is to be storied. We are born into a tradition and come to consciousness in traditions. Our language itself presumes a long history out of which we speak. Cultural anthropologists tell us that we live out of a deep story, and that all our particular stories are located within such a deep story. A lot of people would find moral theology and sacraments a strange twosome to put into a single course, but we have done that in the Institute for Ministry, for example, aware that our moral positions find their moral intelligibility in the narrative structure of the communities in which we live, and that symbol and ritual are also grounded in our narrative structure. People "become people only as they acquire a history through the adventures they share as interpreted through the traditions" (Hauerwas 1981, 13).

Our coming to know anything and everything is part of a dialogic process from start to finish, even when alone. Martin Buber has understood about as well as anyone the defining role of intersubjectivity as a characteristic of humanness. Dialogic community is a place in the world where our intersubjectivity is taken seriously. In church terms, magisterium has tended to belong only to the outpourings of the intersubjectivity of the ordained guild of authoritative interpreters, male and celibate. This description does not mean that the quest for truth here does not count, only that it is conditioned by the range and the limitations and particular vested interests. There is a more complete coming out into the light from hiddenness when the intersubjective space is larger and houses dialogic community. The Spirit of God works everywhere.

Dialogic Community and Praxis

Paul Lakeland's description of the church's weak dialogic process is a good place to start:

> The teaching model in the Catholic church is seriously deficient. Whether this is a product of a system that serves to preserve relations of power and oppression, whether it is a matter of a view of the laity that is simply obsolescent, or whether indeed all are held captive in an outmoded church structure is a matter of opinion. But that, for whatever reason, mature and well informed adult members of the church who are not bishops, and many who are, play no active role in the formulation of ethical or theological thought, is a fact beyond dispute and a scandal of growing proportions. (Lakeland 1990, 92)

Lakeland's proposal is that the critical thought of Jürgen Habermas be brought to bear upon ecclesial praxis, especially his critical theory and ideology critique. The exclusion of knowledgeable laypeople in the formulation of official thought means that the vested lay interests are not regularly represented, while institutional vested interests are. The official church interpretation has been able to silence opposition when the opposing voice calls existing power interpretations into question. Had scientists in the six-teenth century, politicians and political scientists in the eighteenth century, and philosophers of interpretive theory and historical consciousness of the twentieth century been officially at the talking table, we may not have des-perately needed a Vatican II for up-dating the pile up of revolutions. A func-tioning dialogic community might head off a Vatican III made necessary by a new pile up of revolutions. Dialogic community is an appropriate structure for making claims and for meeting claims. "This claiming," says Joseph Dunne, "which is implicitly or intuitively present in the communicative action of everyday life, is the ultimate locus of rationality" (1993, 196). Human rationality is by nature dialogic.

Dialogic community is a place where people meet as equals. When our interests clash, and when we are able to confront and challenge, we stand a chance of being able to act together in the world—but not when some inter-ests are allowed and others not. We may not be able to act on all of them, but they have a right to be engaged and submitted to decision.

The bishops in the U.S. church have experimented in dialogic community in the formulation of two pastoral letters on peace and economics and the informed and courageous decision not to issue a letter on women's issues. Two years before the pastoral letter *The Challenge of Peace,* approximately the same percentage of Catholics and Protestants agreed that too much money was being spent on the military machine and especially on the build up of nuclear deterrents. A year after the letter was issued, there was a 20 per-centage-point increase in the number of Catholics who felt the military expenditures were too high, while the percentage remained about the same among Protestant Christians. Catholics were changed not so much by the letter but by their engagement in its production. Catholics all over the coun-try were able to give input to the bishops. There was discussion between bishops and government officials. A new draft was drawn up, with new input, and still another draft and another draft. The bishops made numer-ous suggestions, many of which were incorporated into the final draft. As a result of the dialogic interaction, there was a far broader ownership of the teaching that was finally promulgated. And it was a politically wiser docu-ment—one which at that point in time had the best chance of making a dif-ference, even if it was not everything some people wanted. It is no surprise that Rome was not comfortable with that process and has also tried to downplay the authority of a national conference of bishops.

Human community is always fragile. Dialogic community even more so because it is open to difference. Its takes strength of character to engage in it, and a trust that can only be engendered over time. But we shall deepen our malaise in church and world alike if we do not master it.

Dialogic Community and Spirit

I have used the Pharisees in ancient Judaism, a century and a half before Jesus, as a metaphor for a future church that might welcome a lay hermeneutic into structured official conversation with the clerical hermeneutic, in a form of life called dialogic or dialectic community. Neither I nor anyone else knows how such a thing might take shape. The shape itself would be a product of dialogue and time.

The immediate situation that prompts this recommendation is the education of many women and men in the sacred sciences, in graduate ministry programs in Catholic colleges and universities, and in many other sorts of programs as well—and the need for rapid incorporation of their gifts into ministry and leadership in the Catholic community. The larger background of a Catholic laity increasingly well educated and sophisticated in the secular sciences also calls for a space where their knowledge and experience can impact upon the praxis of the Christian community.

From time to time in these pages I have proposed that the best reason of all for doing this is pneumatological in character. There is no reason why all of the People of God, moved as they are by God's Spirit, all of them, should not have a place in the pattern of interpretive authority—but for the fact that for most of two thousand years they have not had a place there. That, as I read the early history, is a transcendable later fact.

Lay responsibility for Christian life must be "sensitive to the Holy Spirit who gives life to the People of God" (*Apostolicam Actuositatem* §29). "The People of God believes that it is led by the Spirit who fills the earth. Motivated by this faith, it labors to decipher authentic signs of God's presence and purpose in the happenings, needs and desires in which this people has a part along with other people of our age" (*Lumen Gentium* §11). If in some genuine way, daily life in the world is a special concern of the laypeople of God, then deciphering the authentic signs of God's presence there cannot but be a way in which laypeople, through their intersubjective appropriation of their experience in the world, nudge truth out into the openness of Christian praxis in a way that the clerical hermeneutic is not especially fitted to do.

There was uneasiness when Isaac Hecker spoke on behalf of the lay voice, based upon the work of the Spirit. To take with utter seriousness the Spirit's efficacy among the entire people of God, without privilege or prejudice, has consequences on how power functions in the *ecclesia* under the present dispensation. That it should have these consequences seems increasingly indisputable.

The place to find the new and future church of 140 BCE is not in ecclesiological disputation but in the exploration of Christian praxis. We keep trying until we find the ways we need to find. The subtitle for Paul Lakeland's book *Theology and Critical Theory* is *The Discourse of the Church*. We do not deduce a new future from an ecclesiology. We induce a new ecclesiology from a new future, and that is proper church discourse. His words are helpful:

> The church is . . . made up of individuals living out their lives in the world, as the latest generations in a reality that has a history of other individuals doing precisely the same thing. The church, then, is not an idea but a fact. Ecclesiology, as theological reflection on the church, has to be reflection on the fact of the praxis of the believing community, not reflection on this or that idea of the church. The validation of ecclesiology is to be found in the praxis of the believing community. Disembodied theology would find the validation of the praxis of the believing community in the idea of the church. (Lakeland 1993, 104)

Final Words

I feel the need one last time to say that "lay interpretation" and "clerical interpretation" are typological expressions as I use them. There is a very wide spectrum of experience and interpretation in both groups. Not all laypeople think alike, and not all clerics think alike. The main issue is that the social location of the two is so very different. The clerical social location is more closely related, as it should be, to the concerns of *societas*; and the lay social location is more closely related, as it should be, to *communitas*.

There is more New Testament support for Jesus as the founder of *communitas* than of *societas,* and truth to tell, the teachings of Jesus are more like the teachings of the Pharisees than unlike them. It is a belief in the normative value of an evolving oral interpretation that led the Pharisees and Jesus to say, "You have heard it said . . . , but I say to you. . . ."

I think I hear a lay voice saying about the living praxis of Christian life, "You have heard it said . . . , but I say to you. . . ."

Two Kinds of Power

Bernard M. Loomer

Introduction

This lecture is severely restricted in scope. It is concerned almost wholly with delineations and presuppositions of two conceptions of power. Probably neither form of power actually exists in its purity. To this degree the discussion is more concerned with ideal types than with concrete instances of either form of power.

These two conceptions involve a rather simple distinction. But the implications of the distinction are not simple. This short lecture does not adequately suggest the possible intellectual and practical fertility latent within the distinction. More especially, the social applications of the second conception of power are not explored even in a preliminary manner.

Two Conceptions of Power

The problem of power is as ancient as human life. The presence of power is manifest wherever two or more people are gathered together and have any kind of relationship. Its deeper and sometimes darker qualities emerge as soon as the omnipresent factor of inequality makes itself felt.

If power is roughly defined as the ability to make or establish a claim on life, then the range of the presence of power may be broadened to include the notion that power is co-extensive with life itself. To be alive, in any sense,

*The text has been modified to observe inclusive language and is slightly condensed. The original text appears in *Criterion* (Winter 1976), a publication of the University of Chicago Divinity School, with whose permission Dr. Loomer's lecture appears in this appendix.

is to make some claim, large or small. To be alive is to exercise power in some degree.

The principle involved may be extended still further to the level of metaphysical generality. If value is co-terminous with reality, as it is in all metaphysical systems, then the discussion of power becomes correlative with the analysis of being or actuality itself. In this most general perspective, to be actual means to exercise power.

The following discussion of power is not meant to be primarily metaphysical in generality. The focus is on the human involvement with power. But no idea is self-sufficient in its meaning. Ideas, like people, have their lives only in a community of relations. The understanding and justification of any important idea require an explanatory and relational context within which the idea lives, moves, and has its meaning. This explanatory context includes the immediate neighborhood of other ideas closely related to the concept under discussion. This neighborhood expands until it embraces those notions which constitute the most general description of reality of which we are capable during any particular historical epoch.

It is a presupposed and supporting thesis of this lecture that all understanding of power, and particularly the two views to be discussed, are grounded in conceptions both of the human self and, at least implicitly, of the ultimate nature of things. The possible truth of any conception of power is in part a function of the descriptive adequacy of the views of selfhood and the general nature of things that undergird that particular conception of power. If these more general understandings are inadequate, then the correlative concept of power will also be truncated or inadequate in some other way. Conversely, a basic shift in the conception of power should have consequences for a change in our understanding both of the nature of the self and the basic nature of things. As William James was fond of saying, "There can be no difference anywhere that doesn't make a difference elsewhere — no difference in abstract truth that doesn't express itself in a difference in concrete fact and in the conduct consequent upon that fact" (James 1969, 45).

After all these centuries of the practice of power and of theorizing about its nature and function, what is to be said about it that hasn't been said before many times over? I contend that our lives and thought have been dominated by one conception of power. To anticipate the later discussion a bit, this long-standing tradition has on the whole defined power as the ability to produce an effect. This ability to produce an effect has often been understood to be a capacity to bring something into being, to actualize, or to maintain what has been actualized against the threat of nonbeing. In these terms, at the human level power has been defined as the capacity to actualize the potentialities for good and evil of an individual or a group. But the heart of this traditional view is the conception of power as the strength to exert a shaping and determining influence on the other, whatever or who-ever the other might be.

It would be simply wrong-headed to deny that the tradition has identified one aspect of power. But this viewpoint is not only truncated. It is demonic in its destructiveness. Too often it is the basic criterion by which the status or worth of an individual or group is established and measured. The practice of this kind of power is the primary condition whereby the ineradicable inequalities of life are transformed into life-denying injustices.

The problem of power is finally not just a matter of the actualization of possibilities. The issue lies deeper. It is rather a question of the level of indi-vidual and social fulfillment that is to be achieved. It is a matter of the heights or depths that are to be scaled or plumbed. It is the problem of the kinds of possibilities that may emerge, and the kinds of contexts conducive to the actualization of those possibilities. The key to the emergence and actualiza-tion of possibilities, ranging from the most meager to the richest, is the pres-ence of certain kinds of relationships.

To put the point another way, it could be said that our lives and thought have been dominated by one conception of the nature and role of power. This viewpoint is inadequate for the emergence of individuals and societies of the stature required in today's world. The deepest level of the problem of power is ultimately the problem of size or stature.

Therefore, the over-all thesis of this lecture is that the nature and role of relationships determine both the level of human fulfillment that is possible and the conception of power that is to be practiced.[1]

Many people find it difficult and distasteful to accept the role of power in the living of life. Their sensibilities are offended. They accept the fact of power grudgingly in the manner of making a concession to a necessary evil. I suggest that their distaste is directed toward the traditional conception and practice of power. I do not intend to castigate the role of power. On the contrary. But I am concerned to set forth at least an initial version of a more humanizing conception of power.

The rise of modern science and technology makes this effort at recon-ception mandatory. In addition to improving the lot of modern people, science and technology have contributed to the rise and development of problems we have never had to face before in human history. These prob-lems are of such magnitude and complexity that the quality of the future of our planetary existence now confronts us as something more than just a theoretical or imaginative issue first detailed for us by the writers of science fiction.

The emergence of modern science and its operational offspring, technology, together with the evolution of that mode of thought called "historical understanding," have heightened our modern sense of control and have led us to believe that we are responsible for the shape of history. This situation could constitute a rather grim illustration of Niebuhrian irony in that our very creativity may have resulted in the appearance of destructive historical forces too intractable for our capacities to manage or transform.

The development of science has opened Pandora's Box. Once opened it cannot be closed. The interests of scientists and the theoretical and technological consequences of scientific research have been such that, on the whole, science has become a major contributor to and servant of the traditional conception of power. The continued existence of science as a more constructive force in human life presupposes that a sufficient number of the members of our various earthly societies and religions take on a size never before required with such urgency. The traditional conception of power is inadequate to help us in our possible evolution toward this goal.

The problem of power is the problem of the quality of our lives. Those qualities that make for the most complex and intense enrichment of life may not possess the greatest survival value. But they are not engendered by our dominant conception and practice of power.

The alternative conception of power is indigenous to process/relational modes of thought and action. This viewpoint has been elaborated most fully by Charles Hartshorne in his conception of God. In this discussion, as well as in other matters, I stand gratefully on the minds and shoulders of my very illustrious teachers and colleagues.

A sort of non-biblical text and point of departure for this lecture is to be found in one of the definitions in Webster's Dictionary, which characterizes power as an ability either to produce or to undergo an effect. This is intriguing for two reasons. First, except possibly for certain scientific purposes, power, as commonly understood, is seldom defined as the capacity to suffer or undergo an effect. Second, the conception of power is characterized in terms of either/or and not both/and.

PART ONE: UNILATERAL POWER

Having Effects

The first conception defines power as unilateral in character. Unilateral power is the ability to produce intended or desired effects in our relationships to nature or to other people. More specifically, unilateral power is the capacity to influence, guide, adjust, manipulate, shape, control, or transform the human or natural environment in order to advance one's own purposes.

This kind of power is essentially one-directional in its working. Briefly stated, unilateral power is the capacity to influence another, in contrast to being influenced. The influence may be direct or indirect, coercive or persuasive in nature. It operates so as to make the other a function of one's ends, even when one's aims include what is thought to be the good of the other. If the traditional distinction between the masculine and the feminine is accepted for the moment, the masculine being defined as active and the feminine as passive, then unilateral power is quite thoroughly masculine in character.

This is a one-sided, abstract, and non-relational conception of power. Perhaps it would be more accurate to say that this form of power is nonmutual in its relationality. With respect to the one who is influenced, the relationship is internal. That is, one is altered by the relationship. With respect to the one who is exercising this kind of power, the relationship is external. That is, theoretically such a one is unaffected by the relationship. In actual fact, the exertion of influence on something or someone else may involve some degree of reciprocity. Certainly the exercise of power has some valuational effect for good or ill on the one exerting the power. But the main thrust of this kind of power is to produce a desired effect on the other in accordance with one's own purposes. Ideally, its aim is to create the largest effect on the other while being minimally influenced by the other.

It should be emphasized that many instances of influencing and being influenced do not take us beyond a unilateral practice of power. If you push me after I have shoved you, you influence me in the sense that I must take you into account in trying to accomplish my aim, whatever my aim is. You have resisted my unilateral claim with a unilateral claim of your own. You have made your presence and strength felt. I may be forced to use other means to gain my end. I may even be compelled to redefine my purpose with respect to that particular situation. But in any event, I am basically concerned to shape my world as best I can in order to realize my aims. In this endeavor you exist for me as a positive or negative or ambiguous means.

These are unilateral relations, in short, because the focus is on the individuals and their personal goals and not on relationships conceived as mutually internal and creative. (Analogous considerations would obtain if the units were groups rather than individuals.) This characterization applies with double force if the self is understood in non-communal terms (in a manner to be explained shortly).

Self-Identity and Size

In terms of unilateral or linear power, we set forth our claims on life as individuals and groups against other individuals or groups with their opposing and competing claims. We make these claims and create our influence in order to actualize the values of life, including our status and sense of worth. The greater our capacity to influence others, the larger the claim on life we feel we are entitled to establish. Our more predominant power is our justification, our warrant, for our superior status and sense of importance.

Inequality is a categoreal feature of our experience. We differ in energy, ambition, intelligence, emotional intensity, relational sensitivity, imagination, creativity, addiction to evil and other forms of destructiveness, and the capacity to love. We are strikingly unequal in power, in our capacity to influence others for good or ill, by fair means or foul. In this view our size or stature is measured by the strength of our unilateral power. Our sense of self-value is correlative to our place on the scale of inequality. That is, our size is determined by our ability to actualize our purposes in the context of others with their competing aims. Our strength is measured by the amount of competing power we can resist, control, or overcome. It is evaluated by the amount of pressure others must exert before our claims are curtailed or before we must reach some compromise. The degree of our strength or the level of our size is relative to the degree of pressure we can handle or control.

Another's Gain as Our Loss

When power is defined in a unilateral or linear fashion as a capacity to influence another, it follows factually as well as logically that the gain in power by the other is experienced as a loss of one's own power and therefore of one's status and sense of worth. At the human level, at least, and possibly with respect to nature itself, the other is often experienced as a threat or a potential threat to our ability to realize our purposes. The idea of being influenced seems to connote a loss or lack of power relating to our sense of insecurity. To be influenced by someone or something other is therefore experienced as a weakness, just as dependence on another is a reflection of our inadequacy or lack of self-sufficiency. Within this understanding of things, passivity is no virtue. On the contrary, it is a preeminent symbol of a lack of power.

In this competition of power, our relative strength or size can be ascertained by the degree to which the freedom is an attenuation of power. Consequently, in our struggle for greater power it is essential that the other be as restricted in his power as much as possible, or that the freedom of the other be contained within the limits of our control—whether the other be another person or group or the forces of nature. We hesitate or refuse to commit ourselves to those people or realities we cannot control.

Inequality and the Expansive Character of Freedom

As long as one's size and sense of worth are measured by the strength of one's capacity to influence others, as long as power is associated with the sense of initiative and aggressiveness, and passivity is indicative of weakness or a corresponding lack of power, then the natural and inevitable inequalities among individuals and groups become the means whereby the estrangements in life become wider and deeper. The rich become richer, the poor become poorer. The strong become stronger and the weak become weaker and more dependent. From a deeply religious point of view, and in the long run, this manner of handling the inequalities of life results in an increasing impoverishment for both the strong and the weak.

This link between unilateral power and sense of worth in the eyes of others as well as in our own eyes is one of the important factors involved in the problem that has puzzled and preoccupied ethicists for centuries, namely, that we seldom relinquish our power voluntarily. We loosen our grip and make our concessions only when we are forced to do so by some competing group that has acquired sufficient power to bring us to the negotiating table, as the history of the labor-management conflict and the modern women's movement illustrate. Without interference from this competing group our power tends to become inertial and self-perpetuating. As Saul Alinsky used to insist: people in power will listen only when you have enough political "clout" to make them listen. We tend to trample on or remain indifferent to those people whom we feel we can safely ignore.

This conception of power takes on a darker color if the fact of inequality is united with the restive quality of human freedom. More than any other contemporary thinker it was Reinhold Niebuhr who taught us that the human spirit, which is the unity of the self in its freedom, possesses a transcendent outreach. The self in its freedom can transcend in fact or in imagination any given or proposed limitation on what is regarded as possible with respect to its security or fulfillment. On the basis of insights which he attributed to Kierkegaard, Niebuhr grounded both creativity and sin in the self's basic anxiety or insecurity. In this view, no amount of security with respect to the goods of this life can overcome the self's anxiety, and no level of achievement can exhaust its creative passion. Consequently, the human spirit in its unbounded restlessness moves toward the indefinite or the infinite in its effort to subdue its anxiety or to exemplify its freedom.

This expansive quality of freedom is manifested in every aspect of a person's life. This means that any impulse of a person may become insatiable. This is especially the case with respect to the desire for power. In this way our demands or claims tend to become inordinate. This inordinacy reflects the elements of self-interest which infects every activity of a person. The self's claim to rectitude is pretentious, since the self is often the servant and not the master of its impulses. The children of darkness know all this full well since they recognize no law that transcends their self-interest. The children of light, who do not take sufficient cognizance of the expansive character of the self's freedom whereby an individual's or a group's self-interest may take the form of inordinate or unreasonable claims, believe that our impulses are manageable and amenable to rational control.

The expansive character of freedom means that we tend to over-state the legitimacy of our claims and they become presumptuous. We are prone to overplay our strengths and to refuse to recognize the limitations of our virtues. The result is that they become destructive. While freedom can manifest itself in the form of creative reconstruction, it can also inflate our natural inequalities and thereby provide conditions that lead to greater injustices. This quality of freedom may be one reason for the adversary proceedings in our law courts. For Niebuhr it led to his defense of the system of checks and balances in our form of democracy. As he put it, our capacity for justice makes democracy possible; our capacity for injustice makes democracy necessary.

The Non-Communal Self

It is apparent that this conception of power is grounded on a non-communal or non-relational understanding of the self. In this view, the self lives in a society, but the society does not live in the self as part of the self's inner being. The self has relationships with others, but the others are not constitutive of the self. The self is not created out of its relationships. It has its being within itself. It derives its being from itself (and God).

Consistent with this view of the self, society is conceived as a context within which the self operates. The self has relationships with other members of the society because society is the necessary medium for the fulfillment of the self. There is a movement of the self toward others, but these others exist as a means for the realization of the goals of the self. The goals of the self necessarily include some others, whatever or whoever the others may be. Thus these others exist either as helpers, or obstacles, or possible threats to the full use of the self's power to actualize its purposes.

Furthermore, in this outlook the freedom of the self is in no sense an emergent from the relationships the self has with its society. Freedom is a power inherent within the self in its own individual being. In the same sense, the possibilities of the self are latent within the self in its own life. Society provides the occasions whereby these possibilities are actualized.

In this conception of power the aim is to move toward the maximum of self-sufficiency. The self is to become as self-dependent as possible with respect to its motivation, strength, and resourcefulness. Dependency on others, as well as passivity, are symptoms of weakness or insufficiency. Dependency may become a threat to the integrity of the self. The self is to live as much as possible out of the resources and forcefulness of its independence. It should relate to others out of its strength and not out of its dependency. Communities may exist as cooperative societies made up of essentially independent and self-reliant members who share common concerns. In this view, communities essentially derive from the activities of independent individuals. The less fortunate members of a society, the handicapped and disadvantaged, are the beneficiaries of the charitable and compassionate feelings of the more fortunate, although they are to be praised and prized most honestly when they approximate as nearly as they can the self-dependency of the life of unilateral power.

This viewpoint has its religious dimension, of course, because the independence of the self may be qualified ultimately by the sense of its dependence on God the creator and sustainer. This conception of power is at home with Descartes' definition of a substance as that which requires nothing but itself (and God) in order to exist. The strength of the creative and influential power of the self is derived from itself and from God and not from other members of the society.

I suggest that a unilateral conception of power is a reasonably faithful interpretation of the official creed of the Republican Party in this country. I also believe that it is basically congruent with the traditional metaphysics of substantive modes of thought. This viewpoint is integral to that tradition of Christian theology which has been heavily influenced by this traditional metaphysical outlook. I believe that this conception of power in Christian theology has brought confusion to our understanding of the meaning of Christian character and personality, the nature of salvation, the practice of prayer, and the reality of God.

To push this point a bit further, I think there is at least one strand of the New Testament interpretation of Jesus which illustrates this conception of power. In several passages it is emphasized that Jesus derived his power and size from God, and from God alone. This is the same power that the Gospel of John reports Jesus as prayerfully asking God to grant to his disciples. It is not recorded that Jesus ever acknowledged his indebtedness to his companions and friends for his stature or power. As recorded, the relationship was essentially one-sided. The people were the recipients of the influence of his love, his healing graces, and his teachings. In return they gave him his crucifixion. As Scripture has it, "I came to minister, not to be ministered unto."

Power as Abstract

Partly because of the non-relational view of the self that is presupposed, unilateral power tends to be somewhat abstract in its operation. Unilateral power is an expression of specialized concerns. That is, we deal only with the aspects of the human and natural environment which are relevant to our purposes. Our interest in others is highly selective. We are not concerned to deal with the full concrete being of the other—whether the other be a person or nature in its livingness or God.

This abstract character of unilateral power is not merely theoretical in its import. The fact is that those aspects of people or nature or God which we neglect tend to revenge themselves on us. The energy of ignored or repressed dimensions of the other cannot remain bottled up indefinitely. Sooner or later it will express itself overtly. If it be true that God is not mocked, it is also the case that the concrete life of other people cannot be disregarded with impunity. In due season the harvest is reaped, for good or ill. Surely our contemporary revolutions involving blacks, Indians, women, and the under-developed nations furnish us with more than sufficient evidence on this point.

If individuals are emergents from their relationships, as I believe they are, then the practice of unilateral power blocks the full flow of energy that could be productive of the emergence of greater-sized individuals from these relationships. Unilateral power also blocks the quality of the gift that others would give us out of their freedom.

Lord Acton's principle, that power corrupts, involves what I am calling unilateral power. The practice of power, like the possession of great wealth, tends to corrupt its exponents because it helps to create conditions of estrangement. Unless qualified by compensating qualities, the exercise of power tends to alienate the possessor of power. It attenuates our sense of ourselves as equals. It weakens the communal ties that binds us to each other. It deadens our sensitivity to the fact that we are deeply dependent on each other and that we are creative of each other.

The biblical advice to the rich, that they should give their wealth to the poor, will not solve our economic problems. But it could remove one source of alienation. However, the moral of the principle that power corrupts is not that we should divest ourselves of all power or completely eschew the exercise of power. The total absence of all power is non-existence, and the refusal to exercise the power we possess leads to destruction. The moral is rather that another kind of power is required.

The Religious Inadequacy of Unilateral Power

The point concerning the abstractive character of unilateral power can be expanded. The continued practice of this kind of power breeds an insensitivity to the presence of the other—again, whether the other be a person or nature or God. The sense of the presence of the other involves a feeling of the concrete actuality of others, of being truly present to others, of being less concerned to shape and control others, of letting others be themselves in their concrete freedom.

Perhaps this is one reason why most of the great religious figures possessed qualities that we have traditionally associated with the feminine. They were open to the presence of the other. They were open to being shaped and influenced by the other. Certainly much of what it means to be religious is opposed to the traditional conception of the purely masculine.

The practice of linear or unilateral power is antithetical to many of the deeper dimensions of the religious life. The habit of trying to shape and control our human and natural world in accordance with our own purposes makes it difficult to give ourselves in faithful trust to that which we cannot control and which could transform even our sensitivities. Having been nurtured to be insensitive to the presence of the other, in this instance a concretely actual God, God becomes something abstract and remote. So we sometimes have recourse, in Christian circles, to the "living Jesus" in order to overcome our sense of the abstractness, the remoteness, and the emptiness of what in truth is a living, concrete presence. The purely masculine stance in life tends to substitute ethics for religion. Even this approach may become an ethics of ideals which, after all, are themselves abstractions. They are extensions of ourselves. In this fashion we can shape ourselves in accordance with our own ethical projections, and thereby maintain both our independence and the feeling of self-determination that accompanies our sense of controlling power.

It follows, somewhat inevitably, that a life lived in terms of unilateral power reduces the sense of the mystery of life, the mystery of the other in its freedom, including and especially the divine other. Since the mystery of life cannot be reduced, perhaps it would be more accurate to say that this life-style tends to neglect or be oblivious to the dimension of unfathomable mystery that is present in all our experience. The practitioners of unilateral power may appreciate this depth of existence when their efforts to shape life reach their inescapable limits, with all the frustration, anger, or despair that may accompany such disillusion. The freedom of God and the freedom of the human self are not ultimately subject to human control. The strangeness of life and the hiddenness of its meaning cannot be responded to appropriately by a life-style of unilateral power.

Love and Power

Within the Christian theological tradition love is usually contrasted with power. When this is done, it should be noted that it is the unilateral conception of power that is regarded as the antithesis of love. When Jesus is described as being powerless, and as having renounced power as the world understands power, it is unilateral power that is at issue. In terms of this kind of power, Jesus and other religious leaders (or other "christological" figures) are at the bottom of the hierarchy of power.

The issue between love and unilateral power is not finally the issue between persuasion and coercion. The contrast consists in the direction of one's concern, with power focused on the self-interest of an individual or group, and love concerned with what is thought to be for the good of the other. In some interpretations of love, especially Christian love, it would appear that love is as unilateral and non-relational in its way as unilateral power is in its way. The traditional interpretation of divine love as being a concern for itself (which, ideally, we are to emulate), is the ultimate instance of this understanding of love.

It may be that love has been interpreted in this fashion as a compensatory device to counteract the one-sidedness of unilateral power. Love then becomes one side of the coin that carries the face of power on the other side. This involves the principle that the way to offset one extreme is to introduce a contrary extreme. It would appear that this kind of love, like this kind of power, needs an alternative conception.

Knowledge and Power

This is the basic conception of power that has been controlling in Western historical experience. It has been dominant in political and economic philosophies as well as in ethical and theological systems. Its preeminence in military thought and action is obvious. Its efficacious role in the ordering of social life is no less apparent. It is rigorously operative in certain embodiments of leadership as well as in the relations between the sexes. The American experience in the levelling of a continent, and the partial reshaping of the face of nature, constitutes one large national illustration of this kind of force.

Bacon's aphorism, that knowledge is power, refers in the first instance to unilateral power. It symbolizes a modern transformation in the function of knowledge. In the pre-modern world knowledge had practical applications, to be sure. Artisans, farmers, alchemists, doctors, seafarers, astronomers, and a few physical philosophers had knowledge of various natural structures and processes. Their practical grasp of the ways of things enabled people to carry out the necessary affairs of everyday life in a tolerable fashion. But on the whole the most important function of knowledge was to serve as a handmaid to understanding and contemplation. But in the modern Western world knowledge to a large degree has been conscripted in the service of unilateral power and control, especially as this knowledge and control are shaped by the concerns of theoretical and applied science.

Scientific knowledge is specialized knowledge. This kind of competence and understanding and inquiry is essential. But unless it is related to other forms of knowledge and inquiry, and to other dimensions of life in some integral fashion, specialized knowledge becomes a prime servant of unilateral power with its ambiguous and destructive consequences. Our universities have become major training grounds for the practice of this kind of power.

Karl Marx's contention, that the aim of philosophy should not be the quiescent understanding and acceptance of life as it is, but rather the transformation of nature and society, strengthened Bacon's view of the instrumental relationship between knowledge and power.

One of the interesting implications of Marx's interpretation of the role of philosophic study is that the classical conception of philosophy is essentially traditionally feminine in outlook. By contrast, the Marxist conception of philosophy is essentially masculine in emphasis. The classical understanding of the nature of things as they are in their being, to which we must passively conform, has been replaced by a modern dynamic interpretation of things in their creative becoming, with which we should cooperate, to which we can contribute, and over which many of us attempt to exercise greater control.

The enhancement of unilateral power through the development of scientific knowledge, together with the rise of historical modes of understanding our past, has led to a transformation of our role in history. We now conceive ourselves to be at least partially responsible for the course of history. This unprecedented human situation now confronts us with a pivotal question. In the exercise of our unilateral power, by what star, if any, are we to be guided? As we try to direct the evolution of human society and its pluralistic values and styles of living, by what are we to be shaped and transformed? Or are we to think of ourselves as the directors and agents of our own transformation? Do we, the shapers of human history, need to be shaped by something other than our own desires, dreams, or ideals? With the emergence of our modern self-consciousness, are we to be guided by the achieved states of our self-awareness?

Our universal and more complex quandary was pre-figured when the first medical missionary inoculated a member of a so-called primitive society against a disease that had ravaged the village or the tribe. This benevolent act on the part of the scientifically trained missionary had been undertaken only after an intense ideological or religious struggle with the leaders of the tribe. The missionary attributed their resistance and hesitation to ignorance, to their lack of scientific understanding, and to fear of change (and to the fact that this "stronger medicine" probably constituted a threat to the power and prestige of the tribal medicine figure). It wasn't the case, however, that the tribal leaders wanted to see their people killed by the disease. But they believed that the disease was a visitation from one or more of their gods, and that this disease was one aspect of the total order of nature. They realized that the effort to eradicate the disease was not an isolated act. Their type of organismic and non-specialized understanding led them to sense that the whole order of nature and of their world would be changed. Like William James, in the quotation cited earlier, they felt that all acts and ideas had contextual presuppositions and indeterminable consequences.

They sensed that every so-called advance involved some loss—and had its price. They were fearful of displeasing their gods. Their gods brought diseases and death, but also life. This mixture of good and evil, of life and death, was involved in the order of life whose secret harmony resided within the mystery of the gods they worshiped. Their hesitation about accepting the obvious helpfulness of modern medicine and the good intention of the missionary derived from their doubts that the god of the needle was wiser, more truly beneficent, and better able to organize the order of their world than their traditional gods.

Contemporary issues of ecology (both natural and human), eugenics or "human engineering," medical ethics, governmental structures, urban and regional renewal, and international economics, are heightened manifestations of the consequences of the marriage between science and unilateral power. What is at stake is the quality of life in the face of tremendous quantitative dimensions. The issue is not simply survival, but the survival and enhancement of those qualities that effect people of larger size. The realization of this goal calls for a wisdom beyond anything required of us in our history. Is this wisdom to issue from our self-conscious attempts to shape and direct our destiny? Or shall this wisdom emerge out of creative relationships which we cannot control and which, in turn, should give shape to our directive energies?

PART TWO: RELATIONAL POWER

An Alternative Conception of Power

The second and alternative conception of power is relational in character. This is the ability both to produce and to undergo an effect. It is the capacity both to influence others and to be influenced by others. Relational power involves both a giving and a receiving.

The true alternative to the traditional role of the masculine as the active agent who influences is not the traditional conception of the feminine as the passive recipient of the influence. This is so even if it is acknowledged that the undergoing of an effect influences the producer of the effect. The audience does help to create the actor. But the true alternative to a masculine version of power is not a feminine version of power. This would merely be substituting "she" for "he." With respect to developing a more adequate conception of power, the solution does not consist of choosing between the alternatives of producing an effect or of undergoing an effect. This solution would involve the life-style of either/or, which is a strategy of choosing between equally one-sided truncations.

I do not propose or intend to ground the conception of relational power on the possible distinction and relations between typologically masculine and feminine roles. With respect to the problem of power in relation to human sexual differentiation, I am not concerned to defend either traditional or modern versions of the roles of men and women, or to deny or affirm their distinctive natures, regardless of whether these differences are understood to be inherent or culturally derived. I should hope that a relational conception of power would be applicable no matter how the differences and similarities between the sexes are defined. In fact, the problem of sexual differentiation is finally irrelevant to the principle of power conceived in relational imagery, even though sexual differentiation has a bearing on the specific dynamics of relational power involving the two sexes. I mention this context at some length in order to emphasize the point that the dominant conception of power is describable in terms of qualities that have been traditionally associated with the masculine.

Power as Being Influenced

Without opting for a traditionally feminine version of power, it needs to be stressed that the conception of relational power, in contrast to power conceived as unilateral, has as one of its premises the notion that the capacity to absorb an influence is as truly a mark of power as is the strength involved in exerting an influence. We all know that it takes physical and psychic strength to endure an effect. The immovable object may be said to be as powerful in its way as the irresistible force is in its way.[2] Yet in spite of this we have persisted in attributing power only to the producer of an effect.[3] But the principle involved goes beyond this simple observation.

The idea, that the capacity to receive from another or to be influenced by another is truly indicative of power, is not derived from an arbitrary linguistic decision to extend the term "power" to include the receiving of an influence. The idea rests on more elemental considerations that revolve around the notion of size. The concept of size is taken as fundamental and decisive because it is the most basic criterion by which to make decisions and judgments concerning value. To reiterate an earlier point, the problem of power is finally a problem of value. The justification for any conception of power consists ultimately of principles (or decisions or presuppositions) concerning value.

The term "power" is a value term. It is indicative of worth or significance. Under any conception of power, to refer to a person or group as powerless is to reduce that individual or group on the scale of value. Under unilateral power the worth (or size) of an individual is measured by the range of that individual's ability to influence others. The correlative thesis is that the practice of relational power both requires and exemplifies greater size than that called for by the practice of unilateral power. Since the capacity to receive an influence is a necessary component in the actuality of relational power, the principle of size is applicable to the experience of undergoing an effect. It is the factor of value or size that enables us to attribute power to the experience of receiving an influence derived from others.

Our readiness to take account of the feelings and values of another is a way of including the other within our world of meaning and concern. At its best, receiving is not unresponsive passivity; it is an active openness. Our reception of another indicates that we are or may become large enough to make room for another within ourselves. Our openness to be influenced by another, without losing our identity or sense of self-dependence, is not only an acknowledgment and affirmation of the other as an end rather than a means to an end. It is also a measure of our own strength and size, even and especially when this influence of the other helps to effect a creative transformation of ourselves and our world. The strength of our security may well mean that we do not fear the other, that the other is not an overpowering threat to our own sense of worth.

The world of individuals who can be influenced by others without losing their identity or freedom is larger than the world of individuals who fear being influenced. The former can include ranges and depths of complexity and contrast to a degree that is not possible for the latter. The stature of individuals who can let others exist in their own creative freedom is larger than the size of individuals who insist that others must conform to their own purposes and understandings.

The notion that being influenced may indicate a lack of sufficient self-dependence and that it may tend toward a neurotic dependence on others with its attendant lack of freedom, contains a justifiable point of caution and limitation. This is the possible weakness of the strength of openness. But this contention has its counterfoil in the notion that the unqualified urge to influence or to dominate others may indicate a fundamental insecurity and lack of size. This is the possible weakness in the inner dynamics of the strength of controlling or unilateral power.

Under the unilateral conception of power the desire to influence another may well include a concern for what is thought to be for the good of the other. Or, to invert the point, a love for the other may indeed involve the desire to control the other in a direction that is felt to be for the other's good. But, under this conception of power, the good that directs the exercise of influence on the other has the limitations of a preconceived good. It often exemplifies the conscious or unconscious desire to transform the other in one's own image. It is of the nature of efficient cause to reproduce its own kind.

Under the relational conception of power, what is truly for the good of any one or all of the relational partners is not a preconceived good. The true good is not a function of controlling or dominating influence. The true good is an emergent from deeply mutual relationships.

If power always means the exercising of influence and control, and if receiving always means weakness and a lack of power, then a creative and strong love that comprises a mutual giving and receiving is not possible.

The Constitutive Role of Relationships

The foundation of relational power lies in the constitutive role of relationships in the creation of individuals and societies. The individual is a communal individual, a creature of contexts. Individuals live in society and the society quite literally lives in them. They are largely functions of the relationships out of which they are born. They begin their pulsating, momentary existence as individuals from a set of complex impulses derived from the ongoing energy of past events as they objectify themselves into the present. This qualitative energy is carried by the relations or vectoral prehensions which largely constitute their individual lives which are, for the most part, but not completely, a gift from those others who make up the societal context in which they live. Without these others they would not be. Or as the former manager of the New York Yankees, the late Casey Stengel, said after his team had won still another baseball championship, "I could hardly have done it without the players."

This communal or relational conception of the self stand in marked contrast to the non-relational or substantive view of the self. In this latter interpretation, which, like the unilateral conception of power, has dominated the history of Western thought, the self has relations with others but its inner constitution is not composed of these relations. The influences of these others are not parts of the very soul of the non-relational self. These others, through their objectifications of themselves, are not literally present within the self that is being influenced. In the non-relational conception the self has its inner being within itself. Its essential life and the power of its being are derived from itself (and God). It lives in a context to be sure, but this context is not part of the very warp and woof of its being. To put the contrast in another and perhaps more controversial fashion, in the non-relational view the self has experiences, but the self is to be distinguished from its experiences. In the relational view the self doesn't have experiences. The self is its experiences.

The unilateral conception of power has endured in spite of the point, as noted earlier, that we all recognize it requires strength to absorb an effect. Analogously, the non-relational conception of the self has endured in spite of the fact that thinkers in untold numbers have recognized what most of us are aware of, namely, that everyone and everything we encounter becomes part of the fabric of our lives. "Relation" in the internal sense is a way of speaking of the presence of others in our own being. It is the peculiar destiny of process/relational modes of thought to have transformed this common-place but deep-seated observation into a metaphysical first principle.

In the relational viewpoint the individuals begin life as an effect produced by the many others in the world of their immediate past. But they are not simply a function of these relations. They are emergents from their relation-ships; and in the process of their emergence they also create themselves. Their life as living individuals consists of synthesizing into some degree of subjective unity the various relational causes or influences which have initi-ated their process of becoming something definite. The concrete life of indi-viduals is constituted by a process of deciding what each will make out of what each has received. This is emergent selfhood. What individuals make out of what they have received is who they are. This is also every individual's emergent freedom because they are their decisions. Their subjective life is their process of deciding who they are.

When selfhood has been achieved, the qualitative energy of the individual is released from the individual's self-preoccupation. Having been an emer-gent response to a complex set of causes, the individual now joins with others as a member of a complex set of causes to create the future, where the future may include another momentary occasion of the individual's on-going historical life. In order to become an influence in the lives of others, the momentary individual must "die" as an experiencing subject and become an object to be experienced and received by other momentary subjects in their ongoing lives. Anything that can influence another reality can in turn be influenced at a later stage of itself by this other reality. This is the precise meaning of mutuality.[4]

In some such manner we feed upon each other. We are both cause and effect. We constitute each other in part. We are both self-creative and creative of each other, for good or ill, or for good and ill. We are dependent and yet autonomous. We are at once communal and solitary individuals. But the solitariness of individuality is lived out only in the midst of constitutive relationships.

In the relational, contrasted with the non-communal conception of the self, possibilities do not inhere within the individual as latent entities waiting to be realized. In contrast to the traditional view, which held that the acorn contained all the possibilities that were to flower later into the adult oak tree, the relational viewpoint maintains that possibilities are emergents from relationships. A wife is not the occasion whereby a man actualizes husbandly possibilities that reside or subsist wholly within the confines of his enclosed selfhood. The wifely and husbandly possibilities of the respective partners are peculiar to and are created out of that particular marital relationship in which each helps to create the other. The more deeply mutual and creative the relationship, the wider the range of emergent possibilities for those participating in the relationship. The wealth of possibilities is not simply "there" as a present and completed fact, subsisting as a latent condition that is in some sense independent of the world of actual events. Possibilities are created or emerge as possibilities along with the advances that occur within the natural and historical environments.

Analogous considerations apply to the notion of freedom. The self-creativity of individuals is an expression of the strength of their freedom. Or, more accurately, freedom is a pervasive quality of self-creativity. Freedom, like self-creativity, is an emergent from relationships. To this degree, freedom is not a quality that is derived solely from self as though one were an independent, self-contained, self-derived, and self-sustained individual. The degree and range of freedom is not wholly a function of an individual's own resources. On the one hand freedom is derived from the unfathomable mystery of the emergence of self-creativity. On the other hand this freedom is in part an enabling gift from an individual's society, a gift that is conveyed through his constitutive relationships. Individuals are helped or hindered in achieving greater freedom by the enhancing or crippling relations in which they live. The deeper their involvement in creative and transformative relations, the greater the possibility for the enlargement and empowering of their freedom.

Freedom has several dimensions, and all of them are emergents from the functioning of the constitutive relations in which an individual has being. Certainly one of the strongest components is that of transcendence, which is the capacity of an individual in fact or in imagination to transcend both society and self. There are intimate connections between transcendence and the expansive character of freedom of an individual. Even though individuals' capacity to transcend their society is partly a gift from that very society, they often fail to acknowledge this indebtedness, and they act as if they had somehow outgrown their dependence on that society. The tension between society and the freedom of an individual is abiding and irresolvable, to be sure. But in their pride individuals may come to feel that their freedom is wholly self-derived and a function of their own resources. They can imagine that they are essentially independent of all constitutive relationships. In this mood they tend to use their transcendent freedom to enhance their sense of self-importance and to strengthen their egotistic impulses. Almost inevitably they move in the direction of a more consummate practice of unilateral power. In this fashion they become more fully estranged from all the "others" in their life—which adds to the destructive consequences of our natural inequalities.

In terms of the relational or communal conception of the self, our constitutive relationships enable us to be free.[5] In this sense we are related in order to be free, that is to actualize our highest possibilities relative to ourselves as unique individuals. But freedom does not stand alone as the one absolute or primordial value. Just as fundamentally, we are free in order to be more fully related. We are most free in all the dimensions of our freedom when we enter more deeply into those relationships which are creative of ourselves as people of larger size. The inclusive term is stature. Freedom and relationality are its essential components.

Power as the Capacity to Sustain a Relationship

From this perspective, power is neither the capacity to produce nor to undergo an effect. Power is the capacity to sustain a mutually internal relationship. (Because of their inertial qualities, these relationships may also become the enemies of freedom.) This is a relationship of mutually influencing and being influenced, of mutually giving and receiving, of mutually making claims and permitting and enabling others to make their claims. This is a relation of mutuality which embraces all the dimensions and kinds of inequality that the human spirit is heir to. The principle of equality most profoundly means that we are all equally dependent on the constitutive relationships that create us, however relatively unequal we are in our various strengths, including our ability to exemplify the fullness and concreteness of this kind of power.

It is important to stress the point that in relational power the influencing and the being influenced occur within and are functions of the mutuality of internal relatedness. This kind of mutuality is to be contrasted with the mutuality of external relatedness that is involved in various instances of unilateral power, such as the mutual good of compromise and accommodation, or the mutuality of external cooperation and divisions of labor, or the mutuality of bargaining and a quid pro quo. In the context of relational power, giving and receiving, influencing and being influenced, producing an effect and undergoing an effect, are not only mutually dependent and interwoven. At times they seem to be almost indistinguishable and their roles appear to be interchangeable. Often the greatest influence that one can exercise on another consists in being influenced by the other, in enabling the other to make the largest impact on one's self.

The principles of relational power mean that influencing and being influenced are so relationally intertwined that the effort to isolate them as independent factors would constitute an illustration of either one or both of Whitehead's famous two fallacies: that of simple location or that of misplaced concreteness.

If someone is to talk, someone else must listen. If one is to hear, someone else must speak. The actor in part creates the audience. The audience in its turn partly creates the actor. The drama is an emergent from the interaction between the actor and the audience. In this kind of mutuality of power it is as blessed to receive as it is to give. In our kind of culture, where power is identified so strongly with the exercise of influence upon another, it is often more difficult to receive in such a manner as to enhance and further the relationship. One of the most difficult of all social graces to achieve is the ability to receive in such a way that givers feels honored in the giving and in having the gift received, or in such a way that in giving givers feel that they have received.[6]

The art of receiving creatively the influence or gift of another is difficult to master because our sense of worth and power is identified so deeply with the direct act of creating, or giving, or exercising an influence on others. We have been nurtured to believe that dependence is indicative of a lack of worth. But in relational power the focus is not on any particular member of the relationship or on one side of the relationship. The focus is on the relationship to which all contribute and from which all members are fed. The worth of the one who gives is partly dependent on the worth of the one who receives or the worth of the giving is dependent on the worth that must attach to the receiving. Revelation, to be effective, must be received and made operative in the lives of those who are to be disciples. In fact the cries and prayers of those who need and want to be redeemed in part call forth and create the messiah. The messiah's capacity to influence people is in part derived from being shaped by their need, although the response to their need may take a form which is other than what they want and think they need. The messiah who comes is usually not the one they had hoped for or expected.

In conceiving of relational power as the capacity to sustain a mutually internal relationship, the stress is on the primacy of relationships. These relations include, of course, those entities which are related. In the practice of this kind of power one must trust the relationship. The good is an emergent from the relationship. Except in a negative sense this process of creative emergence lies beyond our ability to direct or command. The attempt to guide or control this process results only in obstructing the emergence or in restricting the worth of the relationship to the level of value which already exists. Those who are fearful of committing themselves to something they cannot control enhance the strength of the forces involved in the practice of unilateral power.

Those who conceptualize within the imagery of non-relational or substantive modes of thought, and/or who find it difficult to transcend the traditional conception of power as unilateral, may also be uneasy with the conception of relational power. They may think that the practice of relational power is too nondirective or untrustworthy. They may feel that this kind of power is, for example, ethically sound only if one's concerns in the relationship are directed toward the other and what is for the other's good. But this possible response misses the whole point concerning the primacy and creativity of the relationship and the process of emergent good.

Being Present to Another

The primacy of relationships and the emergence of possibilities within relationships can be seen in looking at the phenomenon of being present to another, or being a presence to and for another. Being present to another, when this is understood non-relationally as though we were dealing with independent individuals, can mean either that one discloses oneself to another in a deeply personal way, or that one is so fully receptive to the other that the other feels known and understood. When interpreted relationally the phenomenon takes on a different coloration.

The initiating disclosure of one's self to another enables and frees the other to receive the revealing of one's self. This reception in turn enables the revealers to be freer in their self-disclosure. The active openness of the receptive mood of one who listens calls forth the disclosure of the one who would speak. The speaking and the listening are creative of each other in the relationship. Also, through listening the listener discloses self to the one who speaks. In being heard, the one who speaks knows the one who hears. The two disclosures may not be equal in depth and range in that specific instance. Yet there is a mutuality of self-revelation. The knowing and the being known are mutually creative. Presence means that each knows and is known in that relationship. Presence means that both knowing and being known are functions of the creativity of both the speaking and the listening. I would understand this to be the relational version of Buber's I-Thou.[7]

Relational Power as Concrete

Relational power, in contrast to the abstractness of unilateral power, is concerned with the concrete life of the other, whether the other be an individual or a group. One of the important consequences of the major intellectual discoveries in the modern world, from Copernicus to Einstein, is our increased understanding of the detailed empirical processes which shape our thinking, behavior, and being. We are more aware of conditioning contexts, histories, psychological dynamics and relationships, which largely determine what we most concretely are.

The exercise of power must operate with an awareness of these elements. To do otherwise is to relate to each other inadequately in terms of abstract classes, or stereotypes, or groups looked at in a cross-sectional manner without reference to their peculiar histories. In this fashion we fail to deal with the inexhaustible and variegated richness, the confusing complexity, and the omnipresent and intertwined ambiguities present in the concreteness of individual and group life. Transparent clarity, cleanness, and the absence of ambiguity are found only in the abstractions of thought. Power, to be creative and not destructive, must be inextricably related to the ambiguous, contradictory, and baffling character of concrete existence. It must live with regenerative awe and wonder in the midst of the strange turnings that transform victory into defeat and defeat into victory; the humbling ironies, and the intractable conditions within both people and nature that shatter the best laid plans and destroy the bridges of our hopes. It must be rooted in the relative chaos and mess in which we live out our days. In this respect, the concept of relational power is nothing more nor less than a recognition of what has in fact happened in our modern world. It is also a recognition of what is needed in order to respond creatively to what has happened.

As a capacity to sustain complex and mutually internal relationships that encompass more of the concrete lives of individuals and groups, the practice of relational power must confront the whole plenum of psychological and spiritual conditions that characterize the human spirit. This plenum includes the better and the worse, the good and the bad, and their confounding mixture. It ranges from the balanced reasonableness of the mature to the excesses and deficiencies of the immature, and from the dependable goodness of sensitive souls to the demonic irrationalities of the deprived, the frustrated, and the depraved. Doubts, anxieties, inertias, resistances, and multidimensional forms of pride live in all of us.

In and beyond all these and countless other problematic states of the human spirit, along with their opposites, there are the many kinds and degrees of inequality that are present in all relationships. The fact of inequality is not just one consideration among many equally significant facts. It is a bed-rock condition. The failure to recognize its decisive status has confounded many social and political theories and programs. It has been a major basis for the traditional conception of order. It is now one of the strong motivating forces which impels us toward the reconstruction of modern societies. It is an ambiguous factor in all lives. It is at once a basis for compassion and a reason to despair. It is at once a precondition of leadership and a major element in the drift toward social mediocrity. It is the presupposition of messiahship. The inequalities that are crippling and dehumanizing may be reducible in scope and influence, but the general condition of inequality seems not only ineradicable but necessary. It is a necessary component in the division of labor and in the variety of creative capacities. In this respect it is part of the meaning of human finitude.

In the practice of unilateral power many of these natural and cultivated inequalities inevitably result in obstructive and impoverishing structures of injustice. It is the hope that in the practice of relational power we may learn how to interrelate these inequalities so they may become mutually enhancing.

It is possible to have a reasonably well-ordered society (in both large and small sense of that term) as long as we deal abstractly with individuals and groups. The practice of unilateral power can create this kind of society. It has done so throughout history. The price for this ordered life is the neglect or repression of many important dimensions of the human spirit. In moving from this well-ordered but repressive society to forms of societal life which enable these dimensions of the human spirit to emerge in more concrete relationships, we must be prepared to live within conditions which are more complex, confused, and unsettling. The surfacing of repressed forces creates problems which did not exist previously. Roles are transformed. Habitual patterns of behavior and response are no longer appropriate or acceptable. Crises in the areas of personal, professional, and social identity appear. The established order in all areas of life is weakened. Traditional values, all too often grounded on structures of abstract relationships, are questioned. The total situation becomes disruptive and potentially disintegrative. It borders on chaos. The social consequences of the liberation of women and the changed consciousness of minority peoples and under-developed countries (among other factors) have brought us to just such a state of affairs.

This unstable condition holds great promise for the future. A wise man has said that "the great ages are the unstable ages." But not all unstable ages have been great milestones in the odyssey of the human spirit. The price for creative advance is enormous. The challenge may be beyond our strength. There is ground for hope and reason to despair.

It is clear that the continued practice of unilateral power is totally inadequate to the social task that confronts us. But the practice of relational power is an incredibly difficult art to master. This type of power requires the most disciplined kind of mutual encouragement and criticism. The creative openness of this type of relationship involves possibilities of the greatest advance and the greatest risk. It calls for the utmost of energy, patience, endurance, and strength. It can lead to the deepest joys and to the abyss of the agony of suffering. In it will be found both heaven and hell and the bittersweet amalgam of their co-presence.

Relational Power as Size

The ultimate aim of relational power is the creation and enhancement of those relationships in which all participating members are transformed into individuals and groups of greater stature. In this kind of relationship the individuals (or groups) are neither swallowed up in the relationship nor are they absorbed into each other. Yet the relationship, which includes its members, exists only in terms of its members.

The aim of relational power is not to control the other either directly or indirectly by trying to guide and control the relationship. The greatest possible good cannot emerge under conditions of control. The aim is to provide those conditions of giving and receiving of influences such that there is the enlargement of the freedom of all the members to both give and receive. This enlarged freedom is the precondition for the emergence of the greatest possible good which is neither preconceived nor controllable. The commitment within relational power is not to each other but to the relationship which is creative of both. It is a commitment to the relational "us" and not to one or the other.

The elements of the structure of this highly involuted relationship can be stated very abstractly, although it must be emphasized that these elements operate relationally and dynamically. On the one hand, in exercising an influence within the relationship, individuals make their claims and express their concerns in such a style as to enable others to make their largest contribution to the relationship. With this contribution the experiences of all the participants are intensified and broadened. In making one's claims and in exercising one's influence on the other in this fashion, the freedom of the other is recognized and respected. On the other hand, one is to receive the presence and influence of the other within the relationship in such a manner that the other is enabled to enter more freely and fully into the relationship. In being received in this fashion the one who influences may be more open to absorb the influences of others.

The structure of relational power, again defined ideally, is such that the claims of justice (from the perspective of unilateral power) are both included and transcended. From the side of the claimant, some portion of justice is obtained in the very making of the claim or in exercising an influence. But in making the claim relationally, that is by enabling the recipient to respond most freely and creatively, justice is transcended. In this kind of relationship transcendence means that all the parties involved both give and receive more than the requirements of justice demand or permit.

This is a description of the nature of the process of relational power viewed structurally and abstractly. It is also a description of relational power as operating ideally and without reference to the baffling and confounding realities which constitute our empirical existence. When looked at concretely and dynamically, the actual instances of relational power fall far short of this ideal structure. They are incredibly far more complex, ambiguous, and involuted. They involve all the contrasting qualities that are to be found in the endless variety of concrete individuals and social groups. They include the full plenum of conditions the human spirit is heir to. These qualities and conditions, which constitute the materials and contexts with which and in which the exemplifications of relational power must fulfill their ambiguous destinies, run the gamut from triumphant breakthroughs to crippling regressions, from life-restoring laughter to life-denying despair, from the beauty of the gracious heart to the debasing cruelty of the small mind and smaller soul.

Within this larger spectrum of the general human situation there appear to be at least two elemental factors with which the practice of relational power must wrestle in its struggle to create individuals and groups of larger size. These factors are at once the materials for creative advance and the grounds of frustration and persistent smallness of size.

The first is the fact of contrast, which often appears as conflict although not necessarily in the form of overt violence. Conflict more usually exhibits itself under the many guises of competition which infects all the dimensions of our social life. But contrast most generically refers to the inexhaustible differences of otherness. Contrast is the precondition of complexity without which the creation of a larger integrity is not possible. Without adequate contrast the intensity of experience may become too narrowly focused, and may lead to the crippling sickness of moralism or to the more virulent disease of fanaticism.

The second is the factor of estrangement which is the brokenness of life's essential relationships. The umbrella of estrangement encompasses the emptiness of the uncommitted, the heartless shrug of the indifferent and the insensitivity of the unmoved, the inertial smallness of the complacent, the errancy of the unfaithful, the demonry of the prideful and the absolutely certain, and the destructiveness of the hateful. The attempt to overcome estrangement is the "open sesame" to the experience of depth, without which the adventure of greater size loses its foundation of elemental simplicity.

Undergirding these two factors of contrast and estrangement, and remorselessly immanent within all movements toward greater size, are at least four conditions which appear to be unalterable or categoreal in nature. The degree of decisiveness with which our grasp of these conditions permeates our understanding, and the manner in which we deal with them, define and shape the limits of our creative advance.

There are first, and most obviously, the inequalities of energy, vision, sensitivity, maturity, and the capacity and the love to sustain relationships. Inequality of some sort or in some degree is present in every relational situation. As noted previously, in the practice of unilateral power these natural and inevitable inequalities lead to destructive injustices. The strong become stronger, and the weak become weaker. This is a form of mutual impoverishment. In the practice of relational power they create an imbalance that can be mutually enriching. Both the strong and the weak may become not only stronger but larger in stature.

There is, secondly, the puzzling fact of ambiguity, the interpenetrating mixture of virtues and vices. Virtues carried beyond their inevitable limits become demonic vices. The individual's weaknesses are the other side of the strengths. Like the biblical parable of the wheat and tares they grow together. They coexist within an individual. The evil cannot be cut out of a person's spirit without weakening the strength of the goodness. The evil can be lessened only by the transformation of the strength of that person's goodness. The passion that causes individuals to transcend the limits of their virtues, and thereby convert them into vices, is the same strength that gives rise to the virtues originally. The failure to recognize the depth of ambiguity in all matters of the spirit leads us to live moralistically, without compassion, and without adequate understanding of others or, more pitiably, of ourselves.

There is, thirdly, the creative role of evil or brokenness in opening us to greater depths of experience. In the absence of problems or failures we tend to live our lives inertially. Dewey has suggested that we think only when our systems of thought and value break down, when we encounter dimensions of life we cannot handle. We often take the value and services of others for granted. Only when they have departed, leaving a vacant space against the sky, when it is too late to express our gratitude, do we come to acknowledge our indebtedness. An infidelity in marriage can lead to a deeper level of maturity in the relationship than perhaps was possible before. In the biblical parable of the prodigal son the deeply resentful older brother is given the possibility of a growth in stature in the face of the father's joyous welcoming of the repentant younger brother. The naughtiness of young children can call out depths within the parents which were not exemplified previously. The presence of evil does not lead inevitably to a greater good. Obviously. But the actualization of greater good seems to be grounded on brokenness in some degree.

Fourthly, as Reinhold Niebuhr has reminded us, through all the ironies and strange turnings of the human spirit there persists the ineradicable dialectical condition wherein every advance makes possible greater destructiveness, and every gain brings new opportunities and large temptations.

All of these categoreal conditions are dimensions of a web of interrelatedness that constitutes the seamless context within which all human life is lived.

Relational power is the capacity to sustain an internal relationship. The sustaining does not include management, control, or domination. Rather, it involves the persistent effort to create and maintain the relationship as internal. This effort is carried out within the context of the factors and conditions previously described, and in the face of all the dynamic forces which operate to weaken or break the internality and transform it into the predominantly external type of relationship that is characteristic of the practice of unilateral power.

The discipline demanded by the effort to sustain internal relationships is at least difficult. Its cost is large and sometimes enormous. The price to be exacted involves the expenditure of great energy in the form of active patience, physical stamina, emotional and psychic strength, and a resilient trust and faith. Above all, the cost is measured in the coin of suffering. The capacity to endure a great suffering for the sake of a large purpose is one of the decisive marks of maturity. In the Christian tradition the adequate symbol of the cost of sustaining an internal relation is the cross.

With the conception of power as relational, size is fundamentally determined by the range and intensity of internal relationships one can help create and sustain. The largest size is exemplified in those relationships whose range exhibits the greatest compatible contrasts, contrasts which border on chaos (Whitehead). The achievement of the apex of size involves sustaining a process of transforming incompatible contrasts or contradictions into compatible contrasts, and of bearing those contrasts within the integrity of one's individuality.

There are other less inclusive criteria which are applicable to the determination of size. Size may be ascertained by the degree of the concreteness of the other, including the other's freedom, that one can absorb, while attempting to maintain the relationship as mutually creative and transformative. This is especially the case when the freedom of the other moves someone in the direction of indifference, refusal, or estrangement. Size may be measured by the extent to which one has enabled the other to be as large as the other might become, and thereby make the fullest contribution to one's own life as well as to the lives of others. Size can also be determined by the freedom with which one's love of the other transcends the "in spite of" character of the traditional conception of love and moves toward an unqualified "because of."

In our religious tradition the "suffering servant" is an important symbol with respect to our topic of power. It may be used to refer to an individual or a people. The suffering servant has sometimes been interpreted as one who receives an influence without making any claim on the servant's own behalf, as one who passively suffers the effect of self-centered or destructive unilateral influence. In this interpretation the suffering servant is one who exemplifies the purely feminine conception of passive power in contrast to the wholly masculine version of aggressive power. This is a contrast between two unilateral actions.

But from the point of view taken in this lecture, this interpretation is inadequate. The suffering servant is rather one who can sustain a relationship involving great contrast, in this case the incompatibility between love and hate. In absorbing the hate or indifference derived from the other, while attempting to sustain the relationship by responding with love for the other, the extreme of contrasts is exemplified. This contrast is an incompatibility, in fact an emotional contradiction within the integrity of one's own being, and in having the strength to sustain the relationship, the incompatibility has been transformed into a compatible contrast.

This is size indeed. This consideration highlights the principle that the life of relational power requires a greater strength and size than the life of unilateral power. Suffering servants, in returning love for hate, and in attempting to sustain relationships as internal and creative, must be psychically larger and stronger than those who unilaterally hate. Without this greater strength and larger size suffering servants could not sustain such relationships. They would crack psychologically or would break the relationship and revert to the practice of unilateral power.

It follows from all this that a christological figure such as Jesus, who is to be found at the bottom of the hierarchy of unilateral power, stands at the apex of life conceived in terms of relational power. But a messiah of size cannot be created out of the weakness of a Milquetoast.

In considering the topic of size it needs to be noted, again, that inequality is present as an inescapable condition. Because of this inequality there is an unfairness to life. This quality appears to have something like a categoreal status in our experience. Our only choice is to choose between two forms of unfairness. In the life of unilateral power the unfairness means that the stronger are able to control and dominate the weaker and thereby claim their disproportionate share of the world's goods and values. In the life of relational power, the unfairness means that those of larger size must undergo greater suffering and bear a greater burden in sustaining those relationships which hopefully may heal the brokenness of the seamless web of interdependence in which we all live. "To whom much is given, much is expected."

It has been maintained that the contemporary world, which has been so decisively shaped by modern science, requires the presence of groups of people of adequate size. It is the contention of this lecture that the practice of unilateral power cannot create people of a size sufficient to cope with the problems we face. If the quality of terrestrial life is to attain a level which makes it worth the effort of living it, this achievement is possible only in terms of the practice of relational power.

But our situation is deeply problematic. The notion that the life of relational power calls for a stature which transcends the life of unilateral power does not mean, however, that relational power has greater survival capability than unilateral power. The higher forms of life may be less able to survive (as higher forms) than less complex forms of energy. The more sensitive the organism, the more it may need to be protected from some of the rougher and cruder aspects of existence. In terms of permanence, the stone far outdistances a human being. As Whitehead has observed, "The art of persistence is to be dead."

There is another dimension to our problematic situation. It is an issue that has troubled theologians and philosophers of history for centuries. Stated in terms appropriate to this lecture: can the life of relational power be sustained with sufficient strength in the face of perhaps overwhelming unilateral power? Those who live relationally are larger in stature and psychically stronger than those who live unilaterally; nonetheless, can relational power become so efficacious historically that it may at least hold its own if it cannot overcome the destructive forces of unilateral power? The lives of those who live relationally may not be sufficiently efficacious or persuasive with respect to those who live unilaterally. In fact the opposite may and does occur. The behavior of the larger may create a fury in the souls of the smaller and weaker that can eventuate in greater impoverishment and destructiveness. This principle is exemplified in the anti-semitism which is an attitude of the weaker against the stronger.

Who shall inherit the earth? The Bible says it will be the meek. But surely this prophecy is not warranted if the meek are understood to be spineless doormats who live in terms of a unilateral feminine conception of power. If the meek are understood to be living embodiments of relational power, if they are in fact members of a suffering servant people, then the proposition is surely interesting. It may even become true.

The earth belongs, or ought to belong, to those who make the largest claims on life. The largest claims are not made nor are they makeable in the form of unilateral power. They are made by those who attempt to embody most fully the life of relational power, for they are claims made not only for themselves but on behalf of all peoples.

The metaphysical depth and pervasiveness of the primary conditions which constitute the problematic context for the practice of relational power point to a universe struggling toward creative advance. This problematic context confronts us whether we opt for unilateral or relational power. The god of unilateral power is not a tribal deity. On the contrary. It is a universal god. But it is a demonic god, an idol which is not large enough to merit our faith and devotion. The issue appears to be in doubt. But the faith which can live with that doubt is a steadfast and hopeful trust in both the goodness and the power of a relational god of adequate size.

Notes

1. It might be contended that the conception of power determines the nature and role of relationships. However, the textual way of expressing the matter is more in keeping with the overall intent of the lecture that conceptions of power are grounded in conceptions of the self and metaphysical reality. All of these conceptions are, in turn, expressions of value presuppositions.

2. This particular illustration involves complex and ambiguous factors. There is no necessary contradiction involved in recognizing that sometimes we may perform better when playing against players who arc better than we are, especially if we tend to perform somewhat indifferently when competing against normally inferior players. Different people respond differently to the various degrees of competitive pressure.

3. There is the New England short story ("The Great Stone Face") about the influence of a mountain in the shaping of a human face. Beginning when he was a small boy and persisting throughout his life, a certain man developed the habit of spending many hours looking at a stone face which the forces of nature had etched on the side of a mountain. Gradually over the years the man's face took on the character of the great stone face.

4. The methodology of historical understanding is thoroughly contextual in character. Every historical figure (or institution or movement) must be seen and understood contextually, because that individual lived his life in that particular context, and in no other. All historical life is particular in its concrete existence. It is possible to interpret this methodology and its achievements in terms of a non-relational conception of self and society. In this conception a context functions so as to shape and limit an individual's possibilities which are relevant to that particular context. But a relational view of the self and society would seem to furnish a more adequate basis for grasping the significance of the work of historians. In a limited way that particular world shapes that individual. The individual lives in a context of others, but that context lives and has its being only within the individuals, and in the relations between individuals, who partly constitute the totality of that context. The context becomes part of the inner life of the individuals who live in that world.

5. In other words, the mutuality is not simultaneous. The presence of mutuality in the strictest sense requires a crisscrossing interrelationship of cause and effect in

the successive stages in the ongoing lives of two or more individuals. For ordinary practical purposes this strict definition of mutuality need not be insisted on.

6. This view of internal relations includes of course the presence of external relations. The communal individual is also solitary. All partners, especially marriage partners, as Gibran insisted, need "spaces in their togetherness."

7. It is also true that it is often difficult to influence or to give to another in such a way that the other is not demeaned but is in fact enhanced by this aspect of the relationship. The difficulty is due to considerations analogous to those involved in the development of the art of gracious reception.

BIBLIOGRAPHY

Arendt, Hannah. 1958. *The Human Condition.* Chicago: University of Chicago Press.

Bakhtin, M. M. 1981. *The Dialogic Imagination.* Austin, TX: University of Texas Press.

Bausch, William J. 1989. *Pilgrim Church.* Mystic, CT: Twenty-Third Publications.

Becker, Ernest. 1971. *The Birth and Death of Meaning.* New York: Free Press.

———. 1973. *The Denial of Death.* New York: Freepress.

Berger, Peter. 1979. *The Heretical Imperative.* Garden City, NY: Doubleday.

Bernstein, Richard. 1983. *Beyond Objectivism and Relativism.* Philadelphia: University of Pennsylvania.

Bianchi, Eugene C., and Rosemary Radford Reuther. 1992. *A Democratic Catholic Church: The Reconstruction of Roman Catholicism.* New York: Crossroad.

Brown, Raymond E. 1970. *Priest and Bishop: Biblical Reflections.* Paramus, NJ: Paulist.

Brueggemann, Walter. 1987. *Hope within History.* Atlanta: John Knox.

Bruns, Gerald L. 1992. *Hermeneutics Ancient and Modern.* New Haven: Yale University Press.

Burkart, Gary. 1992. *The Parish Life Coordinator.* Kansas City: Sheed & Ward.

Caputo, John D. 1987. *Radical Hermeneutics.* Bloomington: University of Indiana Press.

Chopp, Rebecca, and Mark Lewis Taylor, eds. 1994. *Reconstructing Christian Theology.* Minneapolis: Fortress.

Clark, Eric. 1988. *The Want Makers: Inside the World of Advertising.* New York: Viking.

Crick, Bernard. 1972. *In Defence of Politics.* Chicago: University of Chicago Press.

D'Antonio, William; James Davidson; Dean Hoge; and Ruth Wallace. 1989. *American Catholic Laity in a Changing World.* Kansas City: Sheed & Ward.

Dean, William. 1986. *American Religious Empiricism.* Albany: SUNY Press.

———. 1987. "Hebrew Law and Postmodern Historicism," unpublished manuscript, p. 1.

Donceel, Joseph. 1985. "Catholic Politicians and Abortion," *America*, Feb. 2.

Douglas, Mary. 1982. *Natural Symbols*. New York: Pantheon.

———, and Steven Tipton, eds. 1982. *Religion in America*. Boston: Beacon.

Drucker, Peter F. 1994. "The Age of Social Transformation," in *The Atlantic Monthly* (November).

Dunne, Joseph. 1993. *Back to Rough Ground*. Notre Dame, IN: University of Notre Dame Press.

Edgerton, W. Dow. 1992. *The Passion of Interpretation*. Louisville: Westminster/ John Knox.

Eliot, T. S. 1971. *The Four Quartets*. New York: Harcourt Brace.

Everett, William Johnson. 1988. *God's Federal Republic: Reconstructing Our Governing Symbol*. New York: Paulist.

Faivre, Alexandre. 1990. *The Emergence of the Laity in the Early Church*. New York: Paulist.

Fiorenza, Elisabeth Schüssler. 1993. *Discipleship of Equals: A Critical Feminist Ekklesia-logy of Liberation*. New York: Crossroad.

———. 1983. *In Memory of Her*. New York: Crossroad.

Fleischer, Barbara. 1993. *Ministers of the Future: A Study of Graduate Ministry Students in Catholic Colleges and Universities*. New Orleans: Loyola Institute for Ministry.

Fogarty, Gerald P. 1986. "Dissent at Catholic University: The Case of Henry Poels." *America* (October 11).

Foucault, Michel. 1980. *Power/Knowledge*. New York: Pantheon.

French, Marilyn. 1986. *Beyond Power*. New York: Ballantine.

Gadamer, Hans-Georg. 1975. *Truth and Method*. New York: Crossroad.

Gallup, George. 1993. "Empowering the Laity." In *Religion in America 1992-1993*, ed. Robert Bezilla. Princeton: Princeton Religion Research Center.

Geertz, Clifford. 1973. *The Interpretation of Cultures*. New York: Basic Books.

Gelpi, Donald L. 1994. *The Turn to Experience*. New York: Paulist.

Gerhart, Mary, and Allan Russell. 1984. *The Metaphoric Process*. Fort Worth: Texas Christian University Press.

Gilmour, Peter. 1986. *The Emerging Pastor*. Kansas City: Sheed & Ward.

Glen, Jennifer. 1987. "Rites of Healing: A Reflection in Pastoral Theology." In *Alternative Futures for Worship: Anointing of the Sick,* vol. 7, ed. Peter Fink. Collegeville, MN: Liturgical Press.

Grant, Robert, with David Tracy. 1984. *A Short History of the Interpretation of the Bible*. Philadelphia: Fortress. Esp. the final 3 chapters by Tracy.

Habermas, Jürgen. 1973. *Legitimation Crisis*. Boston: Beacon.

Hales, E. E. Y. 1961. *The Emperor and Pius VII*. Garden City, NY: Doubleday.

Hanson, Paul. 1986. "The Servant Dimension of Pastoral Ministry in Biblical Perspective." In *The Pastor as Servant,* ed. Earl E. Shelp and Ronald H. Sunderland. New York: Pilgrim Press.

Hauerwas, Stanley. 1981. *A Community of Character.* Notre Dame, IN: University of Notre Dame Press.

Hebblethwaite, Peter. 1993. *Paul VI: The First Modern Pope.* New York: Paulist.

Heidegger, Martin. 1977. *Basic Writings,* ed. David Farrell Krell. New York: Harper Collins.

——. 1962. *Being and Time.* New York: Harper & Row.

Heschel, Abraham J. 1962. *The Prophets,* vol. 1. Garden City, NY: Doubleday.

Hillers, Delbert. 1969. *Covenant: History of a Biblical Idea.* Baltimore: Johns Hopkins University.

Holland, Joe, and Peter Henriot. 1984. *Social Analysis: Linking Faith and Social Justice.* Maryknoll, NY: Orbis.

Hollinger, Robert, ed. 1985. *Hermeneutics and Praxis.* Notre Dame, IN: University of Notre Dame Press.

Howe, Reuel. L. 1963. *The Miracle of Dialogue.* Minneapolis: Seabury.

Hughes, Philip. 1978. *A Popular History of the Catholic Church.* New York: Macmillan.

Jabes, Edmond. 1993. *Margins.* Chicago: University of Chicago Press.

James, William. 1967. *Essays in Radical Empiricism.* Gloucester, MA: Peter Smith.

——. 1967. *A Pluralist Universe.* Gloucester, MA: Peter Smith.

——. 1969. *Pragmatism.* Cleveland: World Publishing.

Janeway, Elizabeth. 1981. *Powers of the Weak.* New York: Morrow Quill.

Jaspers, Karl. 1970. *Karl Jaspers Philosophy,* vol. 2. Chicago: University of Chicago Press.

Jeanrod, Werner. 1991. *Theological Hermeneutics: Development and Significance.* New York: Crossroad.

Johnson, Luke T. 1983. *Decision Making in the Church: A Biblical Model.* Philadelphia: Fortress.

Killen, Patricia O'Connell, and John de Beer. 1994. *The Art of Theological Reflection.* New York: Crossroad.

Lakeland, Paul. 1990. *Theology and Critical Theory: The Discourse of the Church.* Nashville: Abingdon.

Lee, Bernard; Barbara Fleischer; and Charles Topper. 1993. *A Same and Different Future: Executive Summary.* New Orleans: Loyola, Institute for Ministry.

Lee, Bernard J. 1991. "Christians and Jews in Dialogic Community." In *Journal of Ecumenical Studies* 28:1 (Winter).

——. 1988. *The Galilean Jewishness of Jesus: Retrieving the Jewishness of Christian Origins.* New York: Paulist.

——. 1992. "God as Spirit" and "The Nature of the Church." In *Empirical Theology A Handbook,* ed. Randolph Crump Miller. Birmingham, AL: Religious Education Press.

——. 1993. *Jesus and the Metaphors of God: The Christs of the New Testament.* New York: Paulist.

——. 1994. "Practical Theology: Its Character and Possible Implications for Higher

Education." In *Current Issues in Catholic Higher Education*. Washington, DC: ACCU. Winter.

——. 1979. "A Process Theology of Religious Discourse." In *Religion and Life* 48:4 (Winter).

——, and Harry James Cargas. 1976. *Religious Experience and Process Theology*. New York: Paulist.

Legrand, Hervé-Marie. 1979. "The Presidency of the Eucharist According to the Ancient Tradition." *Worship* 53/5 (September).

Loomer, Bernard M. 1976. "SIZE." Reprinted in Lee, Bernard J., and Cargas, Harry James, *Religious Experience and Process Theology*. New York: Paulist.

Lundin, Roger; Anthony Thiselton; and Clarence Walhout. 1985. *The Responsibility of Hermeneutics*. Grand Rapids: Eerdmans.

Lyotard, Jean-François. 1984. *The Postmodern Condition: A Report on Knowledge*. Minneapolis: University of Minnesota Press.

Mackin, Theodore. 1982. *What Is Marriage?* New York: Paulist.

Macmurray, John. 1991. *The Self as Agent*. Atlanta Highlands: Humanities Press.

McCann, Dennis. 1987. *New Experiment in Democracy: The Challenge for American Catholicism*. Kansas City: Sheed & Ward.

McCann, Dennis, and Charles R. Strain. 1985. *Polity and Praxis: A Program for American Practical Theology*. Minneapolis: Winston Seabury.

Meier, John P. 1991. *A Marginal Jew: Rethinking the Historical Jesus*. Garden City, NY: Doubleday.

Meland, Bernard E. 1976. *Fallible Forms and Symbols*. San Francisco: Harper & Row.

Metz, Johannes B. 1978. *Followers of Christ*. New York: Paulist.

Miller, David L. 1981. *Christs: Meditations on Archetypal Images in Christian Theology*. New York: Seabury.

Mudge, Lewis S., and James N. Poling, eds. 1987. *Formation and Reflection: The Promise of Practical Theology*. Philadelphia: Fortress.

Mueller, J. J. 1984. What Are They Saying about Theological Method? New York: Paulist.

Murnion, Philip. 1992. *New Parish Ministers*. New York: National Pastoral Life Center.

Myers, Ched. 1988. *Binding the Strong Man: A Political Reading of Mark's Story of Jesus*. Maryknoll, NY: Orbis.

Myers, Ched. 1994. *Who Will Roll Away the Stone?* New York: Orbis.

Neusner, Jacob. 1973. *From Politics to Piety*. Englewood Cliffs, NJ: Prentice-Hall.

——. 1971. *The Rabbinic Traditions about the Pharisees before 70*, 3 vols. London: Brill.

Nyberg, David. 1981. *Power over Power*. Ithaca, NY: Cornell University Press.

Palmer, Richard. *Hermeneutics*. Evanston, IL: Northwestern University Press.

Pelton, Robert. 1994. *From Power to Communion*. Notre Dame, IN: University of Notre Dame Press.

Perlmutter, Hayim Goren. 1989. *Siblings: Rabbinic Judaism and Early Christianity at Their Beginnings*. New York.

Pontifical Biblical Commission. 1994. "The Interpretation of the Bible in the Church." *Origins* 12/29 (January).

Pruyser, Paul W., ed. 1987. *Changing Views of the Human Condition*. Macon, GA: Mercer University Press.

Ricoeur, Paul. 1976. *Interpretation Theory: Discourse and the Surplus of Meaning*. Fort Worth: Texas Christian University Press.

Ricoeur, Paul. 1978. Reagan, Charles E., and David Stewart, eds. *The Philosophy of Paul Ricoeur: An Anthology of His Work*. Boston: Beacon Press.

Ricoeur, Paul. 1977. *The Rule of Metaphor*. Toronto: University of Toronto Press.

Rilke, Rainer Maria. 1977. *Possibility of Being: A Selection of Poems*. New York: New Directions.

Rivkin, Ellis. 1978. *A Hidden Revolution: The Pharisees' Search for the Kingdom Within*. Nashville: Abingdon.

Rorty, Richard. 1979. *Philosophy and the Mirror of Nature*. Princeton: Princeton University Press.

Safrai, S., and M. Stern. 1976. *The Jewish People in the First Century*, Compendia Rerum Iudaicarum ad Novum Testamentum, vol. 2. Philadelphia: Fortress.

Saldarini, Anthony J. 1994. *Matthew's Christian Jewish Community*. Chicago: University of Chicago Press.

———. 1988. *Pharisees, Scribes and Sadducees*. Wilmington, DE: Glazier.

Schama, Simon. 1989. *Citizens: A Chronicle of the French Revolution*. New York: Knopf.

Schillebeeckx, Edward. 1983. *God Is New Each Moment*. New York: Seabury.

Schoenherr, Richard A., and Lawrence Young. 1993. *Full Pews and Empty Altars*. Madison: University of Wisconsin Press.

Schrag, Calvin O. 1989. *Communicative Praxis and the Space of Subjectivity*. Bloomington: University of Indiana Press.

Smith, John E. 1973. *The Analogy of Experience*. New York: Harper & Row.

Snook, Lee. 1980. "The Uses of Experience in Recent Theology." *Word and World* 1/3.

Theissen, Gerd. 1985. *Sociology of Early Palestinian Christianity*. Philadelphia: Fortress.

Thiselton, Anthony. 1981. *The Two Horizons*. Grand Rapids: Eerdmans.

Topper, Charles; Geri Telepak; Rita Walters; and Thomas Walters. 1993. *Education for Ministry: A Survey of Graduate Ministry Programs, 1992-1993*. New Orleans: Loyola Institute for Ministry.

Tracy, David. 1981. *The Analogical Imagination: Christian Theology and the Culture of Pluralism*. New York: Crossroad.

———. 1987. *Plurality and Ambiguity*. San Francisco: Harper.

Tucker, Susan. 1988. *Southern Women*. New York: Shocken.

Turner, Victor. 1977. *The Ritual Process: Structure and Anti-Structure.* Ithaca, NY: Cornell University Press.

Veling, Terry. 1994. "Living in the Margins: The Interpretive Edge of Intentional Christian Communities." Doctoral dissertation, Boston College.

Vidler, Alec. 1961. *The Church in an Age of Revolution.* London: Penguin.

Wallace, Ruth. 1992. *They Call Her Pastor: A New Role for Catholic Women.* Albany: SUNY Press.

Watts, Alan. 1972. *The Book.* New York: Random House.

Wheatley, Margaret J. 1994. *Leadership and the New Science: Learning about Organization from an Orderly Universe.* San Francisco: Berrett-Koehler.

Whitehead, Alfred North. n.d. *Adventures of Ideas.* New York: Mentor.

——. 1928. *Process and Reality.* New York: Macmillan.

——. 1967. *Science and the Modern World.* New York: Free Press.

——. 1955. *Symbolism.* New York: Capricorn.

Whitehead, James D. 1987. "Stewardship: The Disciple Becomes a Leader." In *Alternative Futures for Worship: Leadership Ministry in Community,* vol. 6, ed. Michael Cowan. Collegeville, MN: Liturgical Press.

Wuthnow, Robert. 1994. *Sharing the Journey: Support Groups and America's New Quest for Community.* New York: Freepress.

Index